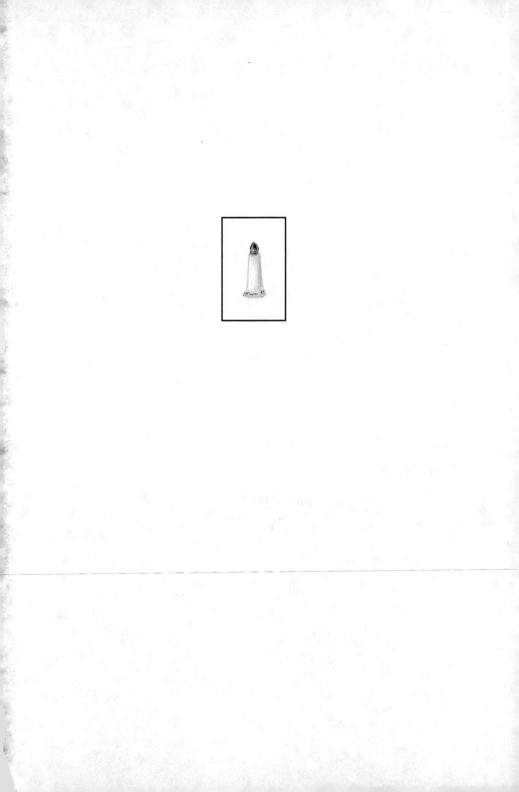

DOUG PSALTIS

with Michael Psaltis

Broadway Books New York

The Seasoning of a Chef

My Journey from Diner to Ducasse and Beyond

BROADWAY

The names of some of the characters and locations in this book
have been changed, as have certain physical characteristics and
other descriptive detail.

PRINTED IN THE UNITED STATES OF AMERICA

BROADWAY BOOKS and its logo, a letter B bisected on the
diagonal, are trademarks of Random House, Inc.

Visit our Web site at www.broadwaybooks.com

First edition published 2005

Book design by Maria Carella

Photo of salt shaker © PictureArts, Corbis. Title page photo by
Tim Hall, Photodisc / Getty Images

Library of Congress Cataloging-in-Publication Data
Psaltis, Douglas.
    The seasoning of a chef: my journey from diner to Ducasse
and beyond / Douglas Psaltis with Michael Psaltis.—1st ed.
        p. cm.
    1. Psaltis, Douglas.   2. Cooks—Biography.   I. Psaltis,
Michael.   II. Title.
TX649.P75A3 2005
641.5'092—dc22
[B]   2005046904

ISBN 0-7679-1968-8

10   9   8   7   6   5   4   3   2   1

For our parents

Contents

The Seasoning of a Chef

"Can he lift the potatoes?"

That was the question that launched me into the world of cooking. My family was sitting in our normal corner booth at the Olympia Diner, having just finished an early dinner, and Poppy was standing by our table as he always did. "Poppy" was what we called my grandfather and Olympia was his diner. That day was unusually tense, as Poppy had fired one of his three cooks that morning. He now needed someone to work Saturdays and Sundays. My parents were obviously off the hook; my older brother Andy had football; and it wasn't a job for my sister. That left my twin brother, Mike, who was too thin and seemed in no way inclined, and me. Of the six of us, I was the only one whose eyes weren't cast down at the table. I just looked up at Poppy, waiting for him to decide. The year was 1984 and I was ten years old.

My grandfather was part of the Old World. He was in his early eighties and had worked his whole life to have and to keep the diner where he spent nearly every minute. He had come to New York in the early 1920s and worked hard for everything he had. The only loyalties and obligations he understood were to his family. He would do anything for us and he expected the same in return. But we all knew he was a tough son of a bitch. Telling him no wasn't easy. Actually, it was difficult to tell him anything. That day it seemed impossible, as his blood was already boiling before we even showed up.

When he first opened Olympia, the entire staff consisted of Poppy, his brother, his cousin, and one outsider—a Turkish guy. When it was his turn, my father also worked for Poppy. Telling Poppy that he couldn't count on one of his grandsons wouldn't be easy. This wasn't a favor; it was expected.

The Olympia Diner was everything to my grandfather. He had worked from nothing to build it. Known to the rest of the world as Andrew George Psaltis (the "p" is silent and the name essentially means cantor, or singer), my grandfather arrived in the U.S. without a cent in his pockets. He had "jumped ship" when he was only seventeen years old and was working on a Greek freighter that picked up wheat from Canada and brought it back to Greece. Without any skills or much education, he worked as a common laborer on the ship. Andros, the island he was from, had very little to offer him. Working on one of the freighters was a chance to earn money, and, ultimately, it was a chance for him to escape a life with few possibilities. During his last trip to Canada, he got off the ship at a port in Halifax, Nova Scotia, and hid in the swamps to avoid being caught. He escaped undetected, but he had nothing and nowhere to go.

With almost as little English as he had money, my grandfather turned to one of the few things he knew he was good at to survive: fighting. He was not a big man; he was only five foot eight. But he was stocky and ferociously determined. And, as he had learned on the long trips on the ship, he had a natural talent for brawling. Not long off the boat, he became part of a group of other Greeks who had pretty much the same skills he had, and soon they found a way into professional boxing and wrestling matches.

Poppy had a big box filled with medals, and he gave us one almost every time we went to his house. There wasn't anything special about the medals. They were just dull metal emblems with red, white, and blue ribbons. But if each medal represented a win, he must have won hundreds of matches. In any case, his success was enough for him to live on, though he knew he couldn't be a fighter for the rest of his life. And, after his success eventually led him to New York, the girl he was dating—a third-generation German-American from Staten Island who would later become my grandmother—wouldn't have a fighter for a husband. Well, at least not a professional one, as he never stopped being a fighter, he just stopped getting paid for it.

Besides carrying bales of wheat and swinging his fists, the only other thing my grandfather knew he was good at was cleaning and cooking fish. He had done it throughout most of his childhood. As it turned out, many of the other Greek men with whom he arrived in New York had the same skill, and they were all getting jobs in restaurants around the city. This seemed to him to be as good a profession as any other, but he didn't want the dishwasher job that most of the other men landed.

Fortunately, he had an edge on the other Greeks: he knew French. His father, who owned a small general store on Andros, had made him take French classes in school. Because of this, instead of working in dives scrubbing dishes, he was able to find work at some of the best restaurants. Back then—as is mostly true today—the money to be made in a restaurant was in the front of the house and the job to have was headwaiter. My grandfather was not the type of man looking to be part of a system. He had made it this far by doing whatever he wanted. Being a waiter was perfect for him. It allowed him to earn a lot of money and pretty much do as he pleased. If he got tired of answering to one boss, he would move on to the next one.

The years he spent working in some of the finest restaurants and clubs in Manhattan were very good to my grandfather, but his pugnaciousness eventually got the best of him. As the story goes, his last job in Manhattan was as the headwaiter at the famous Stork Club. It was the place to see and be seen for New York's elite during the Café Society era. Joe DiMaggio, Frank Sinatra, Marilyn Monroe, and J. Edgar Hoover were among those who were regulars at the nightclub. As the cameras snapped photos of celebrities for the gossip columns, my grandfather made a lot of money wearing a tuxedo and serving drinks and food late into the night. But the job ended abruptly when he got into an argument with the owner, Sherman Billingsley, who was known to watch over everything like a hawk and would toss out bar customers or fire employees for almost any reason or no reason at all.

Billingsley became increasingly unhappy with the amount of money the waiters were making, and in particular was angry with my grandfather because all of the waiters listened to him and not the owner. So, Billingsley came up with what he thought was a clever way to keep some of the waiters' tips and he cut back on everyone's hours. Normally he would issue the new rules in a harshly worded employee memorandum. Instead, to get back at my grandfather directly, he insisted that my grandfather personally tell all of the waiters the new rules. I suppose he figured this would turn all of the waiters against my grandfather, but he never found out if it would work. My grandfather threw him through the restaurant's front window, effectively ending the argument, his job at the Stork Club, and his days waiting tables in Manhattan.

My grandfather and grandmother (now with two sons and a daughter) had been living in Flushing, Queens, for years. So, with Manhattan out of the picture, my grandfather looked in the other direction for work. He soon found that with his Manhattan experience he could easily get a job as a waiter at some of the best and most expensive restaurants on the "Gold Coast" (the north shore) of Long Island. In these restaurants, in exclusive neighborhoods, serving a wealthy clientele, my grandfather found he could make even more money than he could in the fanciest new restaurant in the city.

All of this work finally led to the opportunity he had always wanted: to be his own boss. Even though he had saved a decent amount over the years, he still couldn't open a restaurant like the expensive places he had worked in or one in some rich neighborhood on Long Island. So, he opened a small diner with about forty seats in Jamaica, Queens, not far from where his family had been living for years. Jamaica was really beginning to flourish at this time and the Olympia Diner fit right in. It had a simple motto: "A Good Place to Eat." And, on the sign that hung outside for all of the twenty-five years that he owned and operated the diner, a single phrase described the food: "Steaks and Chops." When I asked my dad what this meant, he said it simply meant they served everything.

On the ride to the diner from our house, we had all piled into my father's big black Cadillac Sedan DeVille—a company car, which was one of the few benefits he received as a salesman and manager at Mitchell Cadillac. The trip out to Queens was a half hour—or with traffic, half a day—and even with the big leather couch that was the sedan's backseat the drive always seemed to take forever.

We lived in Huntington (one of the larger towns on the north shore of Long Island) between extremely nice neighborhoods situated on Huntington Bay and the housing projects that were scattered throughout the south side of town. We were solidly in the middle in a two-story white house with blue shutters framing the five bedroom windows on the top floor, four decorative pillars standing stalwartly but pointlessly in front, and a wooden fence stretching out on both sides. It wasn't a particularly big house, just four bedrooms and one and a half bathrooms for the six of us. But we had other things, like a large yard on the corner of the cul-de-sac and a pool.

While my father backed out of our driveway—right arm on my mother's headrest, slowly over the bump at the end of the driveway—a round robin of arguing, an accepted form of communication in my family, had started. My dad knew that he'd either have to let Poppy down or sacrifice one of his young. We all knew this and each of us was fighting for the best way to handle the situation. During one of the few quiet moments, I put my two cents in. "I'll work for Poppy." The second or third time I said it, they heard.

"Like hell you will," was all my mother said and we all sat in a tense but quiet eye of the storm for the rest of the ride. Even though the "schlepping" (as my mother described it) didn't sound like a pleasant thing, it would just be on weekends and I wanted the job. I was always excited about going to the diner. Besides the fact that Poppy made us whatever we wanted, there was something I loved about the smell of the place and the way it always seemed to be in motion.

From the outside, Olympia was a squat, square building with four large front windows bordered on all sides by panels of chrome. Inside, Olympia's dining room had a white tile floor and an L-shaped row of red vinyl booths. There were only nine booths and as many seats at the counter bar. Poppy worked as the short-order cook behind the bar and on most days Aunt Bessie was the only waitress. Our booth was in the corner across from the griddle.

As soon as we sat down that day, Mike went right to work. As always, he ordered the biggest thing he could—this time a double hamburger with fries. For such a skinny kid, he was a phenomenal eater. Jen sat quietly waiting for her ziti. She no longer ordered, since Poppy knew what she wanted. My mother studied the menu that she must have known by heart, even though she was certainly going to order either a salad or chicken.

My father was talking with Aunt Bessie while she waited for the rest of us to order. Without losing focus on what my dad was saying, she took a pencil out from behind her ear and jotted everyone's order down. She had dark olive skin and a loose cloud of curly black hair.

"Up!" my grandfather called out, followed by a bang on the counter with the palm of his hand, and Aunt Bessie went for the plates. He glared at her as she picked up the plates. While she was busy serving the couple sitting at the table closest to the front door, I watched my grandfather working on our burgers and Dad's steak. The sizzle of the meat on the griddle was just barely audible from where we sat, but we had a good view and I watched a lot of the cooking.

All of the prep work and the heavy cooking was done in the back, but the short-order cooking was done in the front, right behind the counter. There were only a few feet separating the griddle from the countertop, which was nearly as long as the dining room.

While we were still eating, Poppy came over to the table. He had on a white button-down shirt with a large flat collar whose points reached almost to his shoulders. His head was round and bald—except for a gray fringe from ear to ear. His square chin was flat and didn't jut out as far as his boxer's nose. When he smiled, two and sometimes three creases would emerge in his cheeks, as though it was a great strain. He wasn't smiling at that moment.

I was looking at Poppy, but he was staring at my brother Andy. Then my father pointed to me (with my burger in my mouth but ears wide open) and said, "Doug can start coming in." A chain of emotions instantly erupted at the table. My mother, who had been overruled, was red with anger. I was, of course, excited. And everyone else seemed relieved.

My grandfather paused. He ran his hand through the messy white hair on the back of his head. I was the only one looking at him while he decided which of us could replace the guy he fired that morning. Poppy was still watching Andy, who was swirling his spoon in his rice pudding, when he said, "Can he lift the potatoes?" He thought some more. Then finally looking my way, he said, "The rebel." That's what he sometimes called me. I was told that it was because when I was very young I did whatever I wanted. "He'll ride with the Turk," he said, looking back toward my father.

I looked to Aunt Bessie because I knew that she had heard and I knew the "Turk" comment upset her. He was talking about her, even though we all knew she was Greek. When Poppy was angry at her—and there was anger raging between them that day—he always called her a Turk. It was his way of getting her blood boiling. I would soon learn that he had ways to do this with almost everyone and that he was not an easy man to work for.

It was dark when my father nudged me awake the next morning, still in his baggy blue pj's. "Rise and shine," he said, clapping his hands. I sat up and looked over at Mike, who shared the room with me and hadn't budged from a sound sleep.

While I was in the bathroom, I heard the coffee grinder buzzing. When I was in the kitchen, my mom gave me an "everything" bagel with butter wrapped in a paper towel. Then Aunt Bessie's gray Oldsmobile was outside waiting for me. I was out the door at 5:25 A.M. and on my way to Olympia for my first day of work. It was a solid half-hour trip from our house, even this early when there was no traffic.

Aunt Bessie's car was warm and clean, but it smelled of cigarette smoke. She was smiling and kissed my cheek when I got in. She was already wearing the blue dress with a white blouse underneath that she always wore at Olympia. I was still in a sleepy haze and would be for the rest of the ride, but she was wide awake, as though it were the middle of the day.

Aunt Bessie was a big woman, not fat but certainly bulky, with shoulders like rump roasts. She had a big broad smile that showed no trace of concern about revealing a set of stained and jumbled teeth.

She had yet to put on her stockings and I noticed how bad her legs looked. She had purple veins that were like crooked pinstripes leading to her feet. There were days when she could barely walk and now I knew why. I looked away.

"Nice, new sneakers," she said, noticing my bright-white Nikes. They were the newest Nikes, which I had just convinced my parents to buy a few days ago.

It was still dark out and it was cold. I shivered a little bit and tried to get comfortable.

"Twenty-eight minutes is my best time from here," she said. "That gives us about seven minutes to spare. We don't want to be late. Your Poppy will notice and he'll be on us all day." She said this in a defiant way. Working at the diner was her only job, but she always made it clear—especially when she shouldn't have—that she didn't need to work for Poppy. But she really did need to work for him. She owed him that much.

My Aunt Bessie was not really my aunt, but we always called her "aunt" out of respect. She was, however, at one time legally part of the family. Bessie Sartendies was a young Greek girl new to America when she married a tough, heavy-drinking German-American, who was my grandmother's brother. The first time my grandmother and Bessie met was at the wedding and the two became very close friends.

But Bessie and my grandmother's brother were married for only a few (rocky) years. I never once heard her or my grandparents talk about her husband, but, as my father tells it, he was the type of man who drank more than he worked and went out more than he stayed in. When he finally left her (and New York) for good, she had nothing.

She had only been in America for a couple of years before getting married. Like my grandfather, she had left her family behind in Greece. But now that she was no longer young, she didn't have an easy time getting work. Besides my grandmother, she had very few people that she could turn to and eventually she had no choice but to ask her for help. She wouldn't take money; she wanted to work. At the time, though, Olympia only had waiters.

We were stopped at a light a few miles away from the diner when Aunt Bessie lit her first cigarette of the ride. I would soon learn that this was her routine. On the slight hill on Northern Boulevard, whether stopped or not, she would begin smoking her last cigarette and she would put it out on the pavement on her way into the diner after pulling her car into a parking space in the small lot.

I followed behind her as she went through the back door into the kitchen. The first thing to hit me as I walked in was the powerful smell of ammonia. It was strong and unpleasant. Outside it was still somewhat dark, but the kitchen was bright with yellow light. All of the other times I had been in the kitchen it was warm and inviting and smelled of braising and roasting meats. Now it was cold and I was in the way before I was even a foot into the door.

The kitchen was a small rectangle with a worn red tile floor and white walls, which were stained brown in several places. There was a large pot sink immediately to the right as you walked in the back door, then halfway through the room two metal tables lined up parallel to each other. On the other side of the two tables were two sets of four burners and two ovens underneath. To the left of the stoves was a smaller table with a top shelf filled with stacks of plates. Near the swinging door that led to the front was a small table against the wall, which they kept silverware and napkins and glasses on.

Aunt Bessie handed me a white cotton button-down short-sleeve shirt, which is what I'd always seen the men working in the kitchen wearing, and then she was gone. I put on the shirt and had to roll the sleeves up several times as it was much too large for me.

Nick, a middle-aged Greek man with hairy arms that always seemed to be bent into V's, was working the stove. He had a huge stock pot filled with water and some floating pieces of celery and carrots on one burner, and a large cast-iron pan on another. I maneuvered to get a better look, but couldn't see much from the other side of the tables. "Behind," I heard and took a step back. I bumped right into Steve, who was slightly younger, smaller, and less hairy than Nick. He wasn't smiling.

"Onions, salt, sink," he said. I just stared at him. "Bag of onions, downstairs," he pointed toward the basement stairs that were directly opposite the back door. "Box of salt, also downstairs, and sink," he pointed to the other side of the kitchen. "You wash. Understand?"

"Today," he said, and I waited for him to say more until he said it again and I realized that he meant now. I hurried off to the basement. This would be the first time I had been downstairs without following Poppy. The stairs were old, wooden, and grease-stained. As I walked down them, I let my hand drag against the brick wall to keep my balance. There was a single light on in the basement that barely illuminated the shelves. I knew that the box of salt was somewhere on those shelves, but I didn't see it anywhere.

The onions were easier to find. They were in a crate on a table with several other crates. I grabbed one of the red net bags and gripped it tightly by my side. I returned to the shelves and looked for the salt. I wasn't really sure what the box looked like and the limited light didn't help. I scanned all of the shelves and was on my toes trying to see the top shelf when a hand pulled a box down. Steve handed me the box and said, "Salt." He then named the other items on the shelves and pointed to the table, where there were onions, potatoes, and other vegetables, and said, "Veg. Got it?"

He put the salt in my hand and climbed the stairs without me. I followed as quickly as I could, dragging the bag of onions a little. When I reached the long tables opposite the stove, I put the onions and salt on the closest table. Steve quickly moved the onions off the table and put them on a shelf under it. "Not on table, under table," he said and turned to do something else.

I backed away toward the sink but stopped when I felt a hand on my shoulder.

"There's my boy," my grandfather said. "You be nice to my grandson, heh, one day he'll be your boss." He said this to Nick, who nodded his head and turned back to the stove, but I knew he meant it as a warning for Steve. With his arm around me, he told me to listen and that after I helped Steve with the boxes, I'd work with him up front.

I barely got out an "okay" before Aunt Bessie swung through the door into the kitchen. "Orders up," she called and Poppy was gone. Aunt Bessie had a cup of coffee in her hand. She took a long swallow and put the cup down on the small table by the door. She drank coffee all day. One time I counted thirty-two cups.

Steve walked over to me and put his hand on my shoulder. He faced me toward the back door and said, "You see the boxes? They're from today's delivery. After I unpack the boxes, we take them to the Dumpster." This was the most he had said to me at one time and I listened to him attentively. "Carry out those boxes, then I'll give you these," he said kicking the cardboard boxes that were stacked by the table, "then we'll crush them out back, okay? Today."

I nodded.

"Today," he added.

I rushed over to the pile of boxes by the door, grabbed two of them, and burst out the back door. I sped toward the Dumpster that was on the other side of the back parking lot and threw the boxes at it. Some of them were large, but most were fairly small and squat. Some were waxy and some were moist and had spots where something had dripped through them. I carried as many as I could at one time and tossed them at the pile from as far away as I could.

Steve followed me out with the last two boxes and told me to drag over the garbage bags that were leaning against the wall by the door. "Okay, now we flatten boxes and put in a pile." He began pulling the boxes apart and I did as he did. With one I tried kicking through the bottom, but he stopped me, took the box, and cut through the tape with a razor.

"If they're too wet, like this one," he showed me the box he was holding, "just put it in the garbage bag."

We got through the pile pretty quickly, and then he showed me how to tie up the flattened stack. Finally, he tied up the garbage and threw it in the Dumpster.

When we got back into the kitchen, he handed me an apron and told me to go up front. The apron he gave me (like all of the others that I would wear there) fit me like a dress. I had to fold it in half to keep it off the floor.

Nick stopped me on my way out. "Kid," he said with a cigarette hanging out of his mouth, "take this out there and tell your Poppy that this is all the bacon for the day." I took the tray from him. It had big, beautiful thick-cut slices of bacon on it.

When I got out front, Poppy was behind the counter in front of the griddle. "Put the tray here, Dougie," he said, pointing to a spot near him. Poppy was bent over the griddle like he was ready for a wrestling match to start. His back was arched over and his dark, hairy arms were bent at the elbows—ready for action.

"Nick says this is all the bacon for the day."

Poppy nodded and then he told me to stand next to him and watch. He had a few eggs on the griddle and added some of the bacon slices. I stood off to his right, leaning against the end of the counter. The bacon was sizzling and curling up a little. Poppy took the spatula and flattened it down again.

A few times he told me to get things from the kitchen—another flat of eggs, more English muffins, a couple tomatoes—and I rushed to the kitchen and back as quickly as possible. Mostly, though, I just stood and watched. Poppy worked so quickly that his hands always seemed to be moving. I was mesmerized watching him. And, as the orders piled up, he remained calm, even when the whole griddle was packed with eggs, bacon, and pancakes. He was constantly talking to me or to one of the customers. He told me fight stories or talked about what he was cooking. At one point he handed me the spatula and showed me how to slide it under a pancake from the side and on an angle, so that the pancake wouldn't break. To more than one of the customers, he bragged about how he now had his grandson working with him and that someday I'd be running the place.

Even in my new sneakers, my feet hurt a little from standing there, but the time flew by. Before I knew it, my parents and Jen and Mike walked through the door. Poppy waved to them and turned to me. "Just go get more butter from Nick, then sit with them."

I tried not to look at my parents because I knew they were watching me. I went into the kitchen and Nick handed me a towel and a hot pan with butter inside. I rushed back out to Poppy and he took the little pan from me without even using the towel.

"You see the butter is soft?" he asked, tilting the pan so that I could see that the butter was almost melted. "The cold butter will burn too quickly, so you use soft butter." He patted me on the shoulder. "Go sit, I'll get you some bacon and eggs." (I guess he had seen me eyeing the bacon and nearly drooling all morning.) My first day ended with two sunny-side-up eggs surrounded by bacon and toast at our usual booth.

When I arrived at work the next day, Sunday, I wasn't nervous the way I had been the day before; I was excited. Even the offensive ammonia smell didn't seem as bad when we walked in. Instead of standing around waiting to be told where to go, I went over to Steve and asked him if I should start with the boxes. He was already busy unpacking and just nodded when I asked.

Just like the day before, I grabbed as many as I could and threw them by the Dumpster. There were fewer boxes this time, but I still carried them out as quickly as I could. On returning from tossing my last two boxes, I nearly ran into Steve as he came out the back door with four or five boxes in his arms. He walked over to the Dumpster and dropped them into the pile I had made.

"Bring those garbage bags over here," he said, nodding toward the bags that were stacked next to the back door. I dragged them over one at a time. They were too heavy for me to lift and more than one at a time would have been difficult. After I dragged the last garbage bag over, Steve told me to get the string from the kitchen. When I returned, he had finished breaking down the boxes.

"Just tie them up," he said as he lifted the garbage bags into the Dumpster. When I was done, Steve was already smoking a cigarette and leaning against the wall by the door. He stopped me on my way into the kitchen.

"Hold up," he said, "no rush today." He took a cigarette out of the pack that was in his jeans and offered it to me. I shook my head, no. He then leaned back against the wall and closed his eyes. I wasn't sure what I was supposed to do, so I just waited for him. Then the door opened and Poppy was standing there.

"*Blakas*," he yelled, which I knew meant "idiot" and was followed by a string of even harsher-sounding Greek words. Steve jumped up, threw the cigarette down, and rushed into the kitchen. "*Blakas*," Poppy said again, this time to Steve's back.

I followed Poppy back into the kitchen, where Steve was already back to work at the tables near the stove. Almost as soon as the swinging door closed, Steve looked at me and said, "Potatoes." I paused for a second thinking about what he meant. "Today," he said and I realized that he wanted me to get the potatoes from the basement.

I again went slowly down the oil-stained stairs, with my hand along the brick wall, into the dim light of the basement. The potatoes were in huge white dirt-stained paper bags that had a farm's name on them in blue. I grabbed the top of one of the bags sitting on a table and realized why Poppy had asked whether I could lift the potatoes. The bags were almost three feet high and must have weighed fifty pounds.

I put my arms around the bag, wrestled it up to my shoulder, and trucked up the stairs. When I reached the top, I was nearly out of breath and had to put the bag down. I turned around to make sure that no one had seen me struggle, but of course Steve was watching and waved me over.

I started to drag the heavy bag across the red tile floor until I saw Poppy come into the kitchen. I stopped and picked the bag up. "Under that table," Steve said. I dropped the bag on the floor, pushed it onto the table's shelf, and tried to pretend that it hadn't been very difficult.

Poppy came up to me and brushed the dirt off my shirt. "You ask for help if you need it," he told me. "The *blakas* will help." Steve didn't even look up. "Put an apron on and come up front," Poppy said as he left the kitchen.

I grabbed an apron, folded it in half, and tied it on. Then I brushed some of the dirt from the potatoes off my shoes and rushed through the swinging door. Once I was up front, the rest of the day was just like the one before: for the most part I just watched Poppy cook and listened to him talk to me and about me.

My family arrived even earlier that day and my day was over before I knew it. This time my grandmother, who rarely ate with us at the diner, had come along. Smiling broadly, she paused just inside the door before coming over to the counter to kiss Poppy and me.

As we ate our meal, I remember feeling strange sitting in the booth eating after I had spent the last two days behind the counter and in the kitchen. I felt I was now a part of the diner and, possibly because of that, sitting in our booth that day didn't feel as comfortable as it had before—and it never would again.

We were at the top of the hill on Northern Boulevard when Aunt Bessie lit her cigarette the next Saturday. "We're going to be late," she said.

I was finishing a bagel and just starting to wake up. I was looking forward to working again and wasn't concerned if we were late, though it was my fault, as it had taken my dad a few rise-and-shines to get me going. I would make it right, though, by moving quicker once we got there. Of course I didn't expect Poppy would be as upset as he was.

As soon as we walked into the kitchen, Poppy started yelling at Aunt Bessie. I felt bad for her and told Poppy that it was my fault that we were late, that I had overslept. He turned to me with maybe a little less anger than he had shown her. "I already have you late, I don't need excuses too," he said and left the kitchen.

I was pretty stunned. Aunt Bessie, on the other hand, hadn't broken her stride. She was drinking her first cup of coffee before I had even left the spot I felt frozen in.

Finally I got myself together and started on the boxes. I moved as quickly as I could, got through the pile by the door, and went for the pile near Steve's table.

Steve had already unpacked all of the boxes before I had even gotten there and was now helping Nick butcher a side of beef, so I just kept working by myself. I got through these boxes quickly, though a few were wet and difficult to carry. One of the last boxes had been set aside a little and I realized why as soon as I lifted it. It dripped brown liquid right onto my white sneakers and in one splash had ruined them. I carried that box out by itself and threw it right into a trash bag.

I finished taking out the boxes and garbage in record time and was ready to go out front with Poppy. I rushed back into the kitchen, grabbed an apron, and went toward the swinging door. But Steve stopped me and said, "Sink."

This was the pot wash, so there were only large pots and pans in the sink, no dishes. These were the pots and pans that were used and reused all day. Cleaning them would become my least favorite task.

After a while—what seemed like a full day to me—I stopped and turned to watch Nick working at one of the big metal tables opposite the stove. He was tying a string around a loin of pork that was longer than my arm. He kept crisscrossing the string, while dangling a cigarette from his mouth. Then Steve dropped off another stack of pans and said, "More."

I hadn't made much of a dent on the original stack of pans and now the stack was doubled. I turned around and began scrubbing again.

Poppy came into the kitchen and asked for the bacon. Nick looked up and nodded. "Steve, bacon," he said and continued working on the pork loin. But a few seconds later there was a lot of commotion.

"What do you mean you can't find the bacon? You put it away, didn't you?" Nick yelled at Steve.

Steve looked blank then defiant. "I didn't put the bacon away."

"I checked it in this morning," Nick said. "I saw it. Where the hell is it now?"

Steve shook his head. "I didn't touch the bacon."

"Where is it then? Where's the bacon?" Nick yelled, moving closer and closer to Steve. He was only a few inches away from Steve's face when he asked again, "Where's the box of bacon?" Steve looked really nervous, almost frightened, until he remembered.

"The box was leaking. I set it there." He pointed at the floor near the table. In unison their eyes went from the spot on the floor to me. I had been watching the whole thing and now they were looking right at me. Nick turned around and slammed his fist on the table. He stood for a moment looking in the other direction and then he slowly walked over to me.

"Think now, kid, did you take out a dripping box?"

I didn't need to think. I just cast my eyes down (at my brown-stained sneakers).

He shook his head in disbelief and stormed out the back door. I followed close behind him and Steve followed behind me. Nick flung the Dumpster lid open and stared at the four large bags that I had thrown into it. "Which one?" he asked. I had no idea and just shook my head.

The back door flew open. "Where's the damn bacon?" Poppy yelled. The sun was in my eyes, so I could barely see him. He was just a menacing shadow that stood there for a minute taking in the scene and then slammed the door closed. Nick and Steve followed behind him. There was nothing to be done. The box of bacon was in one of those trash bags. But even if we could find it, it had been in the garbage and couldn't be served now.

When I got back into the kitchen, Poppy had taken out a large ham. "Get this thing hot," he said to Nick and stormed out of the kitchen. Nick went right at it and had the ham sizzling in a pan in minutes. I went back to the sink and tried to stay out of the way.

A few minutes later, Nick called to me. "Take this tray out front," he said. There was a stack of thick slices of ham on the tray. I took it from him and walked toward the swinging door, thinking about an explanation or an apology as I made my way up front.

"Where should I put this?" I asked Poppy, who didn't see me until I was at his side.

"Here," he said, taking the tray out of my hand.

"I'm sorry about the bacon," I said.

"Don't be sorry. It happens. You need to listen to what they tell you, okay? Listen," he said, pulling on my ear.

I returned to the kitchen and went right to the sink. The pile was still huge. For the next hour or so, I focused on getting the pans done. I was determined to get something right. Steve told me to take things out front a few times and I hurried back after each trip as though the pans needed to get done immediately. By the time my hands began to hurt, I had almost finished the new stack that Steve had added.

When I took a break from scrubbing, Aunt Bessie was in the kitchen drinking coffee and talking to Nick, who was at the stove adding the back of a chicken to one of the pots (with a cigarette dangling from his mouth). Next, he added salt—a whole lot of salt—and he broke the tops off a few ribs of celery and added the celery to the pot. Then Steve came by with more pans.

I couldn't believe the number of pans that had stacked up, but the pattern was unmistakable. Every time I watched Nick, more pans were dropped off. I was determined to get through the stack, but I couldn't stop my curiosity and virtually every pan in the kitchen was sent my way. This was my punishment. I would have to wash pans all day. As soon as I realized that, my scrubbing went from fast and vigorous to slow and gentle. My hand now circled the pans in big steady circles. I knew I couldn't get through all of the pans and even if I did, more would be added. Now, I just kept working and waiting to be called to run something up front. Bread, eggs, even the ham that represented my failure. The next time was butter.

"Kid," Nick yelled and I shook the soap off my hands and hurried to his side. "Bring this out front," he said and he handed me a small pan with butter in it.

The handle was hot and the pan dropped right out of my hand. He hadn't given me a rag and the pan was too hot for me to hold. Of course it landed butter-side down, mostly on my new sneakers and in a puddle on the red tiles. As if an audience was necessary, Aunt Bessie came in on cue. "Where's the butter?" she asked, before seeing me picking the little pan off my sneaker.

"Here," Nick said, as he placed a big square block of butter in my hand. "Unwrap it before you take it out." I did as he said and hurried through the swinging kitchen door. Aunt Bessie was already

at one of the tables talking to a customer. There were a few tables occupied and several people sitting at the counter. I hurried behind the
counter and over to Poppy with the butter.

"Where should I put this?" I asked.

"Here, here, put it here," he said, tapping with his spatula on a
tray that had remnants of butter in it. I put the butter in the tray and
headed back toward the kitchen. I heard him say, "It's solid," and
turned to see him picking up the block of butter and dropping it back
into the tray. "It's solid," he said again, raising his hands as if to say
he didn't know what the hell my problem was.

"Go back to the kitchen," said Aunt Bessie, who was suddenly
behind me, and she muttered something in Greek to Poppy.

Back in the kitchen, I didn't want to work. I didn't want to be
there. I wanted to go home. I walked slowly back to the sink.

Steve stopped me. "This is the list for the store." He handed me
a small piece of paper. "You know which store?" I didn't know what
he was talking about, but I was certain that it didn't mean washing
more dishes or going back out front. It meant getting out of there.

I followed him out the back door and into the bright sunlight.

"The store is down that way," he said, pointing his thumb over
his left shoulder. "You saw the tomato sign when you got here, yeah?"
I thought for a second—he meant the grocery store up the road—
and nodded. "You go there with the list and they'll give you what you
need. Take this," he swung a tall metal cart to me, "and leave the
apron."

I took the cart from him and started wheeling it toward the
market. It was a wobbly cart that would creak the whole way, but I
was glad to be out of the diner. I looked at my watch. It was already
10:30. I had almost made it through the morning—the worst morn-

ing I had ever had—and I had a plan to make the rest of the day go by as quickly as possible. I would simply take as long as I could to get to the store and back.

I wheeled the cart as though it had a hundred pounds of bricks in it. Slowly, a little slower, almost stopping, and then just a little quicker so that the wheels wouldn't stop moving. I had to pass by the front of the diner on my way up the road and I made certain not to look in the direction of the front windows. I felt Poppy was watching me and I didn't want to see his face. I started to think about how disappointed he must be in me.

Suddenly I was wheeling the cart at a normal rate. I had screwed up pretty much everything I had touched so far that morning, but I was determined not to screw up again. I would get to the market quickly and be prepared to work when I got back.

Nick just stared at me, holding the brown, shredded spinach in his hands. Steve was leaning against the table, running his finger up his forehead and flicking it off, again and again.

The cart had been heavier than I thought it would be, and it seemed to be harder and harder to push it as I made my way back to the diner. I hadn't realized that the spinach box was dragging against the wheel and that I had been hemorrhaging spinach leaves for at least half the trip. When I got to the kitchen, the box was nearly flat and the few leaves left in it were ruined. The tomatoes, the heads of lettuce, and everything else had made it. But, the spinach was gone.

Steve was still running his finger up and off his forehead. I looked at him and Nick, but didn't want to make eye contact with either. I was literally about half their size, but I felt so much smaller than that. Finally, Nick crumbled up the spinach in his hands and threw it in the trash. "They forgot the spinach," he said to me.

"They forgot spinach," Steve repeated, looking at me. I have no idea why, but they decided to save my ass and not a moment too soon. The kitchen door swung open and in walked Poppy. "No spinach," Steve said to him. Poppy looked at Nick.

"Yeah? No spinach?" he asked, and looked at me. "No spinach?"

"They forgot the spinach," Nick said, and banged his open palm against the table. "We'll have to send Bess back to them."

Poppy's face turned a darker shade of olive than I'd ever seen it and he stared at the floor. Then he looked at me. In that instant, I knew that he knew it was my fault. He must have thought that I couldn't get anything right. And I knew that he wasn't going to let me slide.

I took a step back, preparing for him to rip into me. Instead, he launched into a tirade about the market and how they always tried to cheat him. I had heard him go off on people like this before and knew that he wouldn't drop it for the rest of the day.

He stopped yelling and turned to Steve. "I need her up front, you go." Steve took off his apron and headed for the door. "You give them hell, yeah?" Poppy yelled after him.

"Yeah, hell," Steve repeated and was gone.

Nick lit another cigarette and picked up a potato and his knife. I returned to the sink, safely out of the line of fire. Shortly after Steve left, Poppy came over to me at the sink. He put a hand on my shoulder and just stood there watching me scrub a pan. I had a sinking feeling as I realized I hadn't escaped the spinach fiasco after all. My whole day had been one mistake after another. I don't think I did one thing right—well, maybe I didn't screw up the dishwashing, but I definitely didn't do a good job at it. I waited for him to tell me that I couldn't cut it, that I had failed him. I felt certain that this would be my last day.

He just stood there without saying a word. I couldn't turn around to look at him, so I just looked down at my feet. My new Nikes were spotted in bacon juice and covered in dried butter and big chunks of bright-green spinach. I don't know if he noticed this too, but a moment later he patted my back and left the kitchen.

That Saturday wasn't my last day. It was definitely my worst day, but it was just my second weekend of many. My last day came unexpectedly about two years later.

That day began like most others, except that it was the first time Aunt Bessie had picked me up in almost a month. She had stopped working mornings because she was having so much pain in her feet. Her normal shift was more than twelve hours long. She was tough, but her feet and legs were beginning to suffer from a lifetime of waiting tables.

I was glad Aunt Bessie was driving that morning and not just because I had gotten used to taking the ride with her. When she didn't drive me, my dad did and then I was almost assured of being late, as he was a painfully slow driver. Aunt Bessie, on the other hand, was almost never late, except when it was my fault or when she was making a point.

She and Poppy continued their stormy relationship, with her yelling things in Greek and him calling her a Turk or a "phony Greek." It was on the mornings after these fights that Aunt Bessie would take the longer way to work and arrive exactly twenty minutes late. It was as though if we were less late or later, Poppy might not realize she was trying to get back at him.

This morning, though, things were right on track: from the moment she picked me up to the cigarette butt on the parking lot pavement a little more than a half hour later. We had made the trip so many times it was now as much of a routine for me as it was for her.

I no longer rushed about taking out the boxes, but I probably got the task done just as quickly. And I never threw out another box of bacon (or anything else). That's not to suggest that I didn't make tons of other mistakes.

When I think of that kitchen—the red tile floor that shone in the morning and was dull and streaky by the afternoon, and the warm smell of meats cooking—I think mostly about all of the mistakes I made. By the sink I scrubbed a cast-iron pan clean of all the seasoning that had been worked into it; by the oven, I burned eight loaves of bread (half of that day's bread); on the wood cutting board, I forgot to put down paper and stained it orange from the carrots I had peeled. But those mistakes were what motivated me. Not the fear of making mistakes, but the determination not to make them—that and trying to get Poppy to say "good job" at least once.

That morning after the boxes, I continued the routine by asking Steve for the list of items he and Nick needed. "Anything from the basement?" I asked.

He turned to me and said, "Onions, potatoes, carrots, salt, sink." He was still on a one-word-at-a-time basis with me.

After getting the veg and salt and then half-carrying, half-dragging the bag of potatoes, I made my way slowly toward the pile of pots and pans by the sink. I rolled up my sleeves and got to it. But

I was only a pan or two into the stack when Poppy called to me. He needed me up front right away. So, shaking the soap off my hands, I rushed up front.

Poppy was behind the counter waiting for me. "Today, I need you to be a cook," he said. "Just pancakes and toast. I'll do everything else. You ready?"

I was still rolling my sleeves down and just nodded. I had serious doubts—I had never really cooked anything before—but there was no way I would say no. I fixed my apron and moved toward the right side of the griddle. From there, I could see that Aunt Bessie was sitting in the family's corner booth with her feet up. I turned to Poppy and he told me that grandma was coming to pick Aunt Bessie up and that she couldn't work today.

I wondered what had happened, what was wrong. But, Poppy didn't let me hesitate for long. "Okay, to make the pancakes you use this ladle." He then showed me how to dip the ladle into the high, narrow metal bowl, to jerk the ladle at the top of the bowl to spill off excess batter, and then how to pour the batter onto the griddle in a quick upward motion. "Make a few just for me," he said and walked away.

I watched as Poppy started waiting on the tables. There were only a few customers, but soon the morning rush would begin and the tables would fill up. I turned back to the griddle and laid down my first pancakes. The first one was too small, the second was decent, and the third was so big that I had to use the spatula to stop the mix from running too far across the griddle.

"Don't burn them," Poppy said, leaning over the side of the counter. I checked the first pancake and it was already firm enough for me to slide the spatula under it. I gently flipped it over. It was a perfect golden brown. Even if it was a little small and it wasn't exactly a disk, it wasn't bad. The second one was pretty much the same, but the third was a mess: it was big and thin, and it broke apart as I tried to flip it. I grabbed a plate from the shelf to the left of the griddle, as I had seen Poppy do so many times before, and put the first two pancakes and the two halves of the third one on it.

Poppy was talking with Aunt Bessie when I put the plate on the counter. He saw the plate and smiled. "Do it like this one or this one," he said when looking at the plate, "not this one." He then put the plate on Aunt Bessie's table—not so that she'd eat them, but so that she too could see my first pancakes—and came back behind the counter.

"Try to make every one like those two good ones," he said, "and make an extra one, in case one burns or falls apart." He then cracked two sets of two eggs (two in each hand, at the same time), moved some bacon onto the hot side of the griddle, and told me to put down four slices of white bread. The toaster was on the other side of the counter (near the swinging door to the kitchen), as it was usually the waitress's job to make the toast.

Poppy called for me to make an order of pancakes for the first time when my grandma walked in. "Three good ones," he said and walked toward the booth where Aunt Bessie was sitting. I smiled at my grandma and then laid down four pancakes that were almost exactly identical. They were perfect, except when I finally flipped them they had burned a little. I hadn't paid close enough attention because I was watching Poppy lift Aunt Bessie out of the booth and carry her to grandma's car. Whatever was wrong with her feet seemed serious.

I put down four more pancakes, none of which was as perfect as the last set, but they all came out fine. I tossed the worst one into the garbage and handed Poppy the plate of three when he returned. In a fluid motion, he took the plate from me, put four slices of bacon on it, a dab of butter on the pancakes, and then put the plate in front of a customer, a guy who was reading a newspaper at the counter.

That was probably the last time I watched Poppy, because after that the orders started coming in quickly. He was everywhere at once. I'd hear him call out for more toast from a table and then moments later ask me for the two pancakes that I was working on. Two orders of toast, four orders of pancakes, four toast, two pancakes, six toast, four cakes—until he was just pointing toward the toaster or the griddle and saying a number. I ran back and forth trying to get it all done, and trying not to run into Poppy.

Some toast burned, some pancakes stuck, but most of the orders got done in time. When Poppy finally called out the last two pancakes, I started to relax. I flipped the last set as Poppy put his hand on my shoulder. He just stood there and watched me work for a moment. "You did good today," he said. I looked up at him and he was smiling. His thick eyebrows seemed to have grown heavy. "This is for you," he said. I wasn't sure what he meant, but then I remembered how on the first days that I worked with him he told me that one day I'd take over the diner. I smiled and turned to remove the pancakes from the griddle.

It was Tuesday night when our parents sat us down at the kitchen table. I had heard my mother crying earlier that evening, and I expected them to tell us that something bad had happened with Aunt Bessie. I thought about Poppy carrying her out of the diner. There must have been something very wrong with her feet and indeed there was. But as I stared at my hands spread out on the fake-wood Formica table, that's not what my dad talked about.

Poppy had been taken to the hospital earlier that day and his condition was very serious. I wish I hadn't thought about it at the time, but what would happen with the diner was one of my first questions. Olympia would be closed until Poppy got out of the hospital. But Andrew George Psaltis died two weeks later and the diner never opened again.

At the funeral, the one thing I remember the most is what Aunt Bessie told me. I could see that she had trouble walking as she slowly moved up the aisle toward the pew where I was seated in the back of the Greek Orthodox church. I never thought she and Poppy were close, but when she sat next to me I could clearly see her face was crumpled in grief. When she talked, she spoke softly and without the toughness she always exuded.

Most of what she said I just didn't hear, but I remember her telling me how I was lucky to have had the chance to work with Poppy. She told me about how the guy I replaced had always given her a hard time. He had worked at Olympia for years, while Steve did the work I later did, and Poppy knew that he would be hard to replace. But one day Bessie and this other guy had a violent argument and Poppy realized that he had to get rid of one of them. Bessie was the expendable one: she was having trouble working because of her feet and it would be easy to hire a new waitress. Poppy was very angry, but he didn't think there was a choice. He got rid of the other guy for her sake. "It was for me," she said, "but it turned out that it was for you."

This was meant to make me feel better, but it didn't. I did appreciate having had the chance to work with Poppy. People often say that you're born into the life of a cook and I was indeed "born with a greasy spoon." But seeing what it had done to Poppy and watching Aunt Bessie have such difficulty walking away (both figuratively and literally), I was learning that this could be a rough life.

Chapter 2

Hunger

With no need for me to work anymore, I was back to a life of school and sports, which meant primarily football and lacrosse. Most of the school year was filled with games or practices. I coasted along, focusing on sports, not academics. During the summer before my senior year in high school, as a linebacker and lacrosse goalie, I was supposed to spend my time getting bigger, but staying quick. That was the story for most of my teammates. They would spend a lot of their summer vacation training hard, but I had always been big and not because of working out or lifting weights. I got my size from my genes and from the food that I grew up on.

My mother grew up a third-generation Jew in the Bronx, though she tells everyone Queens, where she moved when she was a teenager. When Poppy died, my mother was as devastated as my father. She had lost her own father when she was young and Poppy was in many ways a father for her. Understanding why they got along was easy: they were both volatile—except she saved all of her explosiveness for protective purposes. Once she went head to head in a verbal confrontation with one of my lacrosse coaches, a solid athlete, and left the man cowering. My dad was always the calm, reasonable one; she was the enforcer. When they had a problem with a store, she'd wait in the car while he went in to try to solve it, but if he failed, she would be released in full fury. It could be about almost anything and she'd win. When it was about one of her kids, the outcome was never in doubt. She would do anything for us.

My mother's cooking was simple and repetitive. I wasn't raised a gourmet, eating exotic or expensive foods and trying all kinds of new things. But we did eat well and there was always more food than we could eat. We never ran out of Kalamata olives and often had other Greek food like halava and (after my grandmother would visit) dolmades—stuffed grape leaves—and pastitsio, a macaroni dish resembling lasagna. And we had bagels, knishes, and other Jewish food, like matzoh and matzoh ball soup and latkes and lox and whitefish. Beyond that, my mother kept us on a steady routine that consisted mostly of roasted chicken on Monday, pasta on Tuesday, Chinese takeout on Wednesday, leftovers on Thursday, pizza on Friday, pork chops or chicken again on Saturday, and always steak on Sunday. Most meals also had a heated frozen vegetable or baked potato, and we lived on bagels, Jewish rye, and pumpernickel. Sometimes there was a meatloaf night or the rare taco night—those were the meals that I looked forward to, mostly because it meant no roast chicken for the week.

People cook professionally for many reasons. I suspect that most do because it was just a choice they happened upon or because it was better than doing something else. The great chefs tend to cite a passion for cooking (often stemming from a parent) or say it was because they always wanted to please people. For me, it all started and ended with my love of eating.

Besides working relentlessly for even the slightest sign of approval, I developed a serious love of food from working at Olympia. Not so much a love of cooking, as I only had one short day of actual cooking in the whole time I worked there, but a love of eating. The more I worked there, the more I looked forward to eating during my breaks, if I had time, and always when I was done for the day. It was just like the times we'd go to Poppy's house and he'd cook anything we wanted. I could choose anything, which I could never do at home.

I never really understood why Poppy kept me working at the diner well after he no longer had the urgent need for an extra pair of hands that allowed a ten-year-old to get the job in the first place. But, for my part, I kept going back because I wanted to please Poppy and to eat what I wanted. I loved to eat and I wasn't alone.

My brother Mike had always been a great eater. We are twins but have always looked nothing alike, especially when we were young. He had blond hair as a kid and has blue eyes; I have dark-brown hair and brown eyes. He was always thin, while I was always one of the bigger kids. Aside from the watermelon-eating contests my sister Jen and I had (which, for the record, I never lost), I rarely tried to eat as much as I could. Mike almost always did. When we were twelve years old, many of our summer nights were spent watching *Honeymooners* reruns and seeing who could make the best ice-cream sundae. Mine were better, because at least they didn't quickly dissolve into a sloppy mess, as Mike's did. He would always come up with these monstrous sundaes in a big glass bowl with walnuts, M&M's, peanut butter, chocolate syrup, whipped cream, and virtually anything else that he could add. Of course we had to eat what we made, and most nights when I had finished enjoying my much simpler sundae, I'd look over to see him still working on his, like a skinny white pig at a trough.

Mike also played lacrosse, but he tore his knee up in our sophomore year in high school. After that, he started spending his time on other things, like seeing Grateful Dead shows. Since most of my time was involved in sports in one way or another, we just weren't around each other a lot. But that summer, when my favorite leisure activity became eating out, he was a natural teammate. Since he was not able to play on the lacrosse team anymore, his sport was now eating. But, while I certainly bulked up some over the summer (got bigger, stayed quick: mission accomplished), he stayed skinny.

Besides Mike, Marc Arner—one of our best friends—also went with me to our first no-parents/no-limits meal. We went to the Dragon Gate, a Chinese restaurant in downtown Huntington. We had gone there before with our parents, but we'd never taken ourselves out to eat there, or anywhere else, before. This wasn't just a slice of pizza or a burger; this was a full-blown restaurant meal. The restaurant was all black, gold, and mirrors. Stuck between a stationery store and deli, it was a somewhat narrow restaurant with a few tables in the front, a small bar, followed by a group of five or six tables, and then a slightly raised dining level in the back, which had four tables in it.

We went late in the afternoon and the restaurant was empty. It was a last-minute decision, and we were dressed no differently than if we were going to DiRamio's, one of our favorite pizza joints. Arner, who we met in Hebrew school and who would end up owning a restaurant sooner than anyone else I knew, had on shorts and Teva sandals. His hair was a messy Afro, which was how it always was if it wasn't a tight buzz cut.

Mike and I weren't dressed much better than Arner, and it seemed obvious that the waiters doubted that we'd order much or be able to pay for what we ordered (or both). But we ordered the same way we would have if we were with our parents, and then some: egg drop soup with wontons, fried dumplings, pork fried rice, General Tso's chicken, spare ribs, shrimp with broccoli, and egg rolls. All of the dishes were served family style and each plate had enough for at least two people.

Because we were the only ones in the restaurant, the waiters were standing right near us the entire time—bringing the next dish, filling up water glasses, but mostly just watching us. Typical of waiters at these Americanized Chinese restaurants, our waiters were polite, with an obvious but reserved disdain.

The food was great and it kept coming. We were eating at a very quick pace, as though in a zone. Holding our chopsticks tightly like long, thin shovels, we were simply tearing through the food as it arrived and were barely talking at all. I don't think any of us stopped for anything more than a sip of hot tea or Coke until Mike ate a little pepper by mistake. His face turned red and then he downed his water, and then mine and Arner's. He had sweat on his forehead and was still coughing—and I was still laughing—when the spare ribs arrived. Then we all got back to work.

It was a feast that we'd all remember, but not just because of the great food and not just because it was the first major meal on our own dime. When we were just about done with all of the food that had once filled the table, I distinctly heard one of the waiters turn to the other and say, "Devour, devour!" We all heard it and we all stopped eating.

Then Arner asked, "Did he say 'devour, devour'?" and the three of us laughed. We didn't know how to take this, but I think we all imagined what we must have looked like. Freedom can be ugly, and it would take us a long time before we learned what moderation meant.

Of course once that summer ended Mike and I were back to our family's dinner table and the routine that we'd known all of our lives. But, as school and sports took over again, I started trying food my parents would never even contemplate, like beef patties at bodegas, White Castle hamburgers by the armload, and (eventually) sushi.

A few years later, when Mike moved to Colorado to take an easy sophomore year at Colorado State University, I joined him. I had returned to Huntington, after a short stint at Ohio State University before I realized that college wasn't for me, and was working at a place called Uncle Geoff's Pizza. Geoff was our good friend's uncle and he made some of the best pizza I've ever had. He looked like a young, hippie Santa Claus, but he had a temper. He was big and round and generous, except not always jolly. He made pizzas like potato au gratin or buffalo chicken or steak with Lea & Perrins sauce. Not typical New York pizza slices—and probably blasphemous to some—but most of them were delicious, and they were always made with the best possible ingredients.

But Geoff was a terrible businessman. Except for the plain slices, he couldn't possibly charge as much for a slice as it cost him to make it. And he was living as though he was a big success before his place had any legs underneath it. He was doing great things as far as pizza goes, but his shop was bound for failure.

After Mike had been in Colorado for a few months, he managed to rent a brand-new house and had a job waiting for me if I wanted it. Mike and I had driven out to Colorado together the year before and really liked it out there, despite staying in Greeley, a town filled with fast-food joints, cow pastures, and one of the country's biggest slaughterhouses. It wasn't the mountain town we thought it would be. But Mike was now out in Fort Collins (a big suburb in the foothills) and a few of our good friends were out there too. Laura, a high school friend who always seemed too nice to be a New Yorker, was now living in Fort Collins, and she did a solid job convincing me that I'd love it too. So, without much going on for me in Huntington, I decided to head out west.

Within the first week out in Colorado, I started working at Gibb Long's bagel shop. I worked in the back, baking the bagels, which meant getting there at an inhuman time in the morning. But I got used to the schedule easily enough, especially since it meant having most of the day and every night off. It was a great place to work, but after a few months I realized that this job wasn't really different from what I had left in New York (except the stench of imminent disaster was replaced with the warmth of growing success).

On my last day at Gibb's, I pulled my hand-me-down minivan to a stop behind the bagel store and looked out at the foothills while the engine banged twice more before quitting. There was a big empty field behind the store that seemed to stretch all the way to the mountain range that sits between Fort Collins and the Great Divide.

Gibb Long was an East Coast transplant. He was from New Jersey, but the store was called Gibb's New York Bagels—authentic New Jersey just isn't a strong selling point. But Gibb did study in one of New York's oldest bagel shops before coming out west, and, admirably, he was trying to bring real New York bagels to cowboy land. Like Uncle Geoff, he was a reformed hippie and he was committed to making something he could be proud of, but he was a better businessman and dedicated to making his place a success.

Bagels weren't a big part of Gibb's life until he decided to move to Colorado and realized that was one of the big things they were missing there. His timing was perfect. Colorado was just beginning to figure out what a bagel was, and his shop was greeted as a novelty by the natives and enthusiastically by the transplants from California and back east.

In a town and state where a roll with a hole could pass for a bagel, Gibb could have just made decent bagels by simply baking them, as most places do, but instead he wanted the real thing. His system was to boil and then bake (on burlap, which was probably not entirely health code–compliant but definitely produced a better bagel), the way he had learned in New York.

When I walked into the fluorescent-lit kitchen that morning, Gibb was already in his office and he saw me come in. "Hey, brother," he called out. I nodded a good morning and tied on an apron. The kitchen was a huge square. It had a tile floor, white walls, a walk-in with a thick metal door, and a big commercial mixer to one side. There was a lot of open space, but most of it would fill up throughout the day with the six-foot-high metal racks that held trays of dough. Of course the biggest piece of equipment in the kitchen was the large conveyor oven, which was like the pizza ovens I was used to but with stone shelves that kept rotating around in a circle.

A few minutes later, Shawn stumbled through the back door into the bright kitchen with a hand over his eyes as if he were under attack. He was about five foot seven with messy brown hair and sideburns that ran down his cheeks but stopped short of forming a beard with his goatee. Shawnie Shortbread (as Gibb called him, because he made the shortbread each day) was twenty years old, a year older than me, and had been working at Gibb's since it opened six months earlier. He was by nature a screwup, and most of his hard work only served to balance out his mistakes: he got himself to work even earlier than he had to, but almost always fell asleep after parking the car.

I turned on the bagel cutter—to get the motor warm—then went over to the table where the proofed dough was. It had been kneaded in the machine the night before and then covered with Saran Wrap. I took one of the knives and made a lengthwise cut into the slab of dough, and then wrestled a long strip of dough free. These long pieces were then rolled out and cut into more long strips until they were the right size to go through the cutter. The pieces of dough would begin to resemble a bagel when they were spit out of the cutter.

After we cut all of the dough into strips, the bagel cutter would run continuously, and I would stretch each bagel—a counterclockwise turn with the thumb and first two fingers inside the hole—and then lay the uncooked bagels on trays. We did the same thing each morning, and by now we did most of this work on autopilot, before either of us was fully awake. This just started the process and got us to the point where Shawn would begin working the kettle, flash boiling the bagels that I laid out on the trays. After Shawn began the boiling, I stacked up enough of the trays of uncooked bagels to keep him busy for a while and then started taking back the boiled bagels and laying them out on wooden two-by-fours to be baked. I had finished placing bagels on the third wooden plank when Gibb came up to me.

"So, this is the day?" he asked. He looked tired and his round glasses were smeared with flour. He had on one of the white Gibb's New York Bagels T-shirts, which was a little too tight. He wasn't a big man, but making bagels every day was keeping his arms muscular. "We hardly knew you and we're already missing you." He gave me a look of utter sadness, but I knew that he was just giving me a hard time.

"You'll still have Shawn," I said and laid the last bagel on the fourth wooden plank, brushed all of them with the water-and-oil solution, and sprinkled them with sesame seeds. Then I turned them all over and sprinkled sesame seeds on the other side.

"That and another deadbeat friend from out east, and I'll be all set," he said. I put the four finished planks onto the next rack in the turning conveyor oven. Every rack would fit four wooden planks, and now that Gibb was helping me place and seed the bagels, we'd start filling up the oven quickly.

"What's that, Gibb?" Shawn yelled over the din of the bagel cutter's engine, but didn't stop fishing out the boiled bagels.

"Shawnie Shortbread, you know we love you, bra'," Gibb yelled back with a California surfer accent and flashed him a thumb and pinkie wave. Turning back to me, he asked, "So, where you heading? CooperSmith's?" and handed me a wooden plank with more sesame bagels.

"Yeah, the kitchen in their pub. I got a line job."

He nodded. "They have good beer. I like their Horsetooth Stout. I didn't know they served food." He must have known, though, as CooperSmith's was one of the most popular restaurants in downtown Fort Collins.

"Good artichoke dip," Shawn yelled out. Gibb just smiled at me, as if to say, "We're just ribbin' you, bra'," and we kept working on loading up the oven. As the bagels started to bake, a great aroma began to permeate the air. Later in the day I'd hate that I couldn't get the smell off of me or my clothes, but all morning I enjoyed it. This smell was second only to biting into a golden-brown bagel with a crunchy outside and an inside that was still steaming and very moist. I looked forward to that first bagel of the day all morning and would crack one open as soon I took a break.

I was behind the counter up front, smearing cream cheese onto an everything bagel when Mike came in. The front of the shop had a huge L-shaped counter that began near the front door with a glass case of deli meats and prepared salads and led to two side-by-side registers and then, turning the corner, to a large bagel case. There was a short wall between the counter and the dining room that helped to keep the customers in a single line. The dining room had at least seven tables and was carpeted. The whole place was at least twice the size of a typical bagel store on Long Island.

Mike had been working at Gibb's since they first opened and was essentially the manager of the front. Mike had one of the black Gibb's New York Bagels T-shirts on that morning and had his long, messy hair tied behind his head. He was in full Colorado mode: re-laxed, carefree, and grungy. Along with the farmers and conservatives, the state had attracted legions of grungy freedom lovers. But, like a corked wine aging, the good hippie virtues had soured, and commercialism and selfishness were rampant. (I'll always remember watching a street beggar in Boulder walking with a full handout cup to his nearby Jeep Cherokee with snowboards mounted on top.) The hippie enclaves spread from Boulder to many of the mountain towns and into Fort Collins, and Mike fit right in, though he broke the mold a bit by actually going to school and working for his money.

He was the first counterperson in that day and got to work on his first job right away, his breakfast: a hot poppy-seed bagel with cream cheese and slices of tomato. He had his priorities.

Mike was actually really good at his job—at working under the stress of a line that ran out the door and at making sandwiches. He even had his own sandwich named after him: Mike's Sun-Dried Tomato Sandwich, which was a sesame bagel with one side smeared with hummus, stacked with tomatoes, sprouts, onions, and a little mayo and the other side smeared with sun-dried tomato spread and mozzarella cheese and then toasted and stacked on top of the other half. It was an odd combination that worked well.

While his sandwich was popular and he enjoyed working at Gibb's, it was also clear that Mike treated the job, and everything else about being out in Colorado, as a break from reality. He would eventually get serious and go back east to finish school. For me, Colorado was also a break from reality, but I wasn't as certain of what I'd return to until I started working at CooperSmith's.

CooperSmith's Pub & Brewery was not really like any of the restaurants I grew up eating at. It was a small brewery with two buildings (one a pool hall and the other a pub) right in the middle of Old Town Square. They brewed several different kinds of beer, like Not Brown Ale and Punjabi Pale Ale, and root beer. The pub was all dark wood with yellow lights. It was in the shape of a long shoe box with high ceilings and glass doors that opened on both of the short sides of the building. CooperSmith's was often packed with people, at the bar or at tables in the dining area. The open kitchen served an eclectic menu of mostly pub food, things like hamburgers and bison burgers, Caesar salads and burritos, beer and beer floats made with a midnight-dark stout with a scoop of a local ice cream. They sold T-shirts downstairs.

It was a popular place and had at least a dozen people working in the kitchen at all times. I wasn't carrying potatoes up from the basement all day, but I wasn't given many responsibilities either. My main job for the few weeks that I worked there was the bangers and mash. I would watch over a kettle of sausages simmering in Horsetooth Stout and prepare mashed potatoes. Even though I wasn't doing much cooking, it felt good to be back in a kitchen. It wasn't that I loved every day or even the particulars of what I was doing; but when my first week was over, I knew that I would always work in a kitchen.

I had spent time in one other restaurant kitchen between Olympia and CooperSmith's, but it was in a chain diner during the few weeks I stayed in Greeley. The place was run by a formula that had gone awry: tried and true, and disgusting. Their kitchen ethics weren't great. But even though I didn't feel right about things like running the deep-fry oil under pancakes to stop them from sticking, I enjoyed working through a service as part of the kitchen team—the rush to get many things done at once and at the same time try to make everything perfect. In the much cleaner world of CooperSmith's, doing work that was even simpler, that's what I enjoyed the most.

I was enjoying being in Colorado, but I had figured out what I wanted to do and was now ready to do it. It was time to return to my reality: New York and the kitchen life. After a couple of months of working at CooperSmith's, I packed up my minivan and headed home. Mike followed behind me in his car on what was a rough trip: my minivan had problems partway through Kansas; Mike's car blew a tire while in the middle lane of a highway; and, finally, my minivan gave up in Queens, less than an hour from Huntington.

I don't know if my love of food made me want to work in a kitchen or if working in a kitchen made me love food, but either way I was certain that cooking was what I'd do for the rest of my life. It was good to be home. I had finally found direction, but I still didn't know how difficult that road was going to be.

Chapter 3

From Chopped Liver to Foie Gras

A potato knish is already in the microwave, so the next one has to wait. Two slices of Swiss cheese follow the small mound of sauerkraut that gets placed on top of the slices of corned beef heating up on the griddle—the slices of rye bread are still in the toaster. A quarter pound of chicken salad is needed to accompany the small green salad and the Diet Coke that has already been drunk. Smoked turkey on a roll with oil (no mayo) and tomato and lettuce is up next, followed by an egg salad with light (just a little, not low-fat) mayo on toasted white bread and then a soup-and-salad special. By the time the Reuben and knish are wrapped up and rung up, the line has replenished itself. I take another few orders before rushing back to take the next knish out of the microwave and pull the white bread before it burns.

This is the mad scramble of Frockles during the hour-and-a-half lunch rush. It was a relay race of taking orders, cooking the orders, and ringing them up—and I sprinted through all segments as a team of one. Most days I was the only one working at the small deli in the Katharine Gibbs office building on Melville Road. John, the only other employee, was more of a sometimes worker and rarely worked during the big rushes. He had a lot of problems with his feet and couldn't spend long periods of time behind the counter.

When John did come in, he had a rule that he stuck by: first he had a cup of coffee, then he sat down and relaxed, and then he got to work. Of a dozen tables that were spread throughout the spacious dining room, he always sat at the table closest to the counter, so that he could yell to me things he read in the paper. At sixty-plus years old, he only worked in short bursts, but he did a good job (even though he never stopped talking) and considered the task of keeping me motivated to be his primary responsibility. In the middle of a conversation, he'd interrupt me to say, "Look at the clock," and then a few minutes later he'd interrupt the conversation again: "See that, the clock keeps moving, the clock doesn't wait for you, nothing waits for you."

Coming back from Colorado, I didn't know how to get into a kitchen, but ended up running one. Of course Frockles wasn't exactly what I had in mind. It was just a simple deli on the ground floor of a vocational school, but it was good to me. I was getting paid well and learning how to handle a rush of orders. Although I mostly worked alone, my friends would drop in frequently. I was back together with my high school girlfriend, Nora, who came in at least a couple times a week—and usually with her friends.

Besides Nora, one of my oldest friends, Kirby, was there all of the time. Like a squashed Michelin Man with his tires deflated, there was a lot of Kirby but very little of it stood higher than the counter, which he'd walk behind even when the room was filled with customers. He ordered the same thing every day: roast beef and a Yoo-Hoo. When John wasn't sitting at his table reading the paper and yelling out the latest news, Kirby was. While he talked, I cooked. It was rare that anyone would come in to order anything after lunch, so this was my time to experiment with recipes I'd recently read (in hand-me-down cookbooks like *The New Basics*) and to be creative with the next day's special. I suspect that I surprised at least a few people with some of the specials—like butternut squash soup—and I in turn was surprised when people ordered them.

Even though I was back to living in my parents' house, I wasn't saving a penny. My money was being spent on Nora and food, and not much else. While Mike was off at college, I took over the room he and I had shared growing up and set it up as a (rent-free) apartment, complete with a TV and couch. Nora was a constant fixture in the room. She was a natural book lover, and with her short brown hair and narrow rectangular glasses, she looked like a young librarian. Most of our time was spent with her curled at one end of the couch reading a novel and me at the other end reading a new cookbook or watching shows like *The Frugal Gourmet* on PBS. And, if I wasn't in the room or bumping my mom out of the kitchen, I was out eating or food shopping. I had loved food all my life, but now I was figuring out how to enjoy it. Gone were the requests for my dad to make my steak super well done. Now I was cooking the steaks for myself and was learning quickly that steak tasted better when it wasn't blackened. I also learned that the greatest evil, according to my mom—salt—worked wonders. If I wasn't shy with the salt, the steaks I grilled would come out crispy and taste even better.

I had become entirely absorbed by cooking and eating. Even the vacations I took were now just long versions of going out to eat. The first such trip was with Nora in my nearly decade-old minivan. We went to visit some of her friends in New Orleans, the deep-fry capital of the world. We took the trip with his-and-hers purposes: to eat and drink in the Big Easy for a weekend. While Nora had the look of a librarian, it was most often the look of a librarian who had finally cut loose. We were a good team: she handled the drinking while I took care of the eating, mostly at an oyster bar, where I hit the limit on raw oysters.

My trip with Mike to Memphis had a different focus, the World Championship Barbecue Cooking Contest, which is part of the Memphis in May International Festival. We went to Memphis for an all-out barbecue weekend and we got it. From the rows of barbecue setups that stretched along the Mississippi River as far as I could see to the barbecue restaurant in an alley behind our hotel that filled our room with a constant smoky pork aroma, we were engulfed by barbecue. The weekend was a taxing lesson in overconsumption. I doubt I could have eaten one more rib or pulled-pork sandwich by the time we left Memphis, but as soon as I was back in New York I was thinking about barbecue again.

The Howard Stern show is on as I'm cleaning squid for frying and then cooking and cleaning shrimp for the shrimp cocktails. Then Ron has Rush on while I'm scrubbing oyster shells and clamshells and pulling the beards off mussels. He has the Grateful Dead on while I'm preparing a tub of salad, making Caesar dressing, and filling a bin with shaved parmesan. The Yankees game is on when I'm preparing the hamburger station with patties, sliced tomatoes, lettuce, and onions. In between each of these tasks, I stop for a few minutes to crush ice.

This was a day of prepping at LaMotta's, a seafood restaurant on the north shore of Long Island (a little more than half the drive from Huntington to where Olympia once stood). From Frockles to LaMotta's was a big step: I'd gone from a deli in an office building on a main road in Melville to a line job at LaMotta's Waterside Restaurant on Manhasset Bay in Port Washington. Besides the much-improved setting, after several months of working in a deli, I was back in a real restaurant.

In 1992, three years earlier, LaMotta's had opened on the docks at the head of Manhasset Bay. The spot had once been just a snack bar with a giant red-and-white canopy, which had been built for and taken from the World's Fair site in Queens in 1964. Now LaMotta's was a full-blown restaurant specializing in "American cuisine with a global influence," but most people still sat under the giant canopy. Beyond the flags of the world that circled both the outside and inside, the global influence meant that they served seafood but with Italian, French, and other accents. I had grown up eating seafood, like steamers with butter and fried clams, but a fancy seafood restaurant was never part of my family's dining equation. Parts of LaMotta's menu were completely foreign to me. From opening an oyster to pulling the plasticlike piece out of a squid when cleaning it, the learning curve was high. I had walked into LaMotta's with very little experience but was given a chance—even if it was just during the lunch service.

As I soon realized, I wasn't the only one hired with little or no experience. Most of the cooks in the kitchen were in the same situation. LaMotta's was a seasonal restaurant, open from March to October, so the staff turnover was high at the end of each season. Besides Ron, the chef, and Darrin, a cook who had worked the previous season, none of the other cooks had ever worked at LaMotta's before.

Ronbo, as we called Chef Ron Labo, was a serious cook who ran a seriously relaxed kitchen. The radio was on all the time. Ron was at least six foot two but couldn't have been more than 165 pounds. He was a longhair holdout and the human definition of "chill," even though he oversaw a big and busy restaurant and then went home to a wife and kid (and had another on the way). Ron was a hardworking cook, but for the most part a soft-spoken leader. He'd make sure that everyone's job got done, and he'd mostly laugh and enjoy the work. The only things Ron wouldn't tolerate were a lot of complaining or a cook with a big mouth; otherwise, he was entirely easygoing.

LaMotta's had both inside and outside dining areas. The deck dining area looked out to the marina and wrapped around the building. The last table on the deck was only a few feet away from the kitchen's back door. During the first few weeks, I spent a lot of time staring out that back door watching people enjoy themselves. I couldn't help but wish I was out there, too, eating steamers and drinking beer. But I'd pay a price for this daydreaming, on a busy Thursday afternoon during my third week on the job.

We were in the middle of lunch service and I was shucking oysters by the dozen, crushing ice to serve with them, and then back to shucking more oysters. I grabbed the first of a new dozen and laid it on the counter. The palm of my left hand pressed the oyster to the counter as the oyster knife in my right hand pushed and jerked its way into the shell's opening. It takes a lot of force to open an oyster shell and I'd gotten a lot of little cuts when I paid too much attention to a boat passing by or another rich girl sitting down for a midweek lunch.

As I'm opening the next oyster, I watch Ronbo at the grill. Darrin is helping him—and working the deep fryer—but they're buried in orders. It's an unusually busy Thursday afternoon, and true to form LaMotta's owner, Guy LaMotta (or GLM, as he calls himself), is on the scene. Whenever we are really slammed with orders, he comes into the kitchen to ask us to make him something special. This day he's coming in and out of the kitchen in his aviator sunglasses making sure his table gets whatever they want.

From what I can see, the outside deck is filling up with what looks like a college graduation party. There are several cute girls out there. Then I look down to see blood flowing around my hand. I don't feel much pain, but I can see a tear in the side of my left hand. It's a deep cut and I almost get sick looking at it. I rush over to the sink with a towel pressed to my hand. There's still no pain, but there's lots of blood. Chris, another cook, comes over to help me. Chris is almost always sweating and nervous during service. He gives me more towels and then yells to the chef that I cut myself. Ronbo looks over his shoulder quickly, but he barely has the time to make a grimace before turning back to the grill.

"It looks bad," Chris says. "You should probably get to the hospital."

I remove the towel and look at the cut. It's at least an inch long and deep, but the bleeding is starting to slow down. GLM comes up behind me and Chris disappears. "Let me see," GLM says and I show it to him. I don't know if he even looks at my hand before leading me out of the kitchen and toward the kitchen office. He starts searching around the office, looking, I assume, for the first-aid kit while I stand in the entrance waiting for him to tell me how to get to the hospital. Then he turns to me and takes my hand in his. He removes the towel and starts wrapping duct tape around my hand. He's taping my hand up tight. Around and around, he wraps the tape. I look at him to see if he's serious—his weathered face is expressionless. He keeps wrapping the tape around my hand. Then he stops and grabs my hand firmly. "How does that feel?" he asks.

I look at my hand, and twist my wrist back and forth. Besides the tape being a bit tight, it feels: "Fine," I say.

"Good, let's go back in there," he says, patting my shoulder and leading the way out of the office and into the kitchen. And I'm back to shucking the oysters, except now I have to catch up with the orders I'm behind on, and putting any force on my left hand hurts. I know there's no way to stop doing my job without walking out the door for good, but that's not even an option—actually that thought has never entered my mind. I made a mistake, but I'm definitely not going to quit because of it. The cut—and any pain that goes with it—is just incidental: a small complication to getting my work done.

After the lunch service died down, Ron surprised me by being mostly upset with GLM. While he warned me about being careful and told me to wrap a towel around my left hand instead of just using a bare hand when shucking, he didn't think duct tape was the best way to take care of the problem—even if I didn't need stitches and my hand would end up being fine. As I leaned against the deck outside of the kitchen, Ron smoked a cigarette and told me about the many times he'd gotten cut or burned. With the cigarette dangling from his mouth, he stuck his hands out to me. They were thick and rough—battle scarred. "You've got to remember," he said, "you're here to help the restaurant, but the restaurant isn't always here to help you. You have to take care of yourself, because sometimes no one else will."

I had taken the job at LaMotta's because it seemed to be as good a job as any other, plus I was moving out of an office building and onto a dock on a bay without even taking a pay cut. But I quickly realized that it would take more than just being there to ever really be a cook in LaMotta's kitchen. The clearest of all separations in most kitchens is between the cooks who are there to learn and to be a part of something and the cooks who are there just to work. I wasn't satisfied doing prep work all day, but I was sure that GLM would have been content if I had just clocked in, done that work, and left. That's mostly what I'd done at the other restaurants I'd worked in, but I wanted more. I wasn't there just to work.

I realized that if I wanted to cook there, I'd have to do more than check in and stare out the kitchen door. I was determined that when something was being done in the kitchen that I had never seen before, I'd be among the first to volunteer to help out. And if I got hurt because I wasn't paying attention, my distraction would be something in the kitchen—not a passing boat or beauty.

A few weeks later, pulling into LaMotta's parking lot in Nora's Nissan Maxima, I immediately caught Ron's attention. He was from West Hempstead and of even more modest means than I. As I caught up to him on his way into the kitchen, he said over his shoulder, "It's bad enough everyone I cook for drives a better car than me, now my cooks do too." It was still early morning, but it was June and it was already hot and bright out. I just squinted at Ron and decided to pass on the long explanation for the nice car.

When Ron and I walked into the kitchen, the radio was already playing. I washed my hands, tied an apron on, and got to work. With the faucet running water over clams in a large metal bowl, I started cleaning squid and then cut it into rings for frying. I'd been prepping and working lunch for the last two months, so most of my daily work had become routine. Almost every day, though, I figured out—or I was shown—a more efficient way to do one of my tasks. The list of items I needed to get ready each day had at least doubled since I first started, but I was getting the larger list done in about the same time. Simply knowing where to make a cut or at what angle to hold something increases a cook's productivity, and I was learning rapidly by watching one of the other cooks or just experimenting on my own— and sometimes Ron or Darrin would stop by my station to show me their way of doing something.

Getting my list done before lunch was my job, but it was no longer my goal. I'd get done with my prep work and then move on to help someone else. On this day, Chris was struggling and I helped him by portioning out the salmon for lunch and dinner. Just as I finished, the first orders of the day came in and immediately the kitchen was behind. Chris was still scrambling to finish his prep work when Darrin called out to him for the tray of cod fillets.

"Five minutes," Chris shouted, but I could see that he hadn't even begun to portion out the fillets. He started cutting the cod—his sweaty hands moving quickly to measure his cuts in fingers—while I helped him finish the rest of his prep work. He wasn't late this morning, but he'd been slow all day. More than ten minutes later, he rushed the cod fillets over to Darrin. The kitchen was already hectic, and so loud that I only saw Darrin mutter "five minutes" to Chris but didn't actually hear him say it.

More orders started coming in and waiters were constantly moving in and out of the kitchen. A row of tickets had lined up. We were all working as hard as we could to catch up.

I had two orders of oysters—a dozen each—plated and ready in minutes. That was followed by six Caesar salads and a house salad. Then I crushed ice for the next orders of oysters. Even through the noise of the ice crushing, I heard Darrin bang the bell—once, hard. "Pick up when the bell rings!" he yelled.

I kept my head down and shucked oysters, until Ronbo called out a shrimp cocktail. As soon as I had the shrimp order done, I had more salads to do. The orders kept coming in. It was just a typical busy Saturday lunch, but it didn't feel like we were winning the fight. The kitchen was hot, everyone was yelling, waiters and food runners were streaming in and out, and the pickup bell kept ringing. Then Darrin erupted again. He banged the bell over and over, at least ten times in a row. "Come on Steven, let's go," Darrin yelled at one of the waiters. He was just about throwing plates at waiters.

Then I saw why he was angry: there were several finished plates waiting for waiters and runners. We'd been pushing so hard to catch up that the kitchen was now moving too fast for the front of the house. We were in complete disarray. Ronbo turned to us and waved his hands toward the ground. He was motioning for us to slow down, trying to get us at a good pace.

Rhythm and pace are everything in a kitchen. When we're in sync with the front of the house, everything just flows: orders, cooking, and expediting. This was easily the most chaotic service I'd been a part of and Darrin's bell ringing made things worse. The loud, constant ringing just kept us all frantic.

Once the lunch service was finally over, I took a much-needed break outside the kitchen. The air wasn't much cooler than in the kitchen, but it still felt like a relief. I checked my watch and saw that I only had a half hour before I'd take off for the day. All I had to do was help clean up before I left. I was watching a motorboat coasting slowly toward the fuel dock when Ron walked up to me. He was a completely worn-out version of the fresh, energetic chef I had walked into work with that day.

"Have you seen Darrin?" he asked.

"No," I said, "but his apron is over there."

Ron looked over to the apron hanging off the deck and nodded. It was obvious that the bell had tolled for Darrin. "So, you're working tonight?" he asked through an exhale of cigarette smoke.

"Tonight?" I asked, pausing to think. I had never worked a dinner service and had plans to go out that night, which is why I had driven Nora's car to work that morning.

"I need someone to work the grill with me. Can you do it?"

This is what I'd been waiting for. It would be a challenge, but it was the opportunity I had worked hard for. I would stay and work the dinner service. First, though, I had something difficult I had to take care of: I had to call Nora to tell her the change in plans.

When LaMotta's closed for the season in October, I had no real direction and no leads. The only thing I knew was that I wasn't going back to working in a deli, a pizza place, or a bagel shop. I wanted something close to what I had at LaMotta's: a serious restaurant where I could cook. The problem was that none of the restaurants I knew of were on this level, and that also eliminated all of the chain restaurants that littered Long Island. So, I opened up the Long Island edition of *Newsday* and searched the classifieds. This was pretty much the only way I knew how to find a job, besides just knocking on doors, and I had knocked on the door of every restaurant I knew back when I landed the job at LaMotta's. There were plenty of ads for cooks in the classifieds and scanning through them I circled the one that sounded the most promising: Harrison Conference Center in Glen Cove. They were looking for a garde-manger cook for a busy kitchen and they offered pay that was at least as good as at LaMotta's.

I didn't know what garde-manger meant at the time, but the Harrison Conference Center fit all of the criteria I was looking for: it was a serious restaurant, I would be cooking, and I'd get paid well. But I knew almost immediately that I had made the wrong choice.

The Harrison's main function was to host business conferences, so the kitchen was responsible for large banquets. Working their garde-manger station meant preparing three cold and three hot platters for a few hundred people each day. This was a kitchen run like a corporation, and the only concerns were output and time: clocking in on time in the morning, producing the required six platters on time (without much concern for quality), and clocking out on time each day (to make certain that overtime never came into play). The Harrison served a whole lot of food in its banquet hall, but it wasn't very good food. Within just a few weeks I knew that this wasn't for me, so I decided to quit. I had narrowed my focus a little, but I would still have been directionless when I left the Harrison if it weren't for Jennifer, one of their sous chefs (the second highest position in the kitchen).

During my last week, Jennifer came over to me while I was taking a break. I was staring out one of the kitchen windows watching a man jackhammering into the sidewalk and thinking how even if I didn't want to work at the Harrison, I still had it easier than that guy. I knew before she even spoke that Jennifer would ask me about my plans. She wasn't the first Harrison cook to try to persuade me to stay, but this time I responded very candidly. I told her that while I might not know much about cooking, I knew that this wasn't the place for me to learn. I wasn't interested in cooking a great amount of food; I was interested in cooking great food. I realized right away that what I said probably sounded pretentious, and my delivery must have lacked conviction as I wasn't even sure what I wanted to do. I waited for her to tear into me—to tell me that I didn't know what I was talking about—but she didn't. Instead she seemed to understand what I wanted better than I did.

Jennifer had worked in restaurants all over the country, but first she had gone to culinary school for two years. After school, she worked at some of New York's best restaurants. Most of the restaurants were in Manhattan. She told me about how expensive the restaurants were and how much work went into each dish. And she told me how hard she worked—all day, for little pay—just for the chance to cook at a particular restaurant. It was the first time anyone had told me that they had cooked in a restaurant from early in the morning until late at night just to learn.

The work had been hard and unrewarding, though she had gotten through it and was a better cook because of it. Now she was where she wanted to be. She enjoyed her work and made a good living. She assured me that if I did as she had done, it would be a long, hard road that would eventually lead me right back to where I was. She had finally gotten to the point, trying to convince me to stay. After I left that day, I was upset that I had even listened to her war story. But the next day we talked again, and she loaned me cookbooks to show me what the food was like at the restaurants where she had worked.

These cookbooks weren't like any of the ones I owned. I came home that night, sat down on my couch, and told Mike to kill the TV. Mike was home from college (in Maryland) that weekend and he now stayed in what was once Andy's bedroom. Even so, he spent most of his time on the couch in my room—especially since Nora was rarely on the other end of the couch anymore. I opened one of the books and started flipping through it. It had beautiful pictures of food that looked better than anything I'd ever served or been served. Against clean white porcelain plates, the food was lined up or stacked up or otherwise arranged with intention. The food wasn't just on the plate; it was assembled on the plate. The dishes seemed too perfect to be real. The arching line of red pepper sauce, the bright-green soup, and the dots of mango sauce all looked like paint on a canvas.

I looked over at Mike, who was slowly turning the pages of one of the other books with the same sort of interest and amusement. These weren't cookbooks; they were art books. I thought about what these dishes must be like when they were served in a restaurant. It was obvious that more creativity and effort went into them than into anything we cooked at LaMotta's or anywhere else I'd ever worked. This was food art. I had never thought about food in this way before. By the end of the night, I understood two things: Jennifer had given me these books to open my eyes to a whole side of the restaurant industry that I knew nothing about, and this was the direction I was looking for.

Once the dough is proofed, I portion out thirty-gram pieces. Then I cup a hand over each piece and roll it in small circles on the metal prep table until it's a smooth round ball. Then I place the shaped dough onto a tray to proof again. After several trays have proofed, which takes at least an hour in the winter, I brush each piece with an egg wash and then sprinkle poppy seeds, sesame seeds, or onion onto them, except for the ones that will become plain rolls.

This is what I did each morning at Panama Hatties for the first few months; I made the rolls. I had gone from being the only cook at a deli to part of the line at a middle-of-the-road restaurant to the bottom of the kitchen at a very good restaurant. I had moved up in the restaurant world, but down in importance with each move.

Located in a nondescript strip mall on a main road in Huntington Station, Panama Hatties was about three miles from the house I grew up in, but I never knew it existed. In the mid-eighties, it had evolved from an ordinary pub into a fancy restaurant that was recognized by the restaurant critics at both the *New York Times* and *Newsday* as one of the best on Long Island. But it was never even a distant bleep on my family's radar. At Panama Hatties people were quiet, reserved, and formal. We went to places like the Ground Round, where they let you throw peanut shells on the ground. We didn't wear suits unless we were going to a wedding. And the only time I had ever seen caviar was in an episode of *Three's Company* when Jack crashed a ritzy party.

I found Panama Hatties by again searching the classifieds, but after the Harrison I had some idea of what I wanted. I didn't know what four stars meant in the Panama Hatties listing, but the brief help-wanted description claimed that this was one of Long Island's best restaurants and that was good enough for me.

My interview was about as short as possible. I met Ritchie Gertz, the manager, in the restaurant's entrance late in the afternoon. Ritchie was wearing sharp blank pants and a silver shirt. He was standing perfectly still but seemed impatient, as though he were leaning over the starting line for a race. He rubbed his jaw before shaking my hand and again before beginning a twenty-second speech that served as an introduction to Panama Hatties. I barely had time to notice the green marbled floors or the huge bouquet of flowers in the entranceway before Ritchie showed me through the dining room into the kitchen and out the door I would come through when I started working there. I didn't see much of the kitchen and didn't get to meet the chef I'd be working for. As he walked me around to the front of the restaurant where my car was parked, he told me that I'd be given a few days' trial and, if that worked out, I'd work five days a week, from early in the morning until late at night. We didn't even discuss the salary, but he assured me the pay wouldn't be great. Then he asked me if I could start the next day and that was the end of the interview.

When I entered the kitchen the next morning, I didn't know what to expect. As I walked in, I was greeted with the now-familiar smell of ammonia. It was only 8:00, but people were already working in the kitchen. I walked past the dishwasher's station on my right and a cook working feverishly at a station to my left. Just like at LaMotta's, there was music (classic rock) blaring. The kitchen was a tiny rectangle (probably thirty by ten feet) that may have been as small as La-Motta's but had a much higher ceiling. But there was barely any open space—every inch was filled with a table, a stove, a person, or a stack of supplies that nearly reached the ceiling. I immediately felt in the way as I scanned the room looking for the chef. All of the cooks were wearing the same stiff white jackets and aprons. I singled out a tall guy as the chef—he had short, spiky light-red hair and a beard that was shaved so close that it was barely a beard at all—partly because he looked the oldest and partly because he was giving another cook instructions.

Matt Hisiger was actually the sous chef. He shook my hand too firmly and then showed me around. It was a short tour that consisted mostly of pointing ("that's the dry storage, that's the pastry station") and concluded with him showing me the walk-in refrigerator, which was out the back door and stood alone in the back parking lot. He then gave me a jacket and an apron and told me to help out the garde-manger station (which had just one cook) with the bread. Every other restaurant I had worked in received bread in a big paper bag early in the morning, before any of the cooks got to work. Panama Hatties made their own bread, and my job this morning was to help make it.

When we finally took a break before the lunch service began, I stood outside and thought about how much work I had just done for such a small part of what the restaurant served. This wasn't a bakery. The bread at Panama Hatties was just an accompaniment to the meal—like the butter served with it—yet I had spent the whole morning working on it. As I watched the waiters, in black pants, white shirts, black ties, and black vests, march through the back door, it was clear that even the waiters were in a different league.

Just as I was about to go back into the kitchen a cook who looked about my age came over to me. "How's the first day going?" he asked. Kent Monkan was actually a year younger than me, but he had just graduated from the Culinary Institute of America and had been at Panama Hatties for two months. Monkan was an easygoing guy with a slow smile that never quite became a grin. As we walked back into the kitchen, he pointed out all of the cooks. There were eight in total, and most of them had culinary-school backgrounds or had worked in other serious restaurants. The only other young cook was Nicky Litterello, but he worked in pastry—a skinny guy working with sweets all day. And the short stocky guy who was working across from the dishwasher was the chef, Blake Verity.

Now that the bread was done, Matt told me to just watch the garde-manger cook during lunch and help him with anything he needed. The station was just a table with a portable electric grill. It was obvious that one of the priorities of the cooks in the cramped kitchen was to maintain a place to work and to stay out of the way of everyone else. I watched the cook set up many different containers of various sizes filled with things like mushrooms, thinly diced tomatoes, and vinaigrette. He was rushing to arrange the containers and didn't seem close to being ready for the lunch service. A few minutes later the chef was yelling out the orders. The music was off and everyone was serious—this wasn't LaMotta's at all.

Of course I didn't know any of the dishes they were serving, but even if I had, I doubt I would have understood what the chef was calling out. He called the orders quickly and did so without stopping his mad back-and-forth march from station to station. But the cook I was watching obviously understood and he reacted each time "lobster" was called out. He was already working on six different plates within minutes of the lunch orders coming in, and he was scrambling to keep up.

He turned to me and handed me a mango. "Slice it thinly, quickly," he said.

I put the mango down on the cutting board and reached for one of the station's knives.

"That's my knife," he said as I picked up a chef's knife that was on the table. I looked around for another knife but didn't see any. "Don't you have your own knives?" he asked, and then handed me his chef's knife. In every other kitchen I'd worked in there were always kitchen knives that everyone shared. I didn't even own any knives that would be good enough to bring to work. Looking around the Panama Hatties kitchen, I realized that not only were all of these cooks trained and experienced, but they were also serious professionals who brought their own tools with them to work. I began to feel daunted and started to doubt if this was the right kitchen for me after all. Then I watched the cook plate the lobster and mango salad. He used a metal ring mold with a three-inch diameter and carefully alternated thin slices of mango and lobster meat on the plate. He pulled the ring mold off and topped the round stack of mango and lobster with a perfect lobster claw. Then he passed the dish to the chef, who finished the plate by dribbling a yellow mango sauce around the mold and then took a towel and cleaned around the edge of the plate. The dish looked delicious; it looked perfect; it resembled the photos in Jennifer's cookbooks. I knew then I was in the right place.

A few days later, Ritchie offered me a full-time job, and I accepted it without even caring about the significant pay cut I was taking to work there. I had already decided I'd work at Panama Hatties, if given the chance, and then maybe I would go to culinary school a year later.

Pulling my newly acquired used red Chevy Corsica into the parking lot behind the restaurant, I thought about the sacrifices I had made and would have to make. I had given up a lot to work at Panama Hatties (five full days of nothing but work and for barely half the pay I received at LaMotta's), and I knew I'd have to give up even more, but I was prepared to do whatever was necessary to cook.

I had made one of my first major sacrifices for cooking one Saturday when my minivan refused to start as I was leaving my house to work at LaMotta's. I was left with no way to get to Port Washington. No one was around to give me a ride and the train would take too long. I had no options until Nora decided to help me out. I suppose she loaned me her car to make sure that I'd make it back from Port Washington in time for the party that her family was throwing that night. It was important to her that I come to the party, but she also didn't want me to miss work. It was very nice of her, but I never made it to the party that night. That was the night that Ron gave me a chance to work my first dinner service and going to Nora's party was the plan I had to cancel. The decision to work was the right one, but after that night not only was Nora not on the other end of my couch as often, she was also around a lot less in general. It was my first opportunity to cook at a serious restaurant, and I had made a decision I knew could mean losing someone I cared about. It was a necessary sacrifice and it wouldn't be the last one.

Chapter 4

Four-Star Cuisine
in a No-Star World

I drove the ten minutes it took to get from my parents' house to Panama Hatties under the light of streetlamps and left the restaurant under the same light. The only daylight I would see was during the short breaks the kitchen took or while rushing out to the stand-alone walk-in refrigerator. I was working more than I had ever worked before—fifteen or sixteen hours a day—but now I was dedicated to what I was doing. I wasn't just working because I had to and I never felt overwhelmed by the amount of work.

I was the lowest guy in the kitchen, since I had no experience cooking at this level and had no formal training. Within just the first few days, I saw ingredients like foie gras and caviar that I had never seen before, but the luxury products weren't the most significant difference between Panama Hatties and every other restaurant I had worked at. What Panama Hatties introduced me to was an entirely different approach, where presentation and attention to detail were as important as the right temperature for a piece of meat. I had cooked food before, but now I was part of a team that was presenting food to be admired as well as eaten. Aesthetics were as important as anything else.

Panama Hatties' cuisine was labeled refined American and indeed it was refined. The details for every dish—the precise placement and design of each dish—were more exacting than anything I'd seen before. We didn't just spill the contents of a pan onto a plate or roll food off a spatula and serve it. We hovered over each plate before it was sent out to the dining room. Every step was careful and there were often many steps to complete a dish. One of the signature dishes was foie gras with roasted apple chutney. It required sautéing apples, sautéing foie gras, making apple chutney, and then stacking the separate elements up into a small tower in the middle of a bright white plate. This dish called out to the diner in every way that it could, but especially with its vertical design and strong colors against a clean white background. Many of the dishes were like this and many had vibrant colors, either through the combinations of ingredients or with the addition of one of the many colored oils we used.

This was Blake Verity's food and this is what made the restaurant special. While he didn't own Panama Hatties, it was still Blake's place. He had been the driving force that turned Panama Hatties from a bar into a casual restaurant with food that outshone everything else and finally into a fine dining establishment. Blake was from Long Island and had gone to the Culinary Institute of America, and then worked in Manhattan at some of the city's best restaurants at the time, including Les Célébrités in the Essex House (a premier hotel on Central Park South). Les Célébrités ranked as one of the top restaurants in the country. It was run by Christian Delouvrier, a French chef, and the menu was composed mostly of classic French dishes.

When he returned to Long Island, Blake didn't set out to have an easy life and make money at a hotel or country club. He was out to prove himself. Most cooks would have taken what they'd learned while working in the city and just repeated it. But Blake hadn't made Panama Hatties into a fancy French restaurant; he made it into something that was truly his. Without following any formulas, he turned it into one of Long Island's elite restaurants: a highly acclaimed restaurant (four stars from *Newsday* and "extraordinary," the top ranking, from the Long Island edition of the *New York Times*) in an area with very few restaurants that even aspired to such a level. Blake had accomplished what he set out to do, partly because he was talented, but mostly because he worked incredibly hard.

All the way down the line—from Matt to Monkan and me, and even Nicky on pastries—we all followed Blake's example. He worked harder than any of us, while we only tried to match his efforts. But he wasn't all business. Blake was thirty-five going on eighteen with blond hair, a goatee, and some extra pounds. He was generally a cool guy who got along with everyone, and not just because he was the chef. He was funny and liked to joke around, and then could turn serious in an instant. The restaurant—or rather, the food that we served—was more important to him than anything else. His dedication made the people around him better cooks. He was the first chef I worked for who inspired the kitchen to work hard and to get everything right just by his presence.

There was an energy and a buzz in the kitchen that I had never experienced before. The cooks weren't just completing orders as quickly as possible. They were concerned about every particular and were genuinely proud of the food we were serving. After just a few days of working there, I was dedicated to the restaurant and to the chef. I quickly forgot about the sacrifices I'd made to be there and instead considered myself fortunate.

At the end of my first Friday night, I felt relief more than anything else. It had been my first night working the garde-manger station alone and I hadn't made any mistakes. I had even understood pretty much everything Blake yelled out. He walked very quickly from station to station during service and spoke even quicker.

During my "trial period" and first few days, I had worked on garde-manger with one other cook, but we wasted a lot of time because we were constantly trying to work around each other. There really was only room for one cook on the station. So, after I learned what I had to do, I became the only garde-manger cook and the other guy moved on to another station. Besides the bread, I was responsible for all of the restaurant's salads, canapés, and cheese plates. If I had to use an oven, I'd have to go to another station. And for some dishes I had to rely on another cook for one of the main ingredients, like the shrimp for the Thai Shrimp Salad. To help with the space problem, above my table were several rows of shelves almost as high as the ceiling. The first shelf was used for plates, the next one up had items I'd need for lunch or dinner service (like oils), the one after that had cooking tools (like spatulas), the next shelf had pots and pans on it, and the highest shelf was just for storage (since it was a bit of a climb to reach).

As I was cleaning up my table, Blake came over to me. He was sweaty and his face was flushed, even though his chef jacket was now halfway unbuttoned. He asked me how everything was going and what I thought—still speaking at the breakneck speed he used during service. I responded by asking him questions about some of the dishes. I didn't even think to answer his question about whether working there was working out for me, as I hadn't questioned that since my very first day. So, we skipped that question and got involved in a conversation about Panama Hatties' food. At first Monkan and a few of the other cooks were standing around with us and then it was just me and Blake. By the time we were walking out the back door, we were just talking, and not necessarily about food, though he was still talking quickly.

It was late (or very early in the morning) and a bit cold, but we stood outside talking. Blake was leaning back against his car. After a few minutes he spun the conversation 180 degrees. "Get out," he said. I paused without knowing how to answer him. His face looked weary. He ran the first knuckle of his right thumb across his goatee. "You should get out of kitchen work now while you're young," he went on. I listened as he warned me how hard the life was, how I wouldn't have a life outside of a kitchen, how I wouldn't know anyone but cooks, and I wouldn't even talk to anyone but cooks.

I didn't know how to take all of this. I had finally figured out exactly what I wanted to do and how I'd get that done. And I was at a place that would make that happen. Blake seemed sincere, though, even if it was obvious he was just telling me what he'd do if he were in my shoes. It wasn't the pat-on-the-back motivation that I probably could have used at the end of that night, but it also didn't lessen my own motivation at all. Cooking wasn't a choice for me. It wasn't a last option or a temporary solution. It had become my life.

I kept working at Panama Hatties, completely committed to doing the best job I could and learning exponentially. After six months, I finally got a chance to work on the line (at the meat station). Also, in addition to reading through the piles of cookbooks that were stacking up near the couch in my bedroom, I started going out to eat on the same level at which I was now cooking. I needed to learn more about food and eating was the most direct way. Besides, it was what I enjoyed doing.

Both Kent Monkan and Nicky Litterello were of a like mind. We were the young cooks at Panama Hatties. The three of us shared the same serious ambition to learn about cooking and to explore the food world. But there were very few Long Island restaurants where we could experience a meal similar to those we prepared at Panama Hatties (and going into the restaurant on one of my two days off was out of the question). So, we looked to Manhattan, where there were plenty of places to try.

On a Wednesday when Monkan and I were both off work (and I wasn't working at LaMotta's, which was how I was spending most of my days off during their season), we decided to head into the city for a meal. Monkan was also a Huntington product, and growing up he had about as much experience with fine dining as I had. Neither of us had much of a clue about the restaurants in the city. Several names had floated around the kitchen, but they were just names. So, flipping through the New York City *Zagat Survey*, I started near the beginning: Aureole.

We stood across the street from the brownstone that housed Aureole for a few minutes, waiting to go in. We were killing time, as we'd done for several hours already. Our reservation (the only one we could get that night) was at 10:30. We'd already had drinks at the Monkey Bar—with people who would have been our friends if we were ten years older and had an extra zero or two added to the end of our incomes—and had walked the seven blocks up Park Avenue as slowly as possible. Now, as the last few minutes ticked away before we could go in slightly early, we were staring through the two-story window that was the restaurant's facade. The main entrance and an upstairs dining room were clearly visible. Aureole was nestled into a piece of prime Upper East Side Manhattan real estate—a far cry from Panama Hatties' strip mall on Jericho Turnpike. We took a few more minutes just gazing through the restaurant's window.

As soon as we walked in, I was glad to at least have a sports coat on, even though it was Kelly green and wool. I was wearing khakis and a white button-down shirt. Monkan was dressed about the same, but with a blue blazer that was much more appropriate. We were welcomed warmly by the hostess and led to the upstairs dining room and to a row of tables. Monkan and I were both hovering around the six-foot mark, but I had him beat in the bulk department, so I let him navigate into the inside seat. We were squeezed between two tables, with couples that were, respectively, double and triple our age.

Aureole, as it turned out, was the perfect first choice for us. It served fancy, creative American food, which was essentially the definition of Panama Hatties' cuisine. Even though it was obvious to us that everything (and especially the service) at Aureole was even more refined than at Panama Hatties, this still gave us a good opportunity to see what being on the other end of the kitchen door was like and to understand why people doled out huge sums of money for the experience.

Stumbling out of the restaurant around 1:30 A.M., we were buzzing, and not from drinking (we could only afford one glass of wine each). We had had a great meal and, as we were walking back to my car, were immediately comparing it to the food we'd been cooking. We were confident that Blake's food was in the same league, but there was one inescapable fact: this was a much bigger stage. At Panama Hatties (as at most Long Island restaurants) the flow of customers was erratic. With the exception of Fridays and Saturdays, any given night could find the front of the house with only a few tables filled. And there was absolutely no late-night business. We had just left a restaurant that was still serving customers into the early morning hours in the middle of the week. It was clearly a more successful restaurant than Panama Hatties, but it had some of the same problems we had—like impossible-to-please customers who came just to be disappointed.

In the middle of a dinner service about a year after I first started at Panama Hatties, I had my first dish sent back. It was September 1996 and New York was unusually hot. The kitchen was always unbearably hot in the summer, so an Indian summer was not a welcome thing for us. That night it suddenly felt even hotter.

I was working on the meat station and a lamb dish was returned to the kitchen with the complaint that it was underdone. Blake was standing at the pass (a metal table with an eye-level shelf that stood between the door to the dining room and the rest of the kitchen) and took the plate out of the waiter's hand as soon as he heard the complaint. He picked up the cube of meat with his hand and squeezed it slightly. A drop of juice dripped onto the plate. All of the cooks were watching, especially me and the other meat cook. "It's fine," he said to the waiter. "How did they want it?"

The waiter looked as though he wanted to say the right thing but didn't know what that was. He knew that the obvious response of "cook it more" could make Blake explode. He shuffled his shiny black shoes and straightened his vest. Finally, Blake turned to me and handed me the plate. "Sear it hard," he said.

I took the meat off the plate with a spatula and handed it to the other cook, who put it in a sauté pan and threw it into the back of the oven (the hottest part). I discarded everything else on the plate and began to prepare the dish anew. Even though we had cooked the meat to the right temperature, we knew that it was our fault the guest had sent it back. Blake wasn't going to do anything about this, but we definitely weren't on his good side that night. And for the rest of the night all of the other cooks in the kitchen treated us like enemies.

On busy nights like these, there would be two cooks working on the meat station: one doing the actual cooking of the meat and the other plating. The job of the cook who was plating was to oversee what was being cooked when, to assemble the dish after the meat had been cooked, and to make sure that the station was running effi-ciently. It was the higher position and this was my role at the time, so this was also my mistake.

When I first moved onto the station, I was cooking the meat. Doing a good job meant listening carefully to the orders called out (always at a barely comprehensible speed) and focusing on timing. In the middle of a service, the entire grill would be filled with meat—everything from beef and chicken to venison and rabbit. It was defi-nitely high-energy cooking, both physically and mentally. My hands were constantly moving a spatula or cooking fork across the grill—checking and turning the meat—then I'd be crouching down to fin-ish a piece of meat (with a big tab of butter) in a cast-iron pan in the oven. At the same time, I had a running clock for every order in my head. When I was asked how long on something (like "How long on the chicken and rabbit?"), I'd have to be able to respond immediately with the minutes it would take before it would be ready. The cook who was plating (and Blake and possibly a cook who was expedit-ing—overseeing the flow of orders—that night as well) would rely on my responses. I also needed to be accurate because if the other meat cook had set up plates with all of the other elements that completed the dish (like the tiny tarts of onions and potatoes that accompanied the filet mignon), those plates couldn't wait very long for the meat. Every miscalculation of time on my part would have a domino effect throughout the kitchen and could ultimately impact not only how that one table was served, but the whole service. Small mistakes were a given and a few minutes either way could be made up, but too many small mistakes or a few big ones could be a disaster.

Now that I was plating for the station, I realized that the only way to make the station run smoothly was to be focused and organized. The prep work (or mise en place, as I first heard it called at Panama Hatties) was as important as the actual cooking. Ensuring that we would have enough of everything to get us through the day was the most important part of the morning. It was also the most difficult part of the day, not least because it involved a lot of guesswork on how much of each dish we'd sell and thus how much of each ingredient we'd need for each dish.

Making sure that each vegetable was cut exactly as it was supposed to be and that each sauce or stock tasted and looked as it should was what drove us. It was one thing to get every item on the list done, but it was equally important to do everything as perfectly as possible. It was easy to sear a piece of meat and make it look good, but the secondary components often involved more effort and were just as important in making a dish look appealing.

Focusing on the finest details while doing our prep work was one of the biggest differences between Panama Hatties and the ordinary restaurants that were all around it. The fish station probably involved the most work because it did more butchering than any of the other stations. I had never worked at a restaurant before where they had whole fish delivered and cleaned them in the restaurant. Even at

LaMotta's, a seafood restaurant, they'd receive fish that had already been filleted and just needed to be portioned out. There was definitely more work involved—and more knowledge and skill needed—when the fish came whole, but the benefit of actually seeing what the fish was like before being cleaned made a huge difference in being able to maintain quality. Matt, the sous chef, ran the fish station and he was as gung ho as any of us about making everything perfect.

Matt was also one of the most competitive cooks in the kitchen. I realized this for the first time after a few weeks running the meat station and, in particular, while doing prep work one day. I had my head down, focusing on cutting peppers into julienne when Matt ambled over to me in his virtually spotless chef jacket. He stopped just behind me and picked up one of the slivers of potatoes I had cut and was now soaking in water (which would eventually be used for a potato tart). He turned it around and held it up, then took another. Inspection done, he showed me the potato slice and said, "Not bad. That's not how we do it on fish, but if it's good for you . . . " Then he looked down at the peppers. "If you want to see how to do that, you should see our mise en place."

I didn't say anything. I just nodded my head and then went back to focusing on the peppers.

It didn't bother me at all that Matt ridiculed my prep work. I was doing my best and I was confident that that was more than good enough. Besides, Matt was the sous chef, so he should have been doing better work. I was also learning from him, especially since Blake was starting to let him have a bigger say in the menu and everything else in the kitchen.

In October 1997, about two years after I started cooking there, Blake left Panama Hatties. There wasn't anything more he could do with the restaurant. He next worked as the chef at Enoteca, a restaurant in Locust Valley, and then he opened a bistro called Blake's Place, and then I heard he was at another restaurant. The last I heard, Blake was working at a country club on Long Island—probably making good money cooking for people who didn't care what he served them. He'd gone to culinary school, then worked at an exclusive restaurant in the city, then made a bar into a fine dining establishment, and ended up in a country club. He probably enjoyed his work now, but he had taken a very long road to get to that point, just as Jennifer at the Harrison had suggested I would if I followed the same path.

Of course, Panama Hatties didn't come to a crashing halt when Blake left. There was uncertainty, but then we moved on. Matt was moved up to the chef position and Monkan and I were named co–sous chefs (and when the pastry chef also left, Nicky took over his job). This was the first time I was given a leadership role in a kitchen.

As the months rolled on post-Blake, the restaurant was still a place where young cooks with ambition came to learn in exchange for bad pay. There continued to be a steady flow of new cooks— among them was Nora's brother Danny, who had gone to culinary school and was now working under me. Competition for positions and among cooks remained fierce. Besides some major renovations to the kitchen, the place was as it had always been, and for the most part the food remained the same. But it had changed for me.

After a meal in the city, I finally realized what I needed to do. That night Mike and I met Monkan and Nicky at a swank new place in Greenwich Village called Clementine. It was early winter—cold, gray, and depressing—outside, and coming through Clementine's revolving door was an extreme contrast. The warmth and soft lights put me at ease immediately. The place was awash in orange light. It was like going back in time to the 1940s, except the people were definitely right in style for the day and time (and probably even exact minute) that we were in. We took off our black leather coats, which were cold to the touch, and checked them in with a slender girl who was sitting on a stool inside a tiny closet. We then maneuvered our way through a tight crowd to get to the bar where Monkan and Nicky were having a drink. Our table wasn't ready, so we ordered a round of drinks.

We actually had two rounds before we were shown to our table, but it was a prime table, right next to the waterfall that was placed incongruously in the middle of the dining room. The lounge area was totally my style, but the dining room felt as though it had been thrown together in an attempt to be fancy and at the same time amusing, but it wasn't really either. It was clear before we were even served bread that Clementine was a place that was better to be at than eat at. And indeed by the end of the meal the food was the last thing we were thinking about. Nothing was particularly good or bad, though Nicky's halibut was overcooked and Mike's duck breast seemed to have been cooked at medium heat for a long time, making it soft but not juicy.

That we weren't dazzled by the food didn't matter. We still had a great time, and I ended up going back to Clementine several times (though only for drinks or to eat in the lounge area). Despite the mediocre food and the many cocktails, I left Clementine with a clearer head about cooking than I had had in a while. I was impressed with Clementine because it felt alive. Panama Hatties just didn't have this level of excitement. On Long Island, people mostly went out to eat because they had to eat and to fancy restaurants like Panama Hatties to celebrate special occasions. In the city, Clementine wasn't unique. There were tons of places like it, where people went just as they'd go to a theater to watch a play. It was an exciting and entertaining place to be.

Going out to eat was how I spent most of my days off. Besides Monkan and Nicky, my brother Mike and our friend Ben frequently went with me to try a new restaurant. I went to all types of places, from fine dining establishments to soul food joints in Harlem. Beyond those I went to in the city, I also tried restaurants on Long Island, but none of them was as good as Panama Hatties or even close. It seemed as though Panama Hatties was a four-star restaurant in a no-star world. But for me Panama Hatties was no longer challenging.

Other than the change in chef, Panama Hatties was essentially the same restaurant that it had been when I first started working there. It had earned a reputation and we worked hard to maintain that level, but I needed more. As a diner I enjoyed places with energy and excitement—like Clementine—and I wanted this in the restaurant I cooked in, too.

I wanted a bigger stage and it was clear that the city was the place to be. During our dinner at Clementine, Monkan, Nicky, and I talked about cooking and about the city's restaurants pretty much the entire meal. We were always talking about cooking in the city. All of the big restaurants were in the city. Every restaurant we talked about and every restaurant we wanted to go to was in the city. It was the next level, the next step for us. As I drove north from Brooklyn through the curves of the Brooklyn–Queens Expressway and then emerged from an underpass with Manhattan's skyline on our left—from the Twin Towers to the Empire State Building in the distance, it was majestic—I knew that I needed to stop being on the wrong side of the East River.

It was now clear to me how I should take Blake's advice: Get out . . . of Long Island. I needed to work at a restaurant in the center of everything. One that people would go out of their way to eat in if they had to. I was now certain that I needed to learn what it was like to work in a kitchen that was the best among the best. Blake had learned what it meant to be at a restaurant like that when he worked in the city and then did his best to make Panama Hatties fit that mold. I suppose if I'd known what the finish line of Blake's course would be, I might have been less determined to follow his lead.

When I had first joined Panama Hatties, I planned to work hard at the restaurant and then go to culinary school. I had worked hard and I had essentially gone to culinary school—at Panama Hatties. I had taken more than two years of an advanced course in serious cooking working directly with cooks. How would culinary school help me? I was surrounded by people with culinary-school degrees and most of them worked under me—and some graduates couldn't even handle working at the lowest level at the restaurant. I'd learned a lot through actual cooking, and I had come to doubt that there was much I could learn at a school, besides the French classes I was told I'd have to take—but I was pretty sure I'd never need to learn to speak French.

So, my plan had now changed. I was focused on continuing my education in the classrooms of the biggest culinary university: the kitchens of New York City. But before I could make that giant leap I had to figure out where I wanted to land. I had trouble just getting reservations at restaurants in the city, so I expected that getting a job at the right restaurant would be difficult. I had no idea how difficult it would be.

Chapter 5

March to the City

The road out of Long Island and into Manhattan is unpredictable. In the middle of the day, smooth sailing, it's an hour door-to-door from Huntington. Or it can be a lot longer, no matter what time it is. The Long Island Expressway is no one's friend. One afternoon on our way to a lunch at Nobu—one of the most popular Japanese restaurants in New York—Mike and I were slowly rolling (no acceleration possible or necessary) through traffic. I looked at the radio's clock, which read 1:25 P.M., the same time as the last time I checked.

We still hadn't gone through the Midtown Tunnel. We had just reached the last turn in the expressway before the toll lanes for the tunnel. We were running late. It was hot outside on this bright June day and almost as hot in the car. Mike and I were starting to sweat in our dress shirts, but we had the windows down to escape from the AC for a few minutes.

By 1:40 P.M., we had just gotten off the F.D.R. It would be tight to make our 2:00 P.M. reservation, so Mike called the restaurant on my cell to let them know that we might be a minute or two late as I cut across town on Canal Street and then down Varick. Weaving in and out of lanes, we were in Tribeca in minutes. It was now just a question of getting a parking space. The one-way streets and limited parking of Tribeca were giving us a fight too. With just five minutes to go before 2:00, I let Mike out on the corner of Hudson while I went to park the car. The restaurant had told him that they needed us to arrive by 2:00 to accommodate us, so we weren't going to take any chances. In the rearview mirror, as I continued up the street, I saw Mike jogging to the restaurant—his baggy dress shirt parachuting behind him. It'd been close, but we made it under the wire.

I parked the car a few minutes later and walked the block and a half back to Nobu. I was looking forward to this meal more than I had any other. I was hungry with anticipation. As I approached the restaurant, I saw Mike waiting for me outside. He was sweaty and his size or two too-large white shirt was a mess. We had made it, but we hadn't made it. We had gotten there on time, but they wanted both of us there as the clock struck 2:00. The polite hostess with soft-boiled-egg-white skin, bright green eyes, and chestnut hair had smiled at Mike in a sympathetic way. Then she apologized for the inconvenience, but they couldn't accommodate us. She suggested that we go around the corner to one of the restaurant group's other establishments, an upscale grill. We followed her suggestion and the broken pavement to the very modern restaurant on Greenwich Street. The food was Mediterranean-influenced and the dishes we had were at least good, but the meal was unexceptional. It just couldn't compete with what we had anticipated.

Perhaps it was because Mike looked like a mess or because we were young, or maybe Nobu really was extremely strict with their patrons arriving together and on time for lunch even when they had several open tables. Regardless of the reason, it felt like a door being shut in my face.

I was quickly learning that finding the right restaurant to work at in the city wasn't any easier than it was for me to get in as a diner. But, the difference was that I wasn't willing to make any compromises.

On the day that marked the beginning of the end of Panama Hatties for me, I arrived as early as anyone else in the kitchen. It was just an ordinary Wednesday. I said my hellos, put on an apron, checked my lowboy fridge (a small refrigerator for items that are needed within arm's reach of a station), and started to write the station's mise en place list (the prep items we needed to get done that day). I had done this so many times that I felt I was on autopilot. It really had nothing to do with the restaurant itself. It was just that I had learned all I could there and needed to move on. I was determined to get into a restaurant in the city, but I barely had any time even to make phone calls. I was now working six days a week at Panama Hatties and Sunday was my only day off. That day, though, I had a plan: a way to squeeze in time in a very busy day.

As a sous chef at Panama Hatties, I took part in weekly meetings to discuss the menu with the other sous chef, Kent Monkan, and the chef, Matt Hisiger, and helped oversee the kitchen team. Besides those new responsibilities, I was still on the meat station and working just as hard as the first day I walked into the kitchen.

In order to keep learning on the job, whenever I could order a type or cut of meat or a vegetable, root, or grain that I hadn't used before, I did. Mostly, though, I just used the meat that we regularly had in the restaurant and tried different ways to cook it or used cuts that the restaurant wouldn't ordinarily serve—like duck legs. The first time I cooked duck confit was at Panama Hatties, but it wasn't because it was a new item we were serving. We served only the duck breast at the restaurant, and discarded the other parts of the duck. I made the duck confit (duck legs slowly poached in duck fat) out of duck legs that wouldn't otherwise have been used. The duck confit was never served; it was just a chance to try something new and was eaten by me and the other cooks. These self-tutorials kept me patient while I waited to find a restaurant to work at in the city, but it was frustrating knowing that there was so much more that we could do at Panama Hatties that I hadn't even seen and knew nothing about.

Americo, my partner in escapism, had the same things on his mind. Americo dressed as if he had just come off the set of a hip-hop video, but he was a serious cook. The first time he walked into the kitchen he was wearing baggy jeans and a tight white T-shirt and had yellow goggles resting in his gel-spiked hair. I'm sure most of the cooks thought he was in the wrong place and would soon realize it and go back to the kitchen he crawled out of. They were wrong; Americo came ready to work. He was a stocky Colombian kid a few years younger than I. He also had grown up on Long Island and was a hard worker with a lot of nervous energy. Even when he tried to stand still, his leg would continue to shake as though it had been dipped beneath the ice of a frozen pond. He never stopped moving, couldn't stop moving. In a kitchen, this was a good thing. He didn't fit the mold of most of Panama Hatties' cooks, but he was talented and eager to learn.

Americo was my partner on the meat station and we made a

good team. That morning we got through the mise en place list that I had written earlier in the morning in record time. We'd still done as careful a job as we normally did, but this day we pushed extra hard so that we'd have a longer break before lunch service began. It was just after 11:00 when I put my knife down and Americo looked at me conspiratorially. I nodded at him in acknowledgment. He walked off the station and toward the dry storage. I followed a few steps behind him, nonchalantly, past the other prep tables in the back.

The dry storage was at the end of a narrow hallway off the kitchen. It was just a small space that wasn't very private, but it had a phone that we could use. As I walked back there Americo was standing casually near the phone with his back to me. When he saw it was me, he pulled the thin red Zagat guide out of his pocket and started flipping to the dog-eared pages.

We had figured out a way around not having an opportunity to call restaurants: we worked harder to get our mise en place done before anyone else and then used the dry storage as an office. I used my cell phone and Americo used the restaurant's phone to call restaurants in the city. Since we couldn't make these calls with everyone around us, this was our only option. Any of the cooks—or Ritchie or the chef—could have walked in on us at any minute, but that was a chance we were willing to take.

I called the first restaurant on my list for that day and then waited through the restaurant's general information recording for a live body.

"Excuse me?" a pleasant but clearly irritated-sounding woman asked to my request to speak to the chef. I said his name again and there was a long pause. I heard her inhale and exhale through her nose. Most of the chefs' names at the restaurants I was calling were French and more often than not I butchered the pronunciation.

Eventually I did get chefs on the phone—and made sure I didn't even try to pronounce their names—and many of them had the same response, "We don't need anyone right now, but come in to do a stage and we'll see how you do." The difficulty, it turned out, was getting the chefs on the line. Once I did, several chefs I spoke with were willing to bring me in to work for free for a day. Bringing in a stagiaire is basically a no-risk proposition for a kitchen. The stagiaire isn't paid but is there to work hard and will often do the most menial tasks—the tasks that the other cooks don't want to do (like peel grapes or shell peas). The stagiaire is just an extra set of hands, and most kitchens can always use extra hands. If the stagiaire works well and there is room and a need for another cook, he may get hired. If the stagiaire doesn't work out, he can be thrown out at any time.

For the young cook, a stage in a restaurant provides an opportunity to see what a place is all about—to see what they cook, how they cook, and what their system is like—and to prove yourself valuable to the restaurant. As I looked at it then, a stage was the ultimate job interview, especially if you were confident that you could cook to impress.

As I pressed "end" on my cell phone, I looked over at Americo, who was still waiting for a chef to come on the line. He had heard how my call went and wanted to know where I had called. I was about to answer him when I heard someone coming. Americo hung up the phone and hid the Zagat guide, but there was no one there. I looked at Americo and he grinned. Then we went back into the kitchen.

I woke up early on my next day off and drove my red Corsica through the tail end of rush hour into Manhattan for my first stage in the city. It was a somewhat slow ride, but I was parked and ready to work on time, at 10:00 A.M. I really had no clue about what was on the other side of Patria's glass door. But as I waited for someone to let me in, I looked over the menu that was posted in a Plexiglas case by the door. Despite the restaurant's being downtown (a few blocks north of Union Square), the menu was somewhat formal— only prix fixe, no à la carte—and expensive.

The reason I was waiting outside of Patria that morning was Douglas Rodriguez. Patria was on the food map because of him and his Nuevo Latino cuisine. Unlike most Latin restaurants, Patria was doing fine dining, even if Rodriguez's food was only partly fancy and mostly fun. Dishes like Oysters Rodriguez—a revamping of the classic Oysters Rockefeller (Rodriguez added plantain puree and fried the oysters) that would be copied again and again elsewhere—were just that. They were doing something different and exciting, which seemed to be a good fit for what I was looking for.

Eventually I was let into the restaurant, though I think the woman who opened the door was surprised to find a non-Hispanic guy wanting to work in the kitchen. I would be the only person in the kitchen that day who didn't speak Spanish fluently. I spoke only kitchen Spanish: two- and three-word sentences about plates, food, and other basics. So, I mostly experienced the day as though it were a foreign film without subtitles. I saw a lot, but was involved in very little of the actual cooking. I spent most of the time that day up front in Patria's open kitchen, which was just an extension of the dining room (a rustic room with high ceilings and splashes of color), doing prep work and simple cooking, like sautéing plantains.

As I drove back to Huntington, I felt a little relieved that the day was over. It had been a good day. The work wasn't very difficult or strenuous and for the most part the food was interesting. But I knew within minutes of being in the kitchen that the restaurant wasn't my style. There was plenty that I could learn from Patria—in fact, I saw several interesting things in the few hours that I was there (like duck breast served on top of bananas and lentils, and sugarcane-skewered tuna)—but it was a place that suited my style of eating more than cooking. Patria was concerned with fun more than serious cooking. I was looking for a restaurant that was more refined and intent on being among the best.

The next day I went back to work at Panama Hatties and several days later—my next day off—I was on my way to my next stage. My second stage in the city was all but a waste of time. It was a restaurant that Zagat rated as one of the city's best, but it was just a name-and-numbers place: it seemed as if everything—from the dining room to the menu and, especially, the kitchen—had been left untouched since the decade when the place had first established itself, and now it was just a big antique machine producing mediocre food at chain-restaurant volumes. Besides doing massive amounts of menial work, I mostly saw things being done that I knew weren't right. I kept my head down and did my work in a back corner of their vast kitchen. Usually cooks keep their heads down and work hard to impress a chef with their focus, but I was doing this so I didn't have to pay attention to all of the bad habits—like not wiping the cutting board clean after each use—I glimpsed going on around me.

The next restaurant I went to was the first place I had called that didn't ask me to come in to do a stage. I had spoken to the chef de cuisine—not the chef, who was fairly well known. He had asked me about my background and then told me to come in to observe. The popular restaurant served American food, but it wasn't quiet and refined like Panama Hatties. It was more fun than fancy and the food was about flair rather than finesse.

As I walked through the kitchen with the chef de cuisine, I wondered what I was supposed to observe. The place was big and busy, but mostly it was a mess. There were pots and pans all over the place, and it looked as though the cooks were mainly concerned with getting through everything quickly, but not working cleanly. Like the Road Runner, they moved fast and left chaos behind: a spoon dripping sauce onto a counter, a dirty towel on a cutting board, and scraps piled near the garbage. There was salt scattered all over the floor to provide traction on the grease-slicked tile. Despite the conditions, there was actually a table right in the middle of the kitchen for customers wanting to be part of the action. Apparently a kitchen working at its worst can be entertaining.

After talking with the chef de cuisine, I met with the chef himself. Like his kitchen, he was sloppy, from his stained chef jacket and worn checks (black-and-white checkered cook's pants) to his pushed-back hair and hanging gut. He wiped his brow a few times with a kitchen towel as he told me his plans. He had obviously heard about my background from his chef de cuisine and knew what he was going to say to me before I got there. He told me that I could join the kitchen if I wanted to, but that he needed me for a new place he was opening in New Orleans. Being offered a position right away made it almost tempting, but there really was no contemplation necessary.

The next stage that I went on was a different story. One of the cooks who had recently joined Panama Hatties had told me about a restaurant that wasn't a fancy factory, like many I had done stages in by then. The restaurant was small and elegant and served food that was perfect in its simplicity. Looping around 58th Street after getting off the Queensboro Bridge and heading through a part of town called Sutton Place, I knew what he meant right away. March Restaurant was in a town house that looked just like any other millionaire's home lining the streets of this exclusive neighborhood. It had steps leading up to a wooden door set in a brick facade, behind which was the inviting glow of what seemed like a high-society dinner party.

There were no lights outside and only a small plaque next to the door with the restaurant's name. March had class and it showed from the outside, up the few black metal stairs into the tiny foyer and bar area, through the small dining room, past the armoire filled with stemware, and out into the seating area in the garden.

March bore the personal mark of its creator. Wayne Nish, the chef and part owner, had once been an architect, until a midlife career change turned him into a cook. He had been part of the kitchen team that made Barry Wine's restaurant, the Quilted Giraffe, a legend. Chef Nish was part Japanese, and it showed in delicate items on the menu, such as hamachi (young yellowtail, which is often served raw in a sushi restaurant), the same way his architecture background was apparent in the menu's structure. Unlike most restaurants, which have some form of the appetizer, main course, and dessert organization, March was more about a slow buildup through different-sized courses. Diners chose three, five, or seven courses from the menu, which the kitchen would then construct into a meal that started with plates that could be as small as a canapé and grew to full-size portions. In addition, beggar's purses (a tradition from the Quilted Giraffe) could be added to the meal. The "Holy Trinity," as I would later come to hear Chef Nish refer to the assortment of three beggar's purses, were crepes stuffed with either lobster and black truffle, or smoked salmon and foie gras, or caviar with crème fraîche, then shaped like a tiny change purse and tied with a long green chive. Wayne was not a technically trained cook, but he knew what tasted good. His food was simple—often just three components to a dish— and, for the most part, perfect.

I didn't know what I'd find when I walked through the staff door at the bottom of the staircase, past the coat-check racks and a walk-in on the right, into a cramped kitchen. In the middle and running the length of the kitchen was a three-foot-wide table. On the left side were the dishwasher station and another sink. On the right side were the stoves and countertops, which were on top of lowboys. There was only enough space for one person to stand between the table and the stove or countertop, so we all worked side by side. The kitchen might have had as many as five other cooks in it that morning and it was already packed. I was put in a small corner and was given a list of prep work. As with every other stage I had worked, I was given fairly basic tasks—like doing brunoises (tiny dice) of various vegetables, breaking down lobsters, and straining stocks. One difference at March, though, was that I was doing this work surrounded by all the other cooks doing their mise en place. Even though I wouldn't work the service, I was part of the team doing the work necessary to get the kitchen ready for service—not just off in the corner peeling potatoes and carrots that would be used throughout the day or maybe the next day or into the following week.

As quickly as I knew that the other restaurants weren't right for me, I knew that March was. This food was as pretty as anything we served at Panama Hatties, but it lacked the kind of contrivances that were the hallmark of Panama Hatties' plates, which were decorated with squiggly lines of squirt-bottled sauces and other heavy-handed techniques. Although the food at Panama Hatties was plated as carefully as at March, this food was art because of its elegant simplicity.

While I thought March was ideal for me, they didn't have room for another cook. The kitchen at March was very small and they had a solid crew that had been together for a while. I was of course disappointed, but I didn't give up and didn't stop showing up at March. The chef told me I could continue to "trail" (as doing a stage is sometimes called), and so I continued to go to March just to help out with the prep work. While I didn't cook during service, I was still learning a lot by doing things—such as picking the meat from pigs' feet—that I had never done before, and I had my first opportunity to work with products that were received directly from farms. I continued to work at Panama Hatties and would until I found a restaurant in the city, but for several weeks I spent my days off learning at March rather than searching for a new job.

In the spring of 1998, after six months of doing stages in the city, I finally landed in a restaurant in Manhattan. I found a place that met the criteria I started out looking for: it was several steps ahead of Panama Hatties, I'd have an opportunity to cook, and there was certainly plenty for me to learn. While it had taken me a long time to find a place like this, in the end I actually had to choose between two different options.

I did a stage in the first place and was as impressed as I'd ever been. The restaurant held about seventy-five people (not counting the many private rooms), and they did about 160 covers on a good night. The kitchen was immaculate. It was big and had ten cooks working in it on the day I was there. All of the cooks were required to wear toques and be clean-shaven for work. It was a serious kitchen that was doing challenging food. The chef was a relatively young guy who was extremely energetic and ambitious. The food he was putting out was as creative as any that I had seen. While it had accents from several cuisines, it was not fusion cuisine, where the lines of inspiration are obvious. This was more unique and borderless than that. In just one day of being there, it was obvious to me that this place was going to be successful and the chef was at the beginning of a significant career. He spoke quickly and nodded his head a lot when I spoke with him. It was clear I could handle the work, though I'd have to start at the bottom like everyone else. The pay was no less reasonable than I thought it would be, but the hours would be difficult. I would work six days of six doubles, which meant shifts from 6:00 A.M. until 1:00 A.M. every day.

The other opportunity was considerably different. The place had been open for a few months and they needed one more cook. It was a small place downtown with a kitchen tinier than any I had ever worked in. There would be three cooks working, plus a chef de cuisine and the chef himself, at any one time and that would be tight. Unlike the other chef, this wasn't a young guy who was about to make a name for himself. This was a chef who had run an eponymous restaurant for many years that had been one of New York's best at that time or any other. He was the type of guy who wore a leather jacket and designer jeans. He had closed his successful restaurant about a year earlier and was now poised to take over the world. The restaurant that I was offered a job in was going to be just his first step of many, which included a bakery and a cooking school. The pay was about the same as the other restaurant was offering, but I'd work just five days with one double.

The hours meant nothing to me, as I was committing myself to work as much as necessary (and possible), but I chose the second place. While the almost guaranteed success of the first place and a young, hungry chef might have been a safer move than a new place from a successful chef who was already looking beyond the restaurant, there was something about David Bouley that convinced me he could show me a whole new approach to food.

Joining a serious kitchen in the city meant giving up the position that I had worked hard to achieve at Panama Hatties. It also meant giving up what had become an easy life: a familiar system, having some control and some input on the food that was served, living close to work, and earning a decent salary. It was difficult to get into the right restaurant, but the real hurdle was giving up so much to do it. In addition to the hour commute each way, it meant starting at the beginning again.

Chapter 6

Bouley Bakery

The first days and months of Bouley Bakery were difficult all around. It was a serious struggle for me. Both the hours and the work were as demanding as in any kitchen I'd worked in before, and the commute to the city each day made it even more difficult. One day in late January, when New York got hit with its first big snowstorm of the year, I faced a real test.

Typical of when I worked dinner service, I got to work that day around 11:00 A.M. I had taken a 9:23 A.M. train out of Huntington, an hour-long ride, followed by a twenty-minute subway ride downtown. As I rounded Duane Street off of West Broadway in Tribeca, I enjoyed the last daylight I'd see that day (albeit under a gray and overcast sky). Once I walked through the steel door on the side of the red stone building, I wouldn't leave until after midnight, except for maybe a few breaks, but even those would be in the early evening.

This was an ordinary day for me; the next day, when I'd work a double and get there almost four hours earlier, was much tougher.

Getting to work was a bit of a pain, but the kitchen itself was the biggest challenge—not the equipment, but the size. It was easily the smallest I'd ever worked in. Bouley Bakery was set up to be a bakery and café. It was just going to be the start of a Bouley empire that was planned for Tribeca. The plans included a fine dining restaurant, a noodle shop, a cooking school, and more. Chef Bouley had big dreams. But his big dreams didn't fit into the confines of a café. While Bouley Bakery was making excellent bread, Bouley's vision expanded, and the original plan for the Bakery to be just a bakery and a café was abandoned. It was a full-blown restaurant from the start. Just as Bouley's previous namesake restaurant had been, the Bakery was immensely popular. The problem was that it wasn't full sized, especially the kitchen. There were just four of us working at a time and there was barely enough room for that many. The food we were doing was difficult to cook in those conditions; the food Bouley wanted to do was impossible. It was a trying situation for everyone.

Joining any new restaurant means learning a new system. My first few weeks at the Bakery were similar to when I first started at Panama Hatties, except I was learning a new system while running a station. I wasn't in the background cooking or just doing prep work; I was an important part of the kitchen.

I had started off—and was still—working on the entremetier station, responsible for hot appetizers and garnishes. I was involved in every dish, except for the cold appetizers and salads, which the garde-manger cook prepared by himself. From the first day that I walked through the kitchen door, I was in the thick of it. There was a lot that I was expected to learn, but I was also expected to perform.

Because of the size of the kitchen, the kitchen team was small and every cook played an essential part.

Besides me, there were just three other cooks working in the kitchen: one who cooked all of the meat and fish, one as garde-manger, and a chef de cuisine. I worked alongside the meat-and-fish cook, who worked in front of the only stove and oven in the kitchen. During service he would cook the meat or fish, and then I would plate the dish (which meant adding the garnish—a vegetable, a side, or a sauce—and arranging the items precisely). All of the plating was done on the metal table in the middle of the kitchen. The chef de cuisine, who worked at the head of the table, between the kitchen and the front of the house, would help me plate the dishes while also expediting. All of the orders came out of the kitchen in this way, except for the appetizers and vegetable dishes. Using a small flattop, I was responsible for all of the hot appetizers and veg dishes myself. And, across the table, the garde-manger cook prepared all of the cold dishes. He had the least amount of room. Besides the metal table that we all used, he used a small table, which was against the wall next to two standing fridges stacked on top of each other. In addition to the space the four of us used, there was a separate small area for pastry and a prep area downstairs. That was the entire kitchen.

We worked hard from the moment we got into the kitchen in the morning straight through service. Partly because of the space and the number of cooks, but mostly because of the complex and labor-intensive food that we were preparing, it was a high-octane kitchen. This was the most physically demanding kitchen I had worked in. We were constantly moving to and from work spaces and around each other, producing food that would be a struggle for a kitchen with a team and space twice our size.

The structure and principles of French cooking, which Bouley's cuisine was rooted in, had been entirely foreign to me before joining the Bakery. While Bouley is American, his heritage and experience are firmly rooted in the principles of French cooking. He had spent time in kitchens in France studying under acclaimed chefs, such as Paul Bocuse and Joël Robuchon. When he came back to New York, he helped lead some of the city's most respected French restaurants, including Le Cirque, La Côte Basque, and Le Perigord. He then became the chef at Montrachet, a restaurant owned by Drew Nieporent that pioneered fine dining in downtown Manhattan. In 1987 he opened Bouley, a restaurant that would cement his importance to the New York food world and make him one of the most celebrated American chefs. Among the accolades he received were four stars from the *New York Times* and both best chef and best restaurant from the James Beard Foundation, and the Zagat guide rated his restaurant as the top spot for food for the last five years that the restaurant remained open.

The most overt difference between the cooking I had done before, which was mostly labeled "refined American" (if it was labeled at all), and Bouley's was that the sauce was never an afterthought in Bouley's cuisine. At Panama Hatties the sauce was essentially a decoration, a way to improve how a dish looked, with a few colorful lines or a swirl around a piece of meat added to every plate. Aesthetics dictated the use of sauce more than anything else. The squirt bottles for making dots and swirls made it seem like play. In Bouley's world the sauce is as important, if not more important, than anything else on the plate. While his cuisine is certainly modern, this is true to classic French cooking. The sauce doesn't just highlight a taste or accentuate a flavor; it is a fundamental element of a dish. The sauces I made at Bouley Bakery, especially those for the fish dishes, were the product of thought and consideration. They were often complicated, consisting of many components (more than a dozen in some). The ingredients might be involved (like clam juice from shucked—not steamed, as is common—bivalves) or refined (five gallons of mushroom stock reduced to half a quart) or simple (ketchup), but each played a distinct role. Bouley didn't just reduce a stock to create the base for a sauce; he used several purees, juices, and stocks for one sauce. This was the first time I'd ever seen a chef do this.

The sauces were the focus of much of Bouley's food, but, like every other element of Bouley's dishes, they were constantly changing. Bouley would come into the kitchen, taste the same sauce or dish that he had tried the day before, and then tell us how to change it so that it came closer to his vision. I'd learn a dish—what was needed to make it and how it was done—and then I'd come in the next day and the dish would be different, sometimes completely so. For a couple of months his favorite ingredients were raspberry vinegar and garlic oil. Whatever the change, he was almost always right—the dish would improve—but keeping up with the changes was challenging.

The changes that Bouley made to his dishes always seemed to be made in his head first, before he even came into the kitchen. If he experimented, it was in the kitchen of his mind. He would enter the actual kitchen already knowing how he was going to improve a dish. Tasting something seemed to be just a formality—a step necessary only to confirm what he had already decided. He rarely did any actual cooking in the Bakery's kitchen, except when he cooked for his friends or other VIPs. And he appeared in the kitchen irregularly. One day he might be there at 4:30 in the afternoon to show us something and then not come back in the kitchen for the rest of the night. The next day he'd be in the kitchen at 9:30, in the middle of dinner service, with a chef jacket on over a nice outfit, cooking for a VIP.

To the outside world Bouley Bakery was one of the hottest new restaurants. People couldn't wait to get into the new Bouley restaurant. We were always busy and just about every night a celebrity would come into the kitchen to thank us for his or her meal. But soon after he opened the Bakery, Bouley was already focusing on his next project.

That night in January, while I was rushing about doing several things at once, Bouley came in to cook for a VIP. When Bouley was in the kitchen during service, it meant dancing around him to get our work done. There were several tickets up, and I was busy keeping up with what I needed to do as he came over to me. He was wearing his chef jacket but had on a nice dress shirt underneath. From his short gray hair to the expensive jeans he was wearing, he looked polished. His chef jacket was spotless, but he blended into the kitchen as though he'd been working alongside us the entire night.

We were in the middle of a rush, but he needed to cook salmon for the VIP. He came over to my area and started moving the pans I had on the flattop around, so that he could fit a twelve-inch sauté pan on it. His pan took up much of the flattop. As he cooked, he explained to me what he was doing. Without acknowledging the urgency and activity around him, he made slow circles with the pan and wanted me to pay attention to what he was showing me. Cooking salmon had nothing to do with what I needed to get done during the service, but that meant nothing to him. I couldn't drop everything I was doing, but I also couldn't tell him that. I kept reaching around him for a pan I needed off the flattop while doing my best to listen to him. More than any other chef I'd worked for, I valued what he had to say about food, but there couldn't have been a worse time for him to give me a lesson.

The Bakery was by no means an easy place to work—we were cooking food that far exceeded the physical limits of the kitchen. With Bouley in the kitchen, that night was at least a little more difficult than it would have been otherwise; with the snow beginning to fall outside, getting home would definitely be more difficult.

I made it to Penn Station about ten minutes before 1:00, which gave me just enough time to try to get a seat on the 1:04 train to Huntington. At just over an hour, the 1:04 was the last best option to get home before daylight. It was almost always crowded—on Friday or Saturday it was standing room only with rambling and staggering drunks spread among the completely exhausted. If I missed the 1:04, I had to wait for a 3:00. That had happened, more than once, but after the first time I did whatever I could to prevent it.

Because I had to work a double the next day, it was absolutely essential that I catch the 1:04 train that night. I'd get home around 2:30 A.M., if there were no delays, and have a few hours to sleep. When I worked a double—both the morning and night shift—I got to the restaurant by 7:00 A.M., which required catching the 5:27 Penn Station–bound train, and then racing to the 1:04 train when I was done. One day a week I slept almost as much on the train as I did at home. This was one of those days.

As the train passed by the Long Island Expressway, I saw that snow was building up along the side and even on the roadway. It was a storm that was definitely going to leave several inches behind. Then the train passed into darkness and I couldn't see much through the window. Mostly I saw reflections, like the master of the universe asleep in a blue suit in the three pack of seats across from me.

I thought about my friend Jim, who wore a suit and took the train to work in the city every day. I doubted he ever took the train home this late, unless it was after a night out. That was something I didn't experience often anymore. I was living a different life than most of my friends.

Then we passed by a row of stores and I saw that the cars in the parking lot were covered in snow. The next day's commute wouldn't be easy. Not for the first time, I wished I could afford an apartment in the city.

After getting enough snow off my car so that I could drive, I got home a few minutes before 2:30. The day was finally over. Or it should have been, but I wasn't really tired anymore. I went into the kitchen and stared into the refrigerator, finding among other leftovers a bowl of plain white rice and a cooked pork chop. Immediately, I knew what I'd snack on that night.

I poured a thin layer of canola oil into a Teflon pan (my mom doesn't have any cast iron) and got it hot. After dicing up the pork chop, I dropped the day-old rice into the pan. It hit the oil with a burst of steam. I waited for the rice to crisp up a bit before cracking an egg into it and then I added the pork. I guided the pan back and forth, flipping the rice over and over so none of it stuck. When the rice was crispy enough, I hit it with a few dashes of soy sauce. A whole new burst of steam erupted—smelling salty and sweet. A few minutes later, I ate the steaming bowl of pork fried rice in front of the TV upstairs in my bedroom.

While I ate I watched a tape that a cook at March Restaurant loaned me of Chef Nish on a crazy Japanese food show. It was my first time seeing the *Iron Chef*, which would become popular on the Food Network. It was all in Japanese without subtitles, but I thought I understood what they were saying when they showed Wayne walking through the Union Square Greenmarket and then superimposed the scene with an American flag. On the show, he competed against a Japanese cook in some sort of cook-off. Both cooks had helpers.

Chef Nish's helpers were Japanese, and it didn't seem as though he understood any more of what they were saying to him than I did watching the show. I fell asleep before he lost.

About three hours later, I was awake and standing outside my parents' house. My day began with shoveling my car out of the snow before driving to the train station. On mornings like this it was impossible for me not to question whether commuting to Bouley Bakery, or any other restaurant in the city, was worth it.

But I was learning a lot being around Bouley and cooking his food. David Bouley understood food better than anyone I had ever met. He didn't just put together ingredients and decide how to cook them. His food had a clear logic to it that could often be traced back to his roots in New England (he grew up in Connecticut), French kitchens, or other inspirations, but it wasn't just variations on classic dishes and preparations. The food wasn't strange (like much of the so-called avant-garde cooking), unrecognizable, or even unusual, but it was original: uniquely, purely Bouley.

His food was all about flavor. Certainly presentation was a factor in the plates that we served, but "how it would eat" was the most important part of any dish. Bouley tried to perfect every element of taste in his dishes. His understanding of food made his seemingly straightforward cuisine difficult to classify. There were certainly French dishes or ones that had typical French components, but most dishes only started there and went off in another direction, like the Ocean Herbal (phyllo-crusted shrimp, baby squid, and crab in a broth of emulsified juices, oils, and herbs) or marinated tuna tartare with fennel and champagne jelly, or skate with pine nut dressing.

A Bouley dish, technique, or element is so recognizable it practically has his initials on it. Even a sauce or potato puree (his wasn't mashed; it was passed through a chinois enough times to make it silky smooth and had enough butter that it floated on a plate and dissolved in your mouth) was recognizable. His food makes guest appearances in restaurants all over the place. On many occasions, eating in another restaurant or working in another kitchen, even years later, I'd see his food and wonder if the chef had worked with Bouley at some point (or whether some cook had just passed along the recipe). His influence on the food world was enormous.

A few weeks after that snowstorm in January, less than two years after the restaurant opened, renovations began at Bouley Bakery. The restaurant didn't close down during this time. The renovations began and the kitchen worked around them. I had worked through some tough days at that restaurant, through some significant obstacles, and wasn't inclined to be there while the renovations took place. While I certainly had gained a new understanding of excellence from working with Bouley, I was ready for a break from his chaotic world.

When I left Panama Hatties I felt I had learned all I could there and needed to move on, but this wasn't the case when I left Bouley Bakery. I doubted I'd ever think that and didn't rule out returning. But, as renovations began at the Bakery and an opportunity opened at March (the first restaurant in the city I had wanted to cook in), I knew it was time to move on. I was ready for a new challenge and I would quickly learn that meant starting at the bottom again.

The Bakery would eventually be fully transformed into a fine dining restaurant, complete with a kitchen that would make it possible to do all of the food that Bouley wanted to do, instead of just what we could manage under difficult conditions. It would be a different kitchen in many ways—not just in size and equipment, but in the cooks as well. The renovations were necessary for Bouley Bakery to continue to rise to the top of the New York restaurant world; working at the Bakery during its evolution did the same thing for me.

Chapter 7

Much to Digest

When I left Bouley Bakery in the winter of 1999, as its renovations began, March was the logical choice for me. I had spent many days there, so I knew what to expect. I also knew that it was completely different from the Bakery, and that was a change I needed.

Joining March as a cook—not just a stagiaire—I was back at the bottom again. Starting at the bottom of that kitchen meant working on the beginnings and endings of meals on the garde-manger station, which was responsible for amuse-bouches (hors d'oeuvres presented as a gift from the kitchen at the beginning of meals at fine restaurants), small cold dishes (essentially what would be called appetizers at other restaurants, but March didn't use the common appetizer-then-entrée models), and desserts. The most significant difference between this station at March and a traditional garde-manger station was that we were also responsible for desserts.

There wasn't a separate pastry kitchen or a true pastry chef at March, as there is in most kitchens. At March, the dessert course came off the same line—just as far down the line as possible and in the corner. This was at least partly because of the size of the kitchen. In contrast with Bouley Bakery, March's kitchen felt spacious to me, but really it was just a slightly less tight space. However, there were twice as many people, including two of us on the garde-manger station. I'd never been involved with desserts before. While there was little room to work, there was plenty of room for me to learn.

March's desserts were straightforward. There were no grand or elaborate presentations. It wasn't because desserts were an afterthought; it was just that after an often long multicourse meal that was composed of fine and delicate food, the dessert course was intended as one last languorous note in the same song. We served simple things like a sorbet with marinated fruit or a candied black walnut tart. And we offered a molten chocolate cake, which was easily the most popular order. The molten chocolate cake was the most overexposed dessert at the time, with slight variations featured on menus throughout the city. Just like any other chocolate cake, it was made of flour, butter, sugar, eggs, and chocolate. The one difference was that the cake was baked for about half the time that a normal cake would be, so the inside remained gooey. The cake could even be baked to this half-finished form then reheated later, and it would still be slightly firm on the outside and oozing a hot chocolate interior when a fork broke through.

Besides having the chance to experiment with the ice-cream maker, working on the garde-manger station meant a lot of redundant work. The exception to this was the amuse that we were responsible for. When I arrived at March, there was one amuse that we served: smoked salmon with pickled vegetables on top of a triangle of

Japanese rice. Everything on the station was done the same way each day and little of it was actually cooked—it was just composed. That was the nature of the station, but I thought we could use the amuse as an opportunity to be creative. I felt there was so much we could do with just the restaurant's trim from various products. I wanted to create something new every day. But there was resistance—not from Wayne Nish or Mike Anthony, the chef de cuisine, but from the other cook on the station, Tim Chen.

Tim Chen worked by the books. We called him Mr. Chen as though it were a nickname, because he was so formal. Tall and thin, he had jet-black hair feathered like Rod Stewart's. He would never smile at work. He approached cooking the way a mathematician would solve a problem: he followed a formula and was precise. He was organized and he worked clean, which were strengths that I greatly respected even when I thought that his rigid work ethic muted our limited opportunities for creativity. When I asked if we should use foie gras pieces left over from cleaning a lobe to make a mousse, or short-rib trim for a ravioli filling, or just about any other deviation for the amuse, his answer was, "Why?" It wasn't really a question; it was a statement. He knew that we could do different things but didn't see why we should. Mr. Chen could do everything we were supposed to do perfectly. He didn't see a reason to do anything else. Eventually, though, I broke him down and he let me create a few things.

Learning steps and repeating them is important to cooking in a restaurant, but that's not all there is to cooking. At Bouley Bakery, there was no way to create a Bouley sauce the way it was supposed to be except by following every one of the many steps. To be a solid cook in that kitchen you had to do exactly what you were supposed to do. But becoming a chef in your own right, which was the underlying goal for most of us, means something else: it means understanding why you are doing each step. Not necessarily the science behind it, but the reasoning. The balances between sweet and sour and bitter and acidic and fatty—truly understanding flavor.

At March, Wayne Nish knew how he wanted a dish, but he didn't follow traditional culinary methods to get there. He'd get in a cut of meat he hadn't cooked before and would cook it every way he could before determining what he thought was the best way to do it. I'd watch him grill, steam, and braise the same cut of meat just to try to understand it, and in watching him I learned a lot. There were some cooks at March, however, who were interested only in what they had to do on a given day.

The epitome of this was the meat cook, Hillary, a cranky guy from the Islands whose hair had started thinning years before I started cooking. He had worked with Wayne at the Quilted Giraffe and he was a competent cook. But he never deviated from his routine, getting there at the same time each day to opening his first Corona on the line while the rest of us cleaned the kitchen. Hill cooked every piece of meat the same way every day. Several of the cooks were like this. They knew their job and did it, end of story. But this wasn't the way I approached cooking and it wasn't the reason I was working there. March was continuing education for me and I wasn't alone. Though they were the exception, there were other cooks who were there to learn, including Chef Wayne Nish.

Of course, Wayne didn't need to learn about his own food, and, unlike Bouley, he wasn't continually developing each dish. But Wayne had a constant drive to learn everything about the world of food that was unknown to him, and it was contagious. As is true of any great kitchen, the chef is the source of energy that keeps the place running. While I was there, he was into game. Not just venison, duck, or ostrich (which was briefly in vogue on menus at the time), but things like elk and dove.

Working with these meats and trying to determine how a particular cut should be cooked also gave me an appreciation for elements of an animal that I really hadn't considered before, in particular offal. By strict definition, offal means waste, and in butchery it generally refers to organs and other trimmings. But one man's garbage is another man's delicacy, and several items that are classified as offal are some of the best products for a cook to work with. I had cooked offal before, and it was on the March menu, in items such as a dish consisting of little peas with sweetbreads (thymus glands—in this case, of veal) and cream. Still, when we got a whole animal in, there were always parts of it that we wouldn't utilize. In a restaurant with food that was richer and heavier and less elegant, this might not be so. In this way March was limited by its refinement. In particular, I remember an especially young calf that I utilized in every possible way, but to do so, I had to bring some of it home to cook.

On my way back to Long Island one night after work, I called Mike to wake him up and prepare him for a treat. It was after 2:00 A.M. and, to be fair, he had to get up for work before 6:00, but I knew he wouldn't want to miss this.

When I got home, he had a small Teflon pan, a chef's knife, a cutting board, and a bowl of cold water ready, as I had instructed him while en route. He was the only thing that wasn't ready when I pulled out the fist-size veal brain and dropped it into the bowl of cold water. A fringe benefit of being a cook is bringing home food, which usually means high-quality ingredients that purveyors have dropped off at the restaurant for the chef to try. In this case, I rescued impeccable-quality veal brain from the trash because there were no other takers.

Peeling the membrane (a thin skinlike covering) off the brains, I found that the lobes were clearly separate and easily parted. I sensed that Mike was uneasy as I rolled each half in bread crumbs. His face was all scrunched up and his eyes were just barely open. He was clearly exhausted, but he also seemed skeptical. "How are you going to cook them?" he asked.

"In a little butter and olive oil," I said, and then I put the sauté pan on the stove and got it hot with a little olive oil. Once the oil was hot, I added the brain and a tab of butter. The pieces were moist and sizzled hard in the pan. The aroma was sweet with hints of browning butter. I moved the pieces gently around the pan and occasionally turned and basted them. When the pieces firmed up a little, a few minutes later, I seasoned them with lemon juice, and then coarse black pepper and kosher salt once they were on a plate. They tasted like tiny blocks of creamy cheese with an almost caramelized outside Mike was hesitant with his first bite, but then our forks were dueling for the delicate treat.

Besides learning a new system, a benefit of working at March was that it provided a relief from the Long Island Railroad, as the restaurant was just a few blocks off the Queensboro Bridge and thus easier for me to drive to from Huntington—especially since I rarely had to drive during rush hour—than the other option of taking the train and two subway connections.

Driving to and from March also gave me flexibility. I was no longer dependent on a train schedule, which made it easier to go out after work. Commuting by train, my days off were the only time I had to do anything or see anyone. Even though I was at March until midnight or later most nights, driving allowed me to see friends I otherwise wouldn't have had a chance to. One night in early July, I had plans to see two of my friends: Nora and Americo. After a few years of rarely talking, Nora and I were dating again, which mostly meant my stopping by her apartment in Brooklyn after leaving the restaurant or seeing her on days off. As for Americo, I hadn't seen much of him since I stopped working on Long Island, but now he was cooking in the city.

Arriving at March that morning, I descended the small staircase and went into the doorless coatroom—the only option, besides the hallway—to get changed. I replaced my street clothes, which I carefully folded so that they wouldn't be wrinkled when I wore them that night, with checks and a white chef jacket. Then I made my way into the kitchen. There was no urgency as at the Bakery. For the most part, everyone in the kitchen had been there long enough (some since the place opened in 1990) to just come in and do his job.

As I made my way onto the line that morning, James, who worked next to me, was already there writing up his mise en place list. James is a Filipino from blue-collar Staten Island. He was the only cook on the fish station. He was in his mid-twenties and liked to joke around, but took cooking seriously. Farther down the line my partner, Tim Chen, had already finished our mise en place list and was working on getting our station's prep work done.

Through the morning and afternoon Mr. Chen and I steadily worked our way through our mise en place. In the late afternoon we went upstairs to the dining room to have "family meal" with all of the cooks and waiters, and then worked service. We had a steady flow of customers—there were two seatings at March, an early one at 6:00 P.M. and then one at 8:30 P.M.—and the orders were called out as they were needed. Our station was the first to get busy and the last to finish, since we were responsible for the first and last dishes for all of the tables. When the service died down, we cleaned up our station. This is what cooking is. Much of it is mundane, but there's nothing easy about getting through it. Cooking is being on your feet all day; it's cutting your fingers, wrapping them up, and continuing to fillet a fish; it's burning your hand on a pot handle and still sticking it into the oven all night long. It's not feeling pain and doing what you've learned to do, over and over again, as soon as you're told to do it.

But cooking is also about learning and experimenting. Although I had only been at March for six months, I was already beginning to feel set in a routine, as most of the cooks there were. Mike Anthony, March's chef de cuisine, was an exception. He was always focused on something new. At the end of that night—even though we were tired and drenched in sweat—Mike stood around the metal table that we worked at all day and sampled vegetables that had been sent from a farmer in Ohio.

Mike was what every good chef should be: a professional. He knew everything about the restaurant and worked hard to run it. He was serious, but he rarely yelled. His quiet passion drove that kitchen, which he ran for years before his name was even in fine print on the menu. As with most restaurants, after a few years of serving the same food and firmly establishing an identity, it was a challenge to keep March creatively alive. The restaurant had to continue to grow, even while it was essentially remaining the same, and the responsibility for this lay on Mike's shoulders.

Mike had an innate curiosity about food and cooking, as all great cooks do. It's not always a conscious decision to set out to learn something; instead you find yourself in some kitchen late into the night cooking or eating or just talking about food that has nothing to do with a job. This is what creates the dividing line between someone who's just a cook and a potential chef. It was never a decision for me; I just always wanted to learn. Cooking was just about the only the thing I thought about, which partly explains why I stood around that kitchen talking about vegetables when I was already late to meet Nora and Americo downtown.

James was riding shotgun in my Corsica on our way downtown that night. We had the music on loud and the windows slightly rolled down. As I turned onto First Avenue, I gunned the engine to try to catch the green light. We were in a rush to get James onto the next ferry back to Staten Island and me to the Greatest Bar on Earth to meet up with Nora and Americo and his girlfriend, who were already there. The ferry station is at the very bottom of the island (the southernmost point), and the bar was just a few blocks uptown in the World Trade Center.

There were few cars on the F.D.R. and I cruised down it, along the East River, at an aggressive speed. I saw James off at the pier on time, with a knock of our fists, and then raced through Wall Street for one of the two tallest buildings in the city. The Greatest Bar on Earth was a swank bar near the top of One World Trade Center. It may not have been the greatest bar, but it was pretty damn cool. Several nights a week they had different themes, like swing or reggae. That night, because it was Saturday, it was hip-hop.

I stepped into the elevator, which was almost big enough to fit a car in, and leaned against the shiny metal walls as it shot up. Part of the reason for going to the bar that night was to celebrate with Americo. He had replaced me at Bouley Bakery when I left, and now I was going to return there (they needed cooks who knew their system and had asked me to come back), so we'd be working together again. I learned plenty from working at March, and some of that included the most basic tasks, such as how to organize a mise en place list that would make the prep time as efficient as possible. I learned this from Mr. Chen.

When the elevator finally slowed and then stopped at the 107th floor, I stepped into the black-tiled lobby between the Greatest Bar on Earth and Windows on the World, the fine dining restaurant that shared the floor. As I made my way into the crowded bar, the first thing I saw was the gleaming black water outside the window. So much of the city was visible through these windows. From the bar's windows, all of southern Manhattan, including the Statue of Liberty, was on display, and so was almost all of Brooklyn and, it seemed, even parts of Long Island. (On the restaurant's side of the floor, just about all of Manhattan could be seen.) To me, this was the world. I could see everything that made me who I was.

I could only make out pieces of the landscape, but I knew what was down there. What I didn't know was where my friends were—that is, until they were right in front of me. Nora looked miserable, and Americo and Nicole looked like they'd been arguing. Nora's short hair was plastered to her forehead. She stayed a few feet away, despite the loud music, and said, "What's up?" followed by a shrug. I could tell that she had something else she wanted to say, but she just smiled a little too warmly at me. Americo pounded my hand into a shake and Nicole gave me a hug.

Americo and I immediately started talking as best as we could over the music. He looked the same as when I first met him—still moving a mile a minute even when standing still—but he had obviously advanced as a cook. First making sure Nicole wouldn't hear him, he told me that he was thinking about going to Spain in the summer to do a stage. After just a couple of minutes of talking, we both turned to notice that Nora and Nicole were just standing there watching us. They were ready to leave. The place was crowded and hot, so I was with them in wanting to get out of there, even though I had just arrived.

Nora didn't say much to me the entire trip back to her apartment in Brooklyn. I dropped her off and then got back on the Brooklyn–Queens Expressway. Just after the road turns and then runs parallel with Manhattan's skyline, my cell phone rang. It was Nora. I lowered the music and then answered the call, delaying what I knew was coming. She was fuming and there was nothing I could say. It all came down to the simple fact that cooking comes first for me. This was the reason we had stopped spending time together the last time around. I didn't say this to her, because she knew it. Still she let me know how angry she was before hanging up.

She's given up, I thought, until the phone rang again. I was on the Long Island Expressway, halfway home. She sounded less angry now, just hurt. She was trying to understand, to deal with the situation. She asked me if we could see each other on Tuesday, my next day off. It was the only day I'd have off in the following two weeks. I was doing a stage at a new, fancy Indian restaurant, I told her. And that did it. She wouldn't be calling back.

If there had ever been a decision, it had been made a while ago. The reality of the cooking life is that there are few hours you aren't working that aren't spent sleeping. Holidays aren't spent with the family around a warm fire; those are the busy times. There are no birthdays and few vacations. You might get Christmas or Thanksgiving off, but it would be the first and only day off that week. You don't get off for New Year's Eve and you definitely don't get Valentine's Day. It meant that girlfriends would not stick around long. A relationship was a near impossibility. Your friends were mostly cooks. You went out and talked about cooking. That's all it was—just cooking. That's what it took and there was no looking back.

Of course, there are plenty of cooks who don't live like this. There are cooks who are married and have children. They aren't willing to give up everything. I understand why, but I was willing to give up anything to become the best cook I could be. Occasionally I had regrets, especially that I didn't see my family more and that my relationships with women rarely lasted long, but this was the life I had chosen and I wouldn't give that up for anything.

A few weeks later, on a rare night off from working at Bouley Bakery, I went out with my friends to celebrate. Ben had just graduated at the top of his law class. So, to kick off the beginning of power lunches and unlimited corporate dinners, my brother Mike, our friend Jason, and I took him out to dinner at one of the hottest restaurants in the city. Plus, Mike and I were celebrating our move into the city. We had lined up an apartment in Astoria, Queens, that we were moving into in a few weeks.

Before the desserts came, I made a trip to the restroom to freshen up. It had been a marathon meal, just about three hours, so getting up from the table felt good. I walked unsteadily, partly from sitting for so long in chairs that really weren't that comfortable and partly because my legs were stiff from working several days in a row. In the restroom, I stood in front of the mirror and splashed water on my face. My dark-brown eyes had red in them. I splashed more water onto my face and then pushed back my hair. The water mixing with the gel made it look slick and black. I ran my hands back under the water. Decorated with scars from cuts and burns, they were tough as leather and could clamp down as strong as a vise. I smiled into the mirror; these were the hands of a cook.

Chapter 8

Rapid Rise

Within just a couple of months after I returned to Bouley Bakery, a lot changed. The restaurant received four stars from the *New York Times* in September 1999, and then business increased considerably and so did the number of cooks. The kitchen was considerably bigger than when I first worked there—almost double its former size— and more functional. There were no longer just three of us, plus the chef de cuisine working the pass, as there was when the restaurant first opened. Now there were at least two cooks on every station. I worked on the fish station, but I was no longer the lowest guy in the kitchen. Since I knew the food and the system, I was there mainly to help the other cooks. I was responsible for making sure the station's mise en place got done in time for service, and I worked on new dishes for the tasting menu, which changed each day.

The fish station's mise en place consisted mostly of preparing sauces and vegetables for the fish dishes. We rarely cleaned any of the fish we used, as Bouley always had "the family" do all of the restaurant's butchering. "The family" was a Dominican family who worked together downstairs. They were an excellent team of prep cooks. Besides butchering all of the meat, poultry, and fish, they also cleaned vegetables, made fruit and vegetable juices, and did so much more.

When the Bakery first opened there was just one cook in charge of meat and fish, so there was a lot to do. Now, with several cooks on fish, we were able to focus on making sure everything was done perfectly. Although it was still a challenging place to work, it was considerably less stressful. I was working the same hours as when I first started—five days with one double—but it wasn't nearly as demanding. Also now that I lived a subway ride away I spent many of my days off doing stages in other kitchens around the city.

It was a Thursday in early November, a beautiful fall day in New York. It was windy and the air was crisp. The city felt alive: people were everywhere rushing somewhere. It was a day off for me, but I was on my way to do a stage.

I stopped outside the front window of the sushi restaurant before going in and shut off my cell phone. I had already learned that it shouldn't ring while I was in the restaurant, and it shouldn't even be with me when I was working. This was just a stage, but I was still respectful to the chef and his restaurant. Before entering the front door, I also took off the khaki Polo jacket I was wearing and put it over the knife box I was carrying. The chef's wife—a Japanese woman with a nearly perfect powdered porcelain complexion—was arranging the hostess stand as I walked in. She was wearing a purple floral blouse and black pants. She looked up, ready to greet a customer who had come in too early, and kept her friendly smile for me. "So good to see you," she said.

The room was quiet. It was slightly warm and there was only the faintest scent of green tea in the air. I felt like an elephant at Tiffany. I slowed down as I walked past the four blond-wood tables in the front of the restaurant and the matching sushi bar on the right-hand side. At the sushi bar, there was a chef who had never spoken to me. He had slicked-back hair and a flat mole where his right cheek met his nose. He was wiping down the board in front of him with a rag—over and over, but only in one direction. He didn't nod at me when he saw me; he just looked at me and his head moved like a bobblehead that had been barely shaken.

The kitchen was directly behind the sushi bar. As I entered, Hiro, the chef and owner, looked at the digital watch on his wrist before looking up at me. "You're here, good," he said. I wasn't late; this was just how he greeted me. Hiro is about five inches over five feet. He was born in Japan, but he's American. His kitchen, though, is thoroughly Japanese.

I put my jacket on top of the ice machine and took an apron and a towel from the crate that was on the floor next to it. There were no extra chef jackets, so I just wore an old T-shirt and black pants. I folded the apron in half and tied it on. Then I washed my hands in the small dish sink.

The kitchen was what I'd become used to: tiny. But this one wasn't just small for me; it wasn't designed for me at all. The kitchen was geared toward Japanese cooks, who generally aren't six feet and two hundred pounds. There were three people working in the kitchen that night—usually there were only two. I was an extra and I knew from past nights that there would be times when we'd have our backs against each other. I also knew that we'd all be serious and we'd be quiet, and there wouldn't be any rushing around, which is good because the kitchen is no more than a hallway with appliances. Along the left wall were the dish sink, two stacked lowboy fridges, a wok, and a flattop. The other cook was heating a broth on the wok. He was young and spoke no English. He had come to the U.S. from Japan only a few months before and lived in the apartment that Hiro kept above the restaurant.

On the right side of the kitchen were a thirty-cup commercial rice steamer, a rice warmer, and then a long wooden table. Hiro was working at the table, and on it he had half a side of salmon, which he had cut into four-inch pieces, and a metal bowl filled with water and some lemon slices. He took one of the orange marbleized pieces and floated it gently back and forth in the water, shook it dry, and then he patted it dry with a clean towel on the table. His motions were slow, almost exaggeratedly slow. When he noticed that I was watching him, he said, "Doug, you'll slice the scallions and then cube the tofu, hai?"

"Hai," I replied. ("Yes" was about the only Japanese I had picked up.)

I took out my chef's knife from my knife box. Besides the sharpening rod, the only other tool in the box was a three-dollar paring knife (on stages, knives always seem to disappear, so bringing the cheapest ones was the best move). I learned the first night I did a stage at this restaurant that I wouldn't need any of my other knives. I wouldn't be involved in any cooking. I'd just help with the most basic tasks. During service that usually meant filling bowls with steamed rice, or salting and preparing a portion of edamame (fresh soybeans), or mixing a new batter for the tempura dishes. In this Japanese kitchen, I was only an apprentice. I was lucky to be allowed to use a knife.

Earlier in the week, on Tuesday, we had had one of the first cold days of the year. While I was working on getting the Bakery's fish station mise en place organized for the day, Raphael rushed into the kitchen as though he were fleeing for his life. He had his arms crossed tightly over his chest and his whole body was shaking. "It's disgusting out there, man!" Raphael is thin, bald, and pale. Even though he's Cuban-American, he's whiter than I am. He looked painfully white at that moment. He's from Miami, and he was in no way prepared for the New York winter, which had yet to really begin. Raphie calls brutally hot days beautiful. He's miserable on days with minimal overcast or a slight breeze. New York is not the place for him. He's only here for one reason: to cook.

When Raphie came back into the kitchen, dressed for work but still shaking, he put his hand on my shoulder. "Doug," he said as though in confidence. "Doug, it's cold, Doug."

"Raphie," I turned to look at him, "it's going to get a lot worse."

"No," he said and let out something that was part grunt and part squeal. "Do you need anything, Doug?" he asked, and after I told him no, I heard him asking Jimmy down the line. Raphie is a perfect gentleman. He's pleasant to an almost unbelievable extent.

"Ye-ah!" Jimmy said with an exaggerated "ye" and a rising "ah." Jimmy's eyes were wide open. "Have you seen my Coke?" he asked Raphie, repeating more loudly, "Who took my Coke?" He was asking about a two-liter bottle of Coke he had in his lowboy. Jimmy used his station's lowboy as his own personal refrigerator. It's supposed to hold butter and meat and other things that need to be kept cold and at the station. But Jimmy kept a variety of snacks in his lowboy, which provided for his constant feeding. Besides soda, it wasn't unusual to find cauliflower, celery, chocolate bars, and assorted candies.

Jimmy's snacks are the creature comforts that he counts on. Jimmy worked at the Bakery because it was a restaurant he wanted to be a part of and for no other reason. Most cooks work in kitchens like the Bakery either to learn or to build a résumé. Almost always these cooks struggle through poor pay to be at the right kitchen. For Jimmy, money is never an issue. He's from Wisconsin and because of his family he doesn't have to work. He chooses to be in New York to work in restaurants. Not so that he can take something away from them, but just to be a part of a great restaurant. Jimmy's desire to be in the kitchen is as pure as anyone's. We later called him Jimmy the Saint. He's a hard worker and a very capable cook, though he's rarely focused until service starts. Jimmy loves cooking but hates the discipline that comes with working in a kitchen.

As I was working on a lobster stock, Eric "Greenie" Greenspan trudged into the kitchen. He was the fish entremetier, which meant he cooked the vegetables for the fish dishes, and that meant he had a lot of work to do. Greenie watched me as I dropped a pile of lobster bodies into a stock pot. He was clearly not ready to work yet. Greenie certainly had had worse nights than the previous one, but his mornings are all the same: you can see pain in every movement.

Greenie has been compared to Yoda, and it's a comparison that he enjoys (in his wallet, he carries a folded-up article from a local newspaper that alluded to him as Yoda when he worked espresso magic at a coffee shop while going to school at UC Berkeley). The comparison is not completely off base, because he is wise, but mostly because he's short, his eyes are round and often half closed, and some mornings he's a shade of green that's only a bit lighter than the little guy. Greenie continually surprises people in kitchens because they always underestimate him. Taking a look at him then, you would have seen an unshaven and unkempt guy in his mid-twenties who was likely either to have just gotten off a bender or to be smack in the middle of one. But Greenie is a smart kid and he's quick to remind you of that.

Eric Greenspan, like the Karate Kid, went from being a New Jersey kid to being L.A. cool in high school. He never learned to kick ass (though he has a scar from a good beating), but he was creative and smart. After high school, he excelled throughout a business major at one of the best schools in the country. Then—instead of following his friends to grad school and easy, successful careers—he decided he was going to cook, so he enrolled in Le Cordon Bleu in Paris.

Despite his slow start that morning, Greenie ended up getting his work done on time. Downing espressos all day, he scrambled around the kitchen and managed to have his mise en place complete just as service was beginning. He didn't even have a moment to stop moving. Right from the beginning of service we were getting killed. It was a busy lunch and there was no shortage of fish lovers. Brian Bistrong, the chef de cuisine, called out orders rapidly and marched back and forth to each station.

"Put two lobsters in the butter, fire a tuna and a skate," he called to me, and then, "ten lobsters in the butter." (The lobsters were first steamed and then poached in a pan with a butter emulsion.) We hadn't anticipated so many lobster orders, so while there would be enough lobster if we got more orders, Greenie would be short on the veg prep. When orders come in like this, it isn't that hard on the guy cooking the fish. As long as there are enough portions, it just means firing more. The entremetier takes the hit because most of the veg items take longer to prepare.

Greenie hustled off the line—pulling up his checks, which had six-inch cuffs, to keep from tripping—and ran down the stairs to get more heirloom tomatoes. As he did this, I took care of the fish, the veg, and the sauce. That meant moving quicker and working harder, but I loved it. I was comfortable running the whole station by myself, managing ten things at once and pushing to keep up with the continuing onslaught of orders. There was urgency in every movement I made, but absolutely no panic.

As the service died down, there was a general sense of relief in the kitchen. We continued to work, but the end was in sight, and so everyone relaxed a little—that is, except for Bistrong, who was still marching around the kitchen making sure everything was perfect. Bistrong is relentless. Five foot three and fearless, he's like a culinary Napoleon. As the dictator passed by our station, I saw him watching everything.

Soon after he made it around to the other side of the kitchen, I heard Bistrong yell out, "Damn it, if I see you stick that spoon in your mouth and then back in the sauce again, I swear to God, I'm going to shove it down your throat!"

I didn't see who he was yelling at, but I didn't doubt that it was Zvi. Even though Zvi is one of the toughest guys I've ever met and about twice his size, Bistrong wouldn't hesitate for a moment to use strong tactics to get him to work the right way. All the same, Zvi is Israeli, ex-military, and seemed ready to snap at any moment, so he was not the best person to threaten. Also on the other side of the room were Americo and Albert Wu, one of whom was possibly the true target of Bistrong's reprimand.

Americo had been cooking at the Bakery for about a year. He was still living on Long Island and dealing with the difficult commute. He worked alongside Albert, a serious but relaxed Chinese guy who was cooking in restaurants so that he could use that knowledge in one of his family's restaurants on the Upper East Side. I first met Albert when he was working at March, and then I met him again when he was deciding whether to join the Bakery right before the renovations. He decided against taking the job, but when I rejoined the Bakery he was working there.

These two guys and everyone else in the kitchen were among the many cooks who kept the Bakery running smoothly and at a very high level. Having grown from just a few cooks in a very small space before the renovations, the Bakery was now operating at full speed, and at the four-star level that it had earned. This new team had many different cooks—each there for his own reason—and, partly because there were so many cooks now working there, not everyone was equally dedicated to the restaurant.

There were basically two different types of cooks who joined the restaurant: the ones who would commit to the restaurant, learn the system, and be a part of it, and the ones who were just there so they could say that they had been there. Some cooks were there to learn and left when they thought they couldn't learn any more. Other cooks just checked in and stayed the mandatory minimum, one year, as a résumé builder. This isn't unique to Bouley Bakery. Restaurants all over the world are filled with cooks looking only to add the name of a top restaurant to their résumés.

I had always looked to work in the best restaurants so that I could learn to be a better cook. I worked in or did stages in as many kitchens as I could, so I could learn as much as I could. Learning only one restaurant or chef's system limits a cook. Just as at any school, a good education is a well-rounded one. And, eventually, there has to be a graduation.

Brady was one of the cooks at Bouley Bakery when it first opened, and he was my first friend to cash in his chips. Before I even met him at the Bakery, he had been working hard at restaurants around the city. Like me, he learned to cook and then cooked to learn. He was in his late twenties, had short dark hair, and had a thick wrestler's build. He was vocal and energetic in the kitchen. He was also ambitious, and by the time I met him he was pretty open about being ready to take on his own place. We'd talk about it a lot. Brady was ready, but I knew I wasn't.

We were constantly focused on the world of cooking and restaurants. When we weren't working, we'd read books, magazines, newspapers. There was never enough information, and even after finishing a fourteen-hour day, we still talked about cooking. All of that leads to ideas. They might be the most ill-conceived ideas of all time, genius, or somewhere in between, but they're your own ideas. You start planning the food you'll cook, your menu, and your restaurant. All of the learning and all of the hard work has to lead somewhere.

The last time I saw Brady was when we had a meal together at the sushi bar of a place called Hasake in the East Village. It was a good meal, though I mistakenly tried fish eyeball for the first and last time. Brady was at full throttle the whole time. He had left the Bakery and was about to become the chef at a restaurant called Vox, which would open a few weeks later.

After Vox opened, it was just a few weeks until things fell apart. An initial uneasy relationship with the owners got worse as everyone realized what they were involved in. There was poor planning (from the building and location to the design), poor management, and poor team organization. Soon after Vox opened, Brady was out. After that, he was an ex-chef, and pride alone made it difficult to get back to work on someone else's line. As far as I know, he never did.

As I walked toward the subway at the end of that night, I thought about Brady's move. The following day, the first of two days off, I had a dinner meeting to discuss a chef opportunity of my own.

Another cook with whom I had worked at the original Bouley Bakery was a Dominican guy named Alex. He came to the Bakery when he returned to the city after cooking in Spain for a few months. He was a talented cook, smart and creative. He understood so much about food, and we shared many of the same thoughts on cooking. He came from a humble background and worked his way up to the top of one of the best kitchens in New York. He gained a lot of respect along the way, and certainly mine. Like me, he had worked hard to get as far as he had. Now, he was ready to run a kitchen, and so was I. That's why we were at Peacock Alley with Peter, who was planning to open a new restaurant.

Peter was putting together the pieces for his first restaurant. I'm not certain how he knew Alex, but he had gotten in touch with me through a friend at the Bakery. He wanted to talk to us about running the kitchen in the new restaurant.

Peter had chosen Peacock Alley, a restaurant in the Waldorf-Astoria that was run by Laurent Gras, who had once been the chef de cuisine at both of legendary French chef Alain Ducasse's Michelin three-star restaurants. His food was rooted in classical French techniques but infused with modern imagination. The food was easily some of the best I'd ever had. The crepinette was particularly amazing. It's a traditional dish of braised meats wrapped up in caul fat (the fatty membrane encasing the abdominal organs, usually of pork or sheep). This one contained virtually every rich food—foie gras, short ribs, and pork belly.

Ideas flew around the table. We started with champagne and talked the entire meal. There were so many great ideas that Alex and I knew we could pull off. And Peter seemed to love what we were saying. As we ate and drank, we formulated concepts that would make for a very solid restaurant.

The idea for the restaurant was simple: a neighborhood place that served great food. The food wouldn't be fancy—there would be no luxury ingredients—but it would be a little nicer and more refined than the average neighborhood place. It would be a small and comfortable restaurant, where people would want to become regulars and the prices would be low enough for that to be possible. Peter already had everything lined up, including a perfect spot near Washington Square Park and some invaluable media connections. He just needed a kitchen team. He would own the place (along with his brother), but Alex and I would run the kitchen. Our only concerns would be cooking and running the kitchen. There couldn't be a better first opportunity for two young cooks.

The next night after the meeting at Peacock Alley was that Thursday in early November when I did a stage at the sushi restaurant. Nothing had been decided by the end of the meal, but I was confident that it would work out. It was good for me to be at the sushi restaurant the next night because it brought me back to earth. If nothing else, the sushi restaurant provided contrast. I wasn't the possible co-chef of a new restaurant there; I was just a lowly apprentice.

My nights at the sushi restaurant ended differently from those at any other restaurant I've worked in. Before leaving, all of the cooks sat down to eat together. At other restaurants, everyone headed for the door as soon as they were done cleaning up.

After we cleaned that night, I sat at a table with the sushi chef who didn't speak to me and the young Japanese cook who didn't speak English. In silence we drank tea and ate miso soup and ton-katsu, breaded fried pork cutlets on top of cabbage with a seasoned dipping sauce. I was enjoying the snack and trying not to eat as fast as I normally do when Hiro waved me over to the empty sushi bar.

Hiro turned his back to the table the cooks were still sitting at before talking to me. His hand was on top of a long, narrow box that he had put on the counter. "This is what you want?" he asked me. He didn't remove the three fingers that held the box down. I knew what was in the box, and I knew that he was reluctant to give it to me. He had told me as much when I first asked him. Terrible idea, he had said. I wasn't ready.

I looked at him and nodded.

"Put it with your coat now and take it home." He took his fingers off the box.

"Hai, thank you," I replied and took the box into the kitchen. I resisted the urge to look inside before sticking the box inside my black plastic knife box. It was my first sushi knife, selected for me and given to me with great reluctance.

In the rigid order of Hiro's world, I wasn't ready for a sushi knife. In his world, it would be years before I ever sliced fish. But in my world I was ready to put all of my learning and hard work to the test. I was ready for a new challenge.

Chapter 9

Cooking by the Book

After our meal at Peacock Alley, there were a few other meetings before it was decided that Alex and I would run the kitchen of Peter's restaurant—and then we celebrated with another meal. I wasn't concerned about any of the particulars, except for the freedom to create. I was confident that Alex and I were going to do outstanding food. The decor, silverware, plates, and almost every other element outside of the kitchen had never been a concern of mine before. But now they were, and I would end up being involved in all of them, and in almost every other minute detail. Putting together the restaurant was a cooperative effort in almost every way. It was Peter, his brother, and his brother's wife, and then Alex and me, weighing in on almost every decision. We started working in January, meeting often and taking trips to different suppliers for equipment and serveware. Even though the location was well on its way before I got involved (Peter had used it for his catering company), there was still so much that was needed to make it a restaurant—it was exciting to be a part of the process. It was a lot of work, even before we began to conceive the menu or got into the kitchen, but my excitement never waned. I worked every day, right into February and the restaurant's soft opening.

On a cool, damp night in early February 2000, the restaurant opened its doors for its first dinner service. It was just a friends-and-family service, which meant only invited guests and reduced (or no) bills. This is typical for a restaurant opening. It's a rehearsal that helps to determine if the kitchen and the front of the house are up to speed and whether they're working in tandem. It also allows the restaurant to make sure that its VIP clients get a first opportunity to eat there, and usually there is at least one day devoted to the media.

For these friends-and-family dinners, I invited a few friends—some from Huntington (like Laura and Jason) and some from kitchens (including Greenie)—and just one family member, as my brother Mike was the only one from my immediate family who hadn't left New York. My older brother, Andy, was now living in Colorado and my sister, Jen, was down in South Carolina, along with my parents, who had retired and moved south to be with her. I had always thought about the day when my father would see my first restaurant, when I'd be running my own place just like his father. These special dinners would have been perfect for the occasion, but he wasn't able to come up to New York on the short notice that we had to invite people.

The restaurant was located downtown on a street lined with town houses and other small buildings. It was a prime location for a simple neighborhood restaurant. A few steps led down to the front door, which opened into just one small room. The lights were soft, yellow, and warm. There was a row of high-backed fabric banquettes that stretched along the entire right side of the room, a bar against the wall on the left, which spaned half the distance into the restaurant, then more banquettes, and a few tables in the middle.

Everything in front of the seated guests—white face plates, white tablecloth, silverware, and stemware—was part of the decision process I'd been involved in. To see the restaurant come together as it did was thrilling. Some corners were cut—the limited budget had to be used judiciously—but in a short time we had created a casual but elegant place. By making Alex and me part of the creation of the front of the house, Peter had made us truly feel like part of a team, together with him and his family.

Of course we weren't all equally knowledgeable about everything. We were all involved in the process, but each of us had his own areas of strength. Peter focused on the wait staff and the additional kitchen help. The food and the menu were, of course, where Alex and I concentrated most of our efforts. But we didn't just blindly cook whatever we wanted. The whole team shared a vision and it was our job to create within those boundaries. Even so, this was our chance to prove ourselves as chefs.

The food that Alex and I were cooking was defined by the cooks we were at the time. Almost every dish could be traced back to what we had learned in other kitchens. Breaking down certain dishes could reveal where either or both of us had come from and where we were trying to head. Obviously inspired by his time working at Ferran Adrià's El Bulli in Spain, Alex created an asparagus soup with parmesan foam. The very slowly poached salmon with a pistou of vegetables illustrated a technique we learned while working in Bouley Bakery, when Bouley invited experts to do a presentation for the kitchen on sous vide cooking—which involves cooking in vacuum-sealed plastic pouches, often for several hours at a very low temperature.

Perhaps no dish displayed the evolution of my learning better than the poached duck. It was a skinned duck breast that I poached in a beurre blanc and duck stock, paired with duck leg confit, and crisped up before serving on top of sautéed artichokes. The concept for the dish was firmly rooted in my past. Besides using the duck confit that I had first toyed with at Panama Hatties, it also relied on techniques I had learned at March. Wayne used to skin a duck breast before grilling it. He had shown me that the texture of the duck skin was not always a good thing and that it got in the way of the flavor of the meat, and he also liked to poach skinless chicken breast. My dish combined these principles. It wasn't revolutionary, but it was unique. It was one of my first original dishes.

At the end of the first friends-and-family night, there were smiles all around. The night had gone well. As I was leaving, Peter was leaning against the tiny staircase in the middle of the kitchen, which led to the upstairs office. He looked tired but relieved. He ran his hand through his hair and then shook my hand. His smile was huge; he had the same feeling that I had. It had been a good night. There were problems, including service issues and getting the orders out quicker, but this was normal for bringing a place up to speed. Most important, we now knew that the combination of food and atmosphere was going to be a success. There didn't seem to be any doubt. As sure as we were that there was still work to be done, we were equally sure that we were on the right track. In just over a month of work, we had put together a very solid restaurant.

About a week later, the restaurant was still finishing up with friends, family, and media dinners. Predictably, there were services that went as well as the first night, some that went better, and a couple of near disasters. But we were still confident that the formula was working. It was just a matter of getting the machine to run smoothly and efficiently. This was the agenda of one midday meeting we had. The restaurant would serve only dinner, so—while we took a break from our mise en place—Alex and I joined Peter and his brother and sister-in-law at one of the tables in the empty dining room.

Without the benefit of the yellow glow that was cast over the restaurant at night, the dining room looked plain and ordinary. It was a bit eerie to be in the dining room when it was so quiet and dim. There were shadows in corners where daylight managed to sneak below street level and under the front door. Only a few of the lights were on and they were doing little to illuminate the room.

The fact that Peter had managed to do what he had on little more than a shoestring budget was remarkable. Once the kinks were ironed out, we would have the restaurant that we had hoped for. I sat quietly during the meeting taking in everything that was being said. Much of the discussion focused on identifying the problems and trying to fix them. Alex and I were the only ones at the table with considerable restaurant experience, but that was almost entirely in the kitchen, so we were learning how to run the front of the house as we went.

I agreed with everything that was being said until I heard Peter's brother start talking about the food. We should showcase the chicken dish, he said, as that's what everyone would order. The chicken dish or the hanger steak would be our top sellers. Perhaps if this suggestion had come from someone who had been a cook, I might have taken it better. If I hadn't gotten involved with the restaurant for the opportunity to create my own dishes, I might have just agreed without thinking twice.

Alex and I were trying to make the restaurant's food unique

and extraordinary. Rather than serving the exact same food that most restaurants served, we had created dishes with some distinction, either by preparing the food in an interesting way or using ingredients that were somewhat out of the ordinary in New York restaurants. During the friends-and-family meals, dishes with things like asparagus foam or beets or pork belly had gone over well. But now we were being told that these were the scary things that people wouldn't order and that the most ordinary dishes on our menu were the best.

Peter immediately sensed my displeasure, but neither of us said anything. I don't know what Alex thought, but I just stared through the bleak, magic-less restaurant at the front door.

Following the meeting about showcasing the chicken dish, Peter became considerably more involved in the kitchen. He was no longer just providing input. He was now a much more active member of the kitchen team. Peter, whose experience consisted of little more than a few stages and running a small catering company, was helping us continue to develop the menu. I didn't know it at the time, but he had become one of the chefs.

One morning Peter bounded down the staircase from his office into the kitchen in his spotless chef jacket and black pants. I was behind the line working on a stock and Alex was in the back of the kitchen.

Stopping in front of the pass with a bounce on his heels, Peter looked as excited as if he had just won the lottery. "Let's try these short ribs," he said. Alex came over to the pass and I turned around to face Peter. In his hand was a sheet of paper. "I just found a great recipe for short ribs!" As Alex read the recipe, I turned back to what I had been doing—skimming fat off the surface of a chicken stock. I had never heard of a chef using a recipe for a dish; we were supposed to be creating our own dishes. Certainly there were basics—like a recipe for a corn muffin or a dough—that provided chefs with guidance, but we weren't in the kitchen to connect dots. Everyone reads books and magazines to know what's out there and for inspiration, but not to re-create someone else's food. Alex and I had digested the information we needed from working with chefs in their kitchens, and we were now creating our own food—and we didn't need a script to do it.

I kept working on the stock and pretended I hadn't heard what Peter thought was great news. It wasn't just the issue of putting some random dish on the menu that wasn't ours; I had a pretty good idea whose short rib recipe he had gotten.

"So, why don't we start working on this and see if you can't get it on the menu this week," he continued. When I turned around to get salt off the table, he said, "Doug, check out the recipe." I took the paper off the metal table, where Alex had left it. It was a faxed sheet with what I had suspected: a recipe for a well-known short rib dish from a famous chef who was on hiatus for the last few years while waiting to open a new restaurant.

I put the paper back down on the table and looked at Peter. I didn't meet his smile. Finally, I said, "I hear it's a great dish."

The short rib dish never made it onto the menu, but it was just the beginning of a new regime in the kitchen. I would come into the kitchen in the mornings and see Peter hard at work behind the line.

There would be equipment and food all over the counter and a cookbook open to whatever recipe he was working on. It could be *The French Laundry Cookbook*, which had just been published, or one of the classic Alain Ducasse books, or one of the El Bulli books in Catalan, or just about any other chef cookbook. As the weeks went on, it was clear that Alex and I were losing our creative control.

I'm not sure if Alex was as sensitive to this as I was, as he was focused mostly on doing what had to be done each day. It was just the two of us cooking on the line during service, and there were only two or three other people working in the kitchen at any other time. So, we had plenty of work between the two of us and our small crew. Also, Alex didn't want to make waves. His father had worked in kitchens (as a butcher for one of the city's best American restaurants), so having climbed from the bottom of the kitchen world to the top of this small kitchen, Alex had achieved a significant level of success, and he wasn't willing to jeopardize that.

While the short ribs didn't make it onto the menu, other dishes did, like foie gras, smoked eel, and apples, which was a dish taken directly from a famous chef in Spain. The borrowed creations weren't always complete dishes; most of the time it was just flavor components and combinations another chef had developed. Using these elements made the dishes on our menu nearly surefire successes, but this was essentially passing off another chef's food as our own. There wasn't anything I could say. It was clear to everyone that I didn't support this way of operating—I even openly derided it—but I couldn't stop it. The menu was basically divided (in my mind at least) between the dishes that Alex and I created and Peter's greatest rip-offs. To everyone outside the kitchen, there was no dividing line. The food was getting as good a response as it had when we first opened. Reviews were starting to come in (only one, in *Gourmet*, alluded to the eel dish as reminiscent of a dish created by a chef in Spain), and the early word of mouth supported what we had first thought: the restaurant was on its way to lasting success.

Despite the burgeoning success of the restaurant, I was growing uncomfortable with being a part of it. I had been working for many years nearly nonstop—as hard as I could, as often as I could—because I believed I was on track to become a chef. Having been slowly pushed out of the process of creating the restaurant's food, I was now just a cook in Peter's kitchen. This wasn't the reason I had left Bouley. We were successful: the restaurant was always busy and the reviews had been universally strong. But, eventually, all of that didn't matter.

On the day that I knew was my last, as I came into the kitchen Peter was leaning over a cookbook on the pass amid the general level of accepted chaos around the rest of the kitchen. I had been so focused on running my part of the kitchen that I hadn't even realized just what the kitchen had become. Besides Peter, Alex, and I, everyone else who worked in the kitchen was just a worker. These weren't cooks, they were just guys doing a job. They were all Dominican or Ecuadorian immigrants. None of them had worked in a kitchen before and they seemed happy just to have a job.

This was the first kitchen I had been in since Panama Hatties where no one was there to learn. In all of the kitchens I had been working in since Panama Hatties there was a chef and a team of what were essentially paid apprentices. Almost all of the cooks in these restaurants were there to learn. At Peter's restaurant, even Alex and I were just doing our jobs like everyone else. We weren't learning from each other and we certainly weren't learning from Peter. As the noose on our creativity tightened, I was grasping for a reason to stay in the kitchen.

It had become clear that the chef was Peter. And, perhaps because Alex was less vociferous about his displeasure with the restaurant's direction, Peter had been gracious enough to give Alex co-chef credit. I was fine with not getting any credit for the work I had put in. It even pleased me that my duck dish was praised in almost every review, especially in the *New York Times*. In my head I had already made the dish better, so it didn't bother me that Peter used the dish that hadn't been perfected as a signature. But what was the point of my staying at the restaurant? Peter would have been the first chef I worked for who I couldn't learn from. What he had to show me was out of the pages of another cook's book. If I wanted to learn from those chefs, I might as well be in their kitchen.

I was somewhat angry when I left Peter's restaurant but soon recognized the value in the experience. I understood that even though we were creating something that was often personal, it was still a business. Eventually I even understood that showcasing the chicken dish and other more common dishes was a smart move. In the short time I was part of the restaurant, I had learned I wasn't ready to run a restaurant. Many cooks find themselves in this position. They become chefs without knowing anything about how to run a kitchen, besides the actual cooking. Some culinary schools teach courses on restaurant management; I took this class at Peter's. What the cooking schools don't teach, though, is how to maintain a level of control over the restaurant where you are the chef. That's easy when the chef's an owner, but it's not so easy when the chef is just another employee. I know several cooks who were hired as a chef, created a menu and a system for the kitchen that worked well, and then were replaced by some cook who, for less money, would just follow their menu and system. Getting used was unfortunately a part of the business, but for me it was also an important lesson.

Unlike Brady, who had gotten involved with the wrong people, I was involved with the right people and the place worked. Peter knew what he wanted his restaurant to be, but he didn't have the kitchen experience to get it done. That's where Alex and I came in. I had been sold on the idea of working with Alex to create a menu and to run a kitchen, but once it was up and running Peter didn't need me in a leading role anymore. Alex and I were merely the supporting cast behind Peter's public success. Besides the mostly positive reviews and a nomination for the James Beard award for best new restaurant, Peter received a great deal of recognition for his efforts— he was named one of the best new chefs by *Food & Wine* and part of "the next generation" of cooks by *Bon Appétit*.

When I left Peter's restaurant, I had nowhere to go. I knew finding a restaurant I could run at the level that I aspired to would be impossible. Not given any credit for my role at Peter's, I hadn't developed a name for myself that would attract investors or restaurateurs. It would be hard for me to get another chef job at a place I would want to run, so I was back to being just a cook.

I had no choice but to return to another chef's kitchen. Many chefs have a problem taking this step back, to go from running a kitchen to being a cook on another chef's line. For me, though, that wasn't the problem. I was willing to start at the beginning again, just as I had at every restaurant I had joined, but I felt entirely directionless. I didn't doubt there was more that I could learn; I just didn't know whom I could learn from. Among the top restaurants, there just weren't many left that were right for me and that I would benefit from being a part of. There were new restaurants on the horizon, but they seemed far off or impossible for me to get into. Of all the restaurants that were supposed to open soon, the first New York restaurant of Alain Ducasse, the world's only eight-Michelin-star chef, was the most promising. But the information I had was sketchy at best: Ducasse was supposedly coming to New York with a team in place and no one seemed to know when the restaurant would open.

In New York, which has more restaurants than any other city in the country and many more fine dining establishments, there are only a dozen or two restaurants that fall into the top tier. There have never been as many as ten restaurants that have earned the *New York Times* four-star rating at any one time. Even with the most wildly optimistic count of fifty top-tier restaurants, there are many, many cooks from all over the world vying for those spots.

Even if I got one of those spots, what then? Was my goal to run a top restaurant or to run my own restaurant? I didn't know. I had never thought about it before. I had kept my head down working hard to learn how to cook for so long, but I had never contemplated what I'd do after I had become a chef. I was reluctant to just get back into the trenches without any sense of where it would all end.

About a year after I left Peter's restaurant, Alex followed me out the door, and he was replaced by Mike Anthony, who had been the chef de cuisine at March. Mike took over the role of co-chef with Peter. But as Peter's place grew even more successful, spawning another restaurant, Mike became a ghostlike presence whose efforts were invisible to the outside world. It was just Peter the Great Chef.

Mike had been the chef at March for several years before he had managed to get his name on the menu in fine print. He was a dedicated and talented cook, but even he was lost in the background while working in Peter's kitchen. Maybe that was fine by him. Maybe he was happy with that, but I thought he deserved more. I knew I wanted more, and I now knew that I would have to work even harder to earn it.

Chapter 10

Grilled

After a short pause, during which I took a couple of the vacation days that I had missed over the years, I was back to cooking in a kitchen. I was working for Laurent Tourondel at Cello restaurant. Tourondel is a French chef who is known for his incredible fish dishes. Cello was a restaurant with class. The dining room was low key and sophisticated, decorated in gray and muted colors. Cello was intended for an older crowd looking for luxury in a soothing atmosphere. Tourondel's cuisine was grounded in traditional French styles but with plenty of modern touches. There were a few meat dishes, but the focus was heavily on fish. We were serving very solid food, but for me it was mostly just a job. I respected the food coming out of the kitchen—it was of the same caliber as other great restaurants in the city—but it wasn't anything that I hadn't seen before. I chose to work there because I knew it was a respected restaurant, but really it was a choice made in the absence of a better alternative. The restaurant world was lean in terms of places where I could cook and learn.

Near the end of April 2000, on one of my days off from working at Cello, my friend Laura called to tell me that she was coming to see me. I was still living in the apartment I moved into after getting out of my parents' house on Long Island. I shared the top floor of a private house with my brother Mike and Marcelo, a friend from high school. The apartment, owned by a Greek olive oil importer, was in Astoria, a part of Queens that had once been predominately Greek but had become one of the city's biggest melting pots. The culture of the neighborhood changed just about every block, from Greek to Czech to Mexican to Brazilian to Egyptian to Thai to yuppie, and more. The neighborhood was just a few blocks north of the Queensboro Bridge, so it was very close to Manhattan (a few subway stops or a ten-minute cab ride). Since the bridge led right to 59th Street, it was a short and painless trip from Astoria to midtown, where many of the city's best restaurants are. Because of that, and because the rent was low and the apartments were relatively big, many people in the restaurant industry lived in Astoria.

Laura arrived, as she always did, late but with a huge smile. I had been impatient waiting for her, but quickly forgave her—just as I always did. I've known Laura since high school and she's a good friend, so seeing her made for a good day off. Besides wanting to hang out with me, though, Laura had another reason for coming by. In a few days she was driving to Colorado with one of her friends and they wanted a guy to take the trip with them. It would ease her mom's mind, but Laura also thought it would be good for me, that I could use the break to figure out what I really wanted to do.

Going out to Colorado on her urging had worked well for

me years before, so maybe she was right. I was beginning to lose hope that I would find a restaurant where I could continue to learn. As when I first left Peter's restaurant, I continued to believe that Ducasse's New York restaurant would be the best next step for me, but several months had passed and his plans were still unknown. Earlier that week I had a minor breakthrough: I had managed to get a woman at Ducasse's still unopened restaurant on the phone. The woman politely told me in broken English that I could fax over a copy of my résumé, but that she didn't know when the restaurant would open. It didn't sound as though she thought the restaurant would open in the near future, and after a few days passed and I hadn't heard anything in response to my fax, I started to share her skepticism.

When Laura left that evening, everything was pretty much settled. We were going to leave New York in a couple of days, take a few days to drive out west, and then I'd stay a week or so. In that time, I hoped to have gained some perspective on what I should do. I thought through all the logistics of taking the trip and was certain that it was the right move. Later that night Mike riddled my confidence with questions.

He asked what seemed like every question he could think of and I had an immediate answer for each. He was trying to convince me not to go, but it wasn't working. Finally, somewhat defeated, he said, "You know as soon as you leave, they're going to call you."

"Ducasse? They've had the fax since Tuesday," I replied. "If they were going to call, they would have by now. Besides I can talk to them from the road just as easily as from here."

"Yeah, but you can't go in if you're lost in the sticks in Colorado."

"They're not open. I don't know when they will be open—it

could be weeks from now or even September. Being here isn't going to make a difference." I knew he was right about the restaurant calling while I was away and that I might then lose that opportunity. But it didn't seem likely that I would be getting a call anytime soon.

"I think it's a terrible idea," Mike said.

I looked down at my hands, which were thick with calluses and scarred. "I could use a break. Getting out of New York will be good." For as long as Mike had been in college and through the first few years of his working in the city, I had been on my feet, sweating behind a hot stove—often leaving the house before him in the morning and working past his bedtime.

Mike kept telling me how bad an idea he thought the trip was while I sat there quietly thinking. He kept saying it was a mistake, that I would regret it, until I just couldn't take any more. "You just want me to keep working until I can't work any more," I snapped. My hand had instinctively balled into a fist. I didn't really blame Mike for wanting me to stick to the path I'd been going down, but he didn't understand how tough that road was. The conversation was over; I was taking the trip.

The first thing I thought about when I woke up the next morning was whether I'd hear back from Ducasse that day. That and the grilling Mike had given me the night before left me no longer convinced that Colorado was a good idea.

A few days later—the day after I was supposed to have left with Laura and her friend—I got a call from the French woman I had spoken with at Restaurant Alain Ducasse. They needed me to fax them another copy of my résumé. So, I called Mike at his office to have him fax the résumé to them. About an hour later, I got a call back. She told me to come in to the office at the Essex House. I was given a room number and was asked to be there at noon that day. I had to be at Cello by 1:00, so time would be tight. But I had been waiting for this opportunity and wasn't about to miss it.

The Essex House, on Central Park South between Sixth and Seventh Avenues, is a luxury hotel built in 1931. It's home to two hotels: the Essex House and the St. Regis Club, a separate and even more posh hotel on the top floors. The lobby, which stretches southward an entire block, from Central Park South to 58th Street, is huge. Because of its size, it wasn't crowded even though there were a lot of people moving through it.

I took the stairs because the office was on the second floor. It was a tiny office with a cluttered desk, beige computer monitor, a pile of papers on the floor, and two French guys sitting in chairs in front of the desk. They were both wearing suits. One of them was an inch or two over six feet and had his hair slicked back. He looked younger than the other guy, who was shorter, nearly bald, and wearing glasses. The big guy was also definitely in charge.

Neither of these guys was Alain Ducasse. One guy was Didier Elena and the other was his sous chef Olivier. I sat in front of them, in black pants and a button-down shirt (I had dressed up for the occasion but was still underdressed), as the two of them started talking to each other in French. Not knowing more than five or six French words, I didn't understand anything they were saying. Didier, the big guy with large round eyes, quickly looked up from the copy of my résumé he was holding in his hands, as if to see if I understood what they were saying. Then Olivier suddenly turned toward me. He stared without blinking, with a fierce intensity but at the same time a disinterested air. It almost seemed as though he wanted to hurt me, but was also indifferent to the task. I began to wonder what Mike had faxed them.

"Bouley," he said as though just stating fact. He didn't intone the name as a question, but I quickly realized that he meant it as one.

"Yes, I worked for David Bouley at his Bouley Bakery," I began and then talked about the restaurant and what I did there. I wasn't sure if they knew who Bouley was, so I explained his background a little. Moreover, I didn't know if either of them understood what I was saying. Neither of them said anything while I talked. When I stopped, Olivier turned to Didier and spoke a sentence or two in French. He seemed to be translating what I said, but while I had talked for five minutes or so, he talked for about ten seconds. Didier hadn't spoken English at all and seemed to understand even less of what I said than Olivier. The two launched into a full-blown conversation in French of which I understood absolutely nothing. It wasn't just a few things said between the two of them. They talked between themselves longer than I talked about Bouley.

When Olivier turned and stared at me again with his still, hard eyes through his round glasses, he said, "March." This time I knew he was asking me a question and I talked for a few minutes about Wayne Nish, March, and what I did when I worked there. Olivier translated my few words into a few seconds of French, and then the two again conferred. For all I knew, they were talking about anything but me or what I just said. I sat through several awkward minutes of them talking in front of me and then I was jarred again by Olivier. He asked me another question about my background, translated a few words of my response, and then got into another private conversation with Didier. After the third question, I sat there again uncomfortably while they talked. I tried to check the time on my cell phone without being noticed. I was already running late and wouldn't be able make it to Cello on time, but I couldn't interrupt them. After the fourth and final question, Olivier turned to me.

"Okay," he said in a heavy French accent, "you'll come in to-morrow, yes?"

I was again caught off guard—this time by the fact that the meeting had actually gone well and that they wanted me to come in tomorrow to start. The restaurant wasn't open; it wasn't even finished. I explained that I needed to give Laurent Tourondel, the chef at Cello, at least a week before quitting. They looked at each other and then nodded their heads in agreement. Didier had a huge smile on his face when he shook my hand. Olivier narrowed his eyes a bit, as though to tell me that he'd be watching me. As soon as I was out of the office door, I practically leaped toward the stairs, only partly to make up time.

When I told the sous chef at Cello I would be leaving in a week to work at Restaurant Alain Ducasse, she thought it was great. Like most people, she hadn't heard much more about the restaurant than I had. I really didn't have anything to add. Obviously the restaurant would open soon if they were hiring cooks. Beyond that, I only knew that the chef de cuisine and the sous chef were two French guys— not really surprising news. The fact that I would be working for Alain Ducasse, though, was all that mattered. I would start in his kitchen at the very bottom, as a commis, but that didn't matter to me, as I was willing to prove myself.

That day, though, Laurent Tourondel wouldn't look at me. I knew that he had been told I was leaving, and it was obvious that he was angry about it. I had been working for him for only a few weeks, but he was making it seem like I had ruined everything. I was giving him a week's notice, so it wasn't as though I was leaving him in a bad spot. I thought he might be taking it personally that I was leaving him to work for Ducasse.

That night during service Tourondel worked the pass, but he wouldn't so much as acknowledge me. Finally, toward the end of the night, he came over to me. He put his hand on the counter next to me and just stood there. He had short dark hair, dark eyebrows, and dark eyes. "You know," he said in English only slightly less heavily accented than Olivier's had been, "if it were me, I'd do the same." He then lifted his palm off the table and banged it once as if to say that that was settled. As he was walking away, he turned back to me. He rubbed his chin once, looked at the face on the big metal watch he was wearing, and then said, "Be ready, they're going to have you peeling the almonds in the basement."

Chapter 11

Alain Ducasse
New York

In May 2000, when I entered the kitchen of Restaurant Alain Ducasse (or ADNY, as it was called) for the first time, it was like walking onto the court at Madison Square Garden. This was clearly another league. The attraction for me was, of course, Alain Ducasse himself. He is widely considered to be one of the world's best chefs. Although he operates restaurants all over the world, this project was his first restaurant in the U.S. With ADNY, Ducasse didn't just open a small restaurant to test the waters. ADNY strove to be nothing less than the best restaurant in the city. Its goal was to set the standard that all other restaurants would follow. While this was never stated directly, it was clear from the very first day. This wasn't the first restaurant I joined that had serious aspirations. Bouley Bakery had once been in the same position and I had climbed with it to the top. So, I was ready and willing to play for a team that wanted nothing less than to be the best.

Alain Ducasse wasn't on the scene that first day, but what made me realize I was in the right place, and that I would fight to stay there, was the kitchen itself. It was levels ahead of any I had ever been in. In just about every other kitchen I had worked in at least part of the accomplishment was stretching to overcome physical limitations. There was no creative rearranging to overcome design shortcomings, and no corners were cut in creating this kitchen. It was not nearly the biggest kitchen in New York, but everything from the hundreds of pen-tip-size fiber-optic lights that would provide light above the stations to the hand-crafted stove was designed for excellence. It was clear that the cooks wouldn't be challenged to exceed the limitations of the kitchen, but to reach the level of excellence it made possible.

The first day I was there it wasn't to cook, but to help set up the kitchen. I spent the whole day unpacking supplies and helping out as needed. In addition to Didier, the chef de cuisine, and his sous chef, Olivier, there were a few other cooks around. Besides me, Scott was the only other American there that day—there would be two more in a few days. All the other cooks had come directly from France. Neither Scott nor I could speak any French, so there was a lot of pointing and gesturing being done. One of the first things that we were instructed to do was to unpack and put away the copper pans. Because they're much more expensive than other pans, most kitchens don't use any cooper pans, and those that do often use thin cheap ones just for presentations (for bringing a whole roasted fish to the table, for example). That day I unpacked dozens of copper pans, in just about every size, from small sauce pans to large roasting pans. We unpacked them, and then we were directed where to put them—many were put out of sight in a storage room. Then we moved on to setting up other parts of the kitchen.

The kitchen itself was designed better than any I had ever been in. When you entered from the dining room, the kitchen's automatic swinging doors opened to reveal a dazzling black tile floor and gleam-

ing stainless-steel equipment. It was an open kitchen with a large window that overlooked the main dining room, and there was even a private dining room in the kitchen. The massive stove took up much of
the kitchen. It had three flattops and one plancha, a mirrorlike metal
griddle. All of the stations would work around the stove. The pass
would be on the side closest to the dining room. The chef would stand
between the stove and an island (the servers' pass), and the servers
would pick up plates that he put onto the island. The dishwashers
would be in a separate room off the kitchen, and the front of the
house would have a separate room for its own preparations.

It was hard not to appreciate the stylish side of the kitchen. It is
as much of a show kitchen as those on the Food Network, but this one
is truly functional. As a cook, I appreciated the details more than anything. The stove, made by Molteni, one of the premier manufacturers,
was better than any I had ever used. It could reach and maintain temperatures that most stoves couldn't and was specifically designed not to
give off heat. Then there was the induction wok. This was a bowl-
shaped hole built into the stove top that would not conduct heat at all
unless the right wok was placed in it. You could touch the surface without any fear without the wok in. With the wok in, water would hit a
boil in seconds. It accelerated the heating process and it applied an
even heat throughout the bowl, which was nearly impossible for other
heat sources to equal. These were just some of the pieces of equipment at our disposal that I had never cooked with before; some, like
the induction wok, I had never even heard of.

Attention to detail is what Ducasse is all about. The thought that
went into everything was incredible, and this wasn't just regarding the
kitchen. The day after we unpacked the pans, we started moving in the
products—dry goods, produce, and meats. Also on the scene that day
were some of the staff for the front of the house. Part of their day was

spent being fitted for their uniforms, which had been specifically designed for the restaurant. The uniforms, custom designed for Ducasse, were both elegant and stylish. The front of the house would also have a second set of custom-designed uniforms that were to be worn when they were setting up. For a restaurant to purchase uniforms for servers for preservice work was unheard of. These weren't just aprons. They were full outfits, nearly as fancy as their serving attire.

The first two weeks at ADNY were a blur. From the very first day, though, everyone knew his place in the kitchen. There was a solid chain of command, a rigid order. The positions in Ducasse's kitchen are based on the traditional French model. There was, of course, Alain Ducasse at the top, then Didier as the chef de cuisine, then Olivier as the sous chef, then there was a chef de partie of each station: the entremetier (in charge of hot appetizers in Ducasse's kitchen), the garde-manger (cold apps), the *poissonier* (fish), and *rotisseur* (meat)—the pastry station, which also baked all of the bread, was separate. On all of these stations, the chef de partie was the saucier (in charge of the sauces) and the manager. He was truly the chef of the station, responsible for everything and everyone, from ordering, receiving, and evaluating the principal products for the station, to the dishes we sent to the pass, to how we cooked and dressed. Then there was a demi chef de partie, who did most of the actual cooking during service, and then there were a few commis—the lowest-level cook, who did whatever was needed. Everyone knew his position, and everyone answered to the man above him and for the man below him.

At least part of the reason that the kitchen team consisted largely of cooks Ducasse had brought with him from France was because the French cooks already understood his system. Besides me and Scott, a boy in an oversized man's body, there were two other American cooks: Brent, a perfect soldier in appearance—tall, thin, and athletic—and Brendan Sodikoff (Soda Pop), who had worked at Ducasse's top restaurant in Paris (ADPA).

A lot of kitchens are focused and competitive, but this was more like the marine corps than a restaurant. We were there to do a job and to do it absolutely perfectly. It didn't matter if you were good buddies with the guy working next to you or if you absolutely hated him. All that mattered was doing more than was expected of you.

The first time I heard the sous chef yell in his harsh broken English, "What the fuck is this! You insult me with this shit! This is shit!" it was over a broken sauce, in which the elements hadn't emulsified correctly. It was a scream of incomprehension, something that you might expect from someone who had just watched a stranger walk up to his mother in public and slap her. This was in the middle of the day when we were only cooking through the menu and plating the dishes so that we could understand them and perfect them. The recipient was a French cook who was the chef de partie of the station I was working on. He hung his head a bit but kept working. The restaurant wasn't open. We weren't even serving special guests.

Then we started doing private dinners. The first two weeks we cooked just for Ducasse and VIPs. Those were tough weeks, or so I thought until we opened. The restaurant was open Monday through Friday and all of the cooks worked all five days together, from 6:00 A.M. until about midnight each day. The intensity made you alert all the time, but that didn't mean mistakes weren't made.

As much as I tried to avoid them, mistakes were a part of the learning process. One of the first big mistakes I was involved in was a joint failure with Scott (or Scotty-do, as we called him). We were both working on the entremet station and one of the dishes we were responsible for was potato lasagna. It was a dish that required several layers of thin sheets of potatoes and alternating layers of spinach, tomato, and eggplant fillings and then was topped with a glaçage, in this case, a broiled béchamel sauce. It was just an accompaniment to another dish, but it took a considerable amount of time to prepare the potatoes and the fillings and then to layer them, glaze the top, and then bake them to make a gratin. During service that night, I bent down and pulled the potato lasagna out of the oven to find a complete mess. Scotty-do had forgotten to put on the last layer of potato and the glaze.

I didn't have time for more than a short, stunned pause before the lasagna was needed. Our chef de partie, a young French guy with light-brown hair and an expression of constant disbelief on his face, called for the lasagna twice before seeing the burned mound in front of me. He banged the base of his hand on his forehead. Didier was then calling for the dish. There was no hiding the mistake. There was no way to rush to put together a new one. Then Olivier was right next to me looking at the failed dish. He looked utterly disgusted and was just slowly shaking his head. He seemed ready to erupt. I was surprised he hadn't already.

The chef de partie bumped me out of the way as he tried to salvage what he could of the dish. He was picking burned potato off the top while Olivier was standing right over his shoulder. He was working as quickly as he could to do something about the lasagna. Then he reached over and moved a pan he had on the heat off the flattop. "Hey you, *vas-y*, huh?" Olivier yelled into his ear. "Come on, let's go."

The young French guy was shaken, but he was doing his best to clean up the mess that Scott and I had created while we just stood off to the side of the station—out of the line of fire. While he hadn't been involved with the mistake, the station was his responsibility, and so it was his fault that we had failed. This mistake didn't lead to anything more than anger, but mistakes like this could instantly move a cook back down the line. Our chef de partie could have ended up being replaced on our station, or Scott or I could have been bumped down to not cooking at all and just being a commis who assisted with the preparations.

Being moved down was the greatest threat in the kitchen. I learned very quickly that, for the most part, the policy wasn't to fire cooks; it was to keep moving them down the line and keep working them until they just gave up. Brent Johnson was a perfect example of this. He was a constant target of attack. I doubt it was because of his work; Didier just didn't like him. He had been completely moved off any station within the first few weeks and was put on butter and bread service. His job was to help with the most basic prep work, like picking herbs (which involves selecting the best leaves and separating them from the stems), and then during service he would plate butter and do the toast for the foie gras course.

I thought that was the worst job in the kitchen. A lot of cooks would be broken by having to do such a job all night. Like me, Brent wasn't new to working in restaurants. He had a decent amount of experience and would be leading in many other kitchens. But while many cooks would have placed their toque on the counter and walked out after a few nights on butter and bread, Brent was a lot tougher than most other cooks. He was ready to endure whatever they threw his way, and even seemed to enjoy it. Then he burned a whole lot of bread and Didier moved him down again.

Below butter was the basement, cleaning mushrooms and beans. This humiliating and painfully boring work was made worse by the fact that there was a video intercom system from the kitchen to the basement prep room. Didier would check in on him and yell through the intercom, "No time to sleep, huh, Brent? *Vas-y*, Brent." In the prep room downstairs, Brent would prep throughout service and then come upstairs to clean up. After that, he was put on candy, making the lollipops that were offered to each patron as part of a dessert cart at the end of the meal. He'd come in early in the morning and work in the basement so he had as little interaction with the rest of the team as possible. But Brent "Sugar" Johnson (as we came to call him) didn't give up.

I didn't know much more than *oui* and *merci* when I joined ADNY. I had started at the bottom of the kitchen, as a commis, but after just a few weeks I was moved up. The French guy who had been our chef de partie was suddenly moved off our station. Now I ran the station as the unofficial demi chef de partie, even though I didn't know French and that was the only language used during service.

For the first few days running the entremet station, I'd hear Didier call an order and I'd have to pause as I tried to figure out what he said before reacting. Olivier stayed near me most of the service to translate. "Hey, *homard*, lobster, *vas-y*," he'd say. I was constantly behind, almost unable to keep up. I had to pick up French right away— *à la minute*—or I'd be gone. So, I took one of the first printed menus home. I translated as much of it as I could (mostly by calling Greenie, who had returned to Los Angeles after giving up on a small restaurant in the West Village that he helped run), and after the first service I had learned at least the main ingredient in every course that I was involved in. I went back to work the next day ready to listen for *homard*, *petits pois*, *poularde*, and more. But the menu had changed and only a few of the words I knew remained useful. I was back to memorizing in the time between work and sleep.

Learning French was difficult, but it was not the only learning I was doing. It had been a while since the food I was cooking was new to me, but ADNY was eye-opening in terms of ingredients I had never seen before—like spiny lobsters and squid smaller than a pinkie nail—and new ways of using common ingredients. The Ducasse method was based on cooking with the finest ingredients in the clearest way. Clams, for example, were steamed then taken out of their shells, and their bellies, the pillowlike part, were trimmed off, leaving just the tiny edge (technically the umbo, but called shark's fin). That was all that was served, even of the tiny clams. The rest was discarded or used for "family meal."

Only the best parts of the best ingredients were used, even with expensive ingredients. Ducasse demanded to receive foie gras wrapped in paper instead of plastic—as all other U.S. restaurants received it in accordance with FDA regulations—because that way the blood didn't soak and ruin the texture of the liver while it was in transit. Many restaurants would serve portions of either of the two lobes of a foie gras, but at ADNY only the better (large) lobe was used for the plate and the other lobe was used for sauces. The best black truffles I had worked with in other restaurants were the size of plums and often barely fragrant. We were using black truffles the size of fists that would overpower just about every other smell in the kitchen.

The food costs of a restaurant are watched over more than anything else. There are fixed costs to a restaurant—like rent and utilities—but one thing that can be, and often is, tweaked is the amount that each dish costs the restaurant, and correspondingly how much is charged for the dish. Using a cheaper cut of meat is a surefire way to reduce the food cost on a dish, but it sacrifices the quality. The cost of a luxury ingredient dish, such as one served with foie gras, truffles, or caviar, is often adjusted by decreasing the amount or the quality of the luxury ingredient. Another option that is common is cutting back on the quality of the background ingredients, such as butter, oil, vinegar, or other basics. Since something like celery is used for the base of a stock and will thus not be served to a customer, there is some sense in not using expensive organic celery. At ADNY, this type of thinking just didn't apply. Cost was never an issue. The restaurant served the best food in every way possible.

The most prominent example of this was the butter. Before working at ADNY, the butter I'd worked with was ordinary American butter. At ADNY, we used excellent and expensive French butter. We used the same butter we served on the table to cook everything from poached lobster to toast points. It was like cooking with fine wine. There is a huge difference, I learned, between cooking with butter that tastes great completely unadorned and butter that is barely pleasant to taste straight up. We cooked with fine cognacs and wines for the same reason.

There was a lot for me to learn, and just as I picked up on the French that was yelled out or at me the minute I needed to, I was learning all of this while pushing to work as fast and as efficiently as I ever had before. Over and over, Didier would scream "*allez, allez, allez*" or "*vas-y!*" both of which essentially meant let's go, move, faster. If you weren't frazzled by all of the work and the learning overload, the tension to move faster—to get everything right at a breakneck pace—would do the trick.

There was a true fear of failing everywhere in the kitchen—not just of letting down the guys, but of being humiliated and ridiculed in front of everyone because of a mistake. Working clean took on a whole new meaning, and not just because during the first two weeks we were open we were also responsible for washing our pots and pans. I learned to not leave my knife on the cutting board. It was used and then it was put away. Dish towels were tucked into your apron, never left on the counter. Chef jackets should be spotless. Aprons should be clean or another one should be used. You didn't just show up to work. You were clean shaven before you got there. This was a serious professional kitchen that demanded the cooks be serious professionals.

The first few months at ADNY were a difficult time, but I was part of a kitchen that was striving to be one of the best in the city. At this restaurant I didn't have to seek out things to learn; I only had to try to keep up with all that I could see. It took time to get up to speed, but eventually I became a solid Ducasse cook. Instead of just observing at ADNY, I started truly helping the restaurant succeed.

Halloween 2000 was in most ways like every other holiday for me: I was working. What made this day different, though, was that by midnight we'd be certain of our fate. I knew by the time service was over that night, when the *New York Times* was first available on the newsstand, we'd either be celebrating or facing changes.

Tension in the kitchen may have been cranked up a little bit, but it was hard to tell. The tension was always high. You didn't sleep much outside the kitchen and you definitely didn't sleep your way through your time there either. But while the intensity hadn't leveled off in any way, a forced camaraderie had developed. We had all been shuffled around the kitchen so much that we had had a chance to work with cooks throughout the kitchen.

By now, although the kitchen was still French in every way possible, slightly fewer than half the cooks were American. A few of the French cooks who had come in the beginning had now left and we had several new cooks. A couple of months after ADNY opened, Joel became one of the first new cooks to join the restaurant. He was a shirt-tucked-in, clean-cut Republican from Rochester. Naturally, he was a hard worker, so he fit right into the rigid system. He seemed to love the ferocious battle that each day brought, except he hated the way the French cooks pronounced his name. They said it like "Noël." The Americans, of course, also called him "Jo-el." Besides me, Jo-el, Scotty-do, Sugar, and Soda Pop, the Americans in the kitchen by October also included a country boy from Mississippi named Rusty "Rustang" Barlow, and Greenie had come back from L.A. just to join the team.

There were still several French cooks, including Armand, who came from a wealthy family in Paris, and Florent—who we called le petit fleur, because in many ways he was like a delicate flower. But few of the French cooks were as experienced as any of the American cooks. Most had worked in Ducasse's kitchens but nowhere else. All of the American cooks had worked in many restaurants before and had been cooking for a lot longer. So, there was a great deal for the two different groups to show each other.

Then there was our dishwasher team. I had been looking forward to their being hired, and not just because we wouldn't have to wash our own pans. I had assumed they'd speak either English or Spanish, so I'd have more people to talk to in the kitchen. But they were a team of Africans. Most dish rooms in New York restaurants were populated by Spanish-speaking workers. The reason ADNY hired Africans was because they all spoke French. They had no problem communicating with the French cooks. But, like the French cooks, most of them spoke little or no English. The head dishwasher, Stephen, spoke the most English, but mostly he'd just say "hey."

Stephen was a huge man, nearly a giant. His hands were incredibly large and heavy. He was a family man with a few small children, but I couldn't imagine him holding a baby without crushing it. He was a great guy and we got along well, considering how little each of us understood of what the other was saying. Stephen liked to joke and liked to punch me when I was off guard to see how tough I was. More than once, he gave me a shot in the shoulder or back that just about dropped me. I'd laugh it off and try to get him back later on, though he'd just laugh when I did. Punching and getting punched by Stephen was one of the rare examples of joking around in that kitchen. For the most part, that just didn't happen.

That Halloween morning, though, one of the least likely sources managed to get the whole kitchen to relax a bit—if just for a second or two. Olivier, the sous chef, always skirted the line between aggressive and dangerous. He was maybe half a foot short of six feet, but stocky. Around thirty-five years old, he had probably been cooking for at least twenty-five of them. He understood exactly what Ducasse meant by perfection. It almost seemed odd that he wasn't the chef and Didier, who was a few years younger, the sous chef. Regardless, together they managed to control every last detail of that kitchen.

Olivier loved it when things were toughest. He thrived, even seemed to enjoy himself, when everyone else was miserable. During his normal weaving in and out of the stations to check that all of them would be *en place* (ready) for service, he passed by one of the dishwashers. All of a sudden he broke into a song. To the tune of Bob Marley's "Buffalo Solider," Olivier started singing: *Flown in from Africa, to wash dishes in America, woo-oh-oh, African dishwasher in a French kitchen in America . . .* Most of us stopped working for a moment in amazement, then the moment passed and we went back to work.

By Halloween, I'd been in charge of the entremet station for a few months, even though I still hadn't been given the official title. Just before service that night, while I was working with Soda Pop to finish the entremet station's mise en place, Didier came by the station. "*En place,* Doog?" he asked. "Doog" was how all the French guys said my name. But I didn't mind, as it was a lot better than "dog," which is what they thought my name was for the first two weeks.

"*Oui, chef,*" I replied.

We were indeed ready, but I kept going over every detail to make sure the service would run smoothly. As I would learn later that night, it didn't matter how careful you were about getting everything right, something could always go wrong. Our station was responsible for two pastas. One was a ravioli made out of spinach dough and the other a spaghettini, a very fine spaghetti made with egg dough. Since the two pastas used different types of dough, we had to make each separately. Making the dough was somewhat time consuming, because you had to let it rest for at least an hour before rolling it out and cutting it. We always made double the amount of dough we needed so that if we ran out of the pasta we had cut, we could roll and cut more pasta *à la minute*—at the last minute. That night, about halfway through service, we did run out of ravioli.

At ADNY just as the service began, while all of the cooks were checking over every little detail, the kitchen's lighting was changed. All day the room was brightly lit, but for service only the lights that were necessary were used. The lights accentuated our focus. Hundreds of little fiber-optic bulbs shone in the precise locations where we would work while the rest of the space was unlit. All of the distractions were removed. The stage was set, the show was about to begin. Didier began to call out the orders—no one else spoke—and we all moved. First just a few of us and then everyone. There was little noise, except the sounds of cooking.

The level of focus in the kitchen that night, as on most others, was extremely high. I was managing all of the orders we had coming in to our station and what we were sending to the pass, and I realized that we were running out of ravioli. As soon as I recognized that, I had Soda Pop start rolling out dough. It would take only a few minutes to get the dough rolled out and cut, so we wouldn't miss a beat in the service. But, while running the dough through the machine, Soda Pop mangled it. A pasta machine has several settings, with the highest number being the largest space between rollers and the lowest number being the smallest space. When you first start running the dough through the pasta maker you start with the highest number. Then, as the dough is being rolled out and thinned by the machine, you decrease the setting. The process is gradual. If you start by rolling the dough through a low setting, you will likely shred it. When you're done, you must always turn the dial back up to the high setting so the next person doesn't ruin his dough. No one had done so on this machine and Soda Pop was left with a mess of green dough.

Having no more spinach dough to make the ravioli with, Soda Pop started rolling out the egg dough. Within a few minutes, he had enough ravioli to get us through the night.

I knew that Didier had seen what was going on; he didn't miss anything. When I sheepishly sent the first egg dough ravioli to the pass, Didier immediately yelled out to me, "*Doog, qu'est-ce que c'est cette merde?*" (Doug, what is this shit?) He pushed the plate with his hand and nearly knocked it off the pass. His face was bright red. Just then

Ducasse, who was with us in the kitchen that night, started yelling his name from another side of the kitchen. I had gotten used to hearing Ducasse yell "Didier" rapidly about ten times whenever he was unhappy with something. That was his way of calling him over to fix something, which could be anything from how a cook was searing a piece of meat to how something was being stirred. The new ravioli were reluctantly used and we were off the hook. They weren't spinach dough ravioli, but at least we had some and we hadn't lost more than a beat or two.

What Soda Pop couldn't have anticipated—mostly because I was keeping track of the order tickets for the station—was that we were about to run out of spaghettini as well. So, when he used the egg dough for the raviolis, he had closed the door on making new spaghettini. Telling Didier that we had no more spaghettini for the night, as Ducasse stood right behind him, was easily the hardest thing I had yet to do in that kitchen. I knew nothing about tension before I stood in front of the two of them as they exchanged several heated words in French. I stood there waiting for a verdict. While I hadn't been directly involved in the pasta fiasco, I was running the station and so this was my fault. A handful of painful minutes later, an alternative was found—we would stretch each portion of pasta that we had and add more veg to the dish—and we moved on.

After service that night, Brendan was very apologetic and thanked me for being in the middle of the fire. I understood what he meant, but all the same I told him his thanks weren't necessary. We had withstood the heat, so it really didn't matter as long as we did better the next time. Regardless of how hard you try, how much work you put in, everything can't always go as planned. Later that night, when the newspaper came out, the news we were awaiting only confirmed that fact.

When I started at ADNY it really was like being back at the beginning. I was learning so much that it was as though I were back in my grandfather's diner. This was also the first restaurant I had been in that reminded me of my childhood. The olives, peppers, and olive oil were elements of the food my grandma used to cook. I was at home at ADNY, with its Mediterranean flavors, in many ways. It was the perfect restaurant for me, but not everyone was as welcoming.

When Ducasse came to New York, he was under attack within days of being open. Many critics decided that ADNY was the personification of Ducasse's arrogance before they even set foot in the restaurant. Word had it that the place was too expensive and its many accoutrements were ridiculous. The extreme level of detail that I admired so much in the kitchen was mocked in the dining room. Perhaps for diners some of these details were over the top—like a selection of unique cutlery to choose from for the squab or a selection of the best pens to sign the check with—but few critics noted that ADNY gave New York its first restaurant that was comparable to Europe's Michelin three-star restaurants. If for nothing else, ADNY was on the same level because of its policy not to turn tables. For diners this meant the table that they were seated at was theirs for as long as they wanted to stay that evening. No diner at ADNY was put on a clock, which isn't true for any of the other top restaurants in the city.

Most restaurants are given the benefit of getting up to speed before being critiqued, but ADNY was written about almost immediately. Critics generally visit restaurants several times before reviewing them, but some publications didn't wait to have well-researched, official reviews written. Instead, they quickly published articles that fully critiqued the restaurant under the guise of news. When the *New York Times* review finally was published on November 1 (six months after ADNY opened) and the restaurant received only three stars (and not the four stars that it had set its sights on), it seemed unjust to all of us in the kitchen.

After the disappointing review was released, the restaurant continued on as it had been doing. It lost no momentum; if anything, it gained more steam. In the kitchen there had been concern that the place might change drastically, but it didn't. Some minor changes were made in the front of the house (eventually the knife and pen options and other luxury amenities that were deemed pretentious were done away with), but otherwise the restaurant remained the same. The tense air of disappointment turned back into the tension of getting everything perfect. While there were no immediate changes in the kitchen, over the next few weeks and months change occurred slowly. Some cooks were gone, including Soda Pop, who left New York for his home in California, and some new ones came on board. The biggest change, though, was that Olivier left. More than anything, I think, he had grown uncomfortable being second in line. He had earned, and deserved, his own kitchen.

It wasn't by any means a happy time, but we put our heads down and got back to work. The tension may have increased after that point, but it was impossible to tell. We were focused on changing perceptions. With hard work, we were certain that the restaurant would become great in everyone's eyes and not just our own. I didn't think ADNY could be more intense than it had been when we first opened, but now we were set on getting the respect we knew we deserved.

Chapter 12

In the King's Palace

Although I was determined to work harder than anyone else in Ducasse's kitchen, this meant outworking the hardest-working man there, Didier Elena. Didier led by example and by instilling fear. He was a large man with a thinning patch of combed-back hair and round bulging eyes, and when he got angry his face turned deep red and his veins looked like they were trying to escape his forehead. He looked as though he had lost all control. On those occasions, he would slam plates down on the pass, throw them across the room, and even bump people out of the way. For the most part, though, even when you knew that he was raging inside, he just flashed his unnaturally big smile. This always seemed more threatening than anything else.

From the very first day, Didier established a rigid order in the kitchen. Absolute perfection was the rule. He kept his eyes and hands on every dish before it left the kitchen and aggressively pursued any-one who performed less than perfectly. If you weren't dedicated to perfection, you'd have to watch someone else who was, and if you didn't catch on, eventually you'd be in the basement cleaning mushrooms during service. And Didier was everywhere.

Working shifts that started at 6:00 in the morning and ended at midnight was brutal, but I was determined to be the first one in and the last one out. But, no matter what I did, Didier was always there first. I'd come in at 6:00 one day and he was already there, 5:45 the next day and he was there. He didn't sleep there—as far as I knew—but I couldn't get there early enough to beat him. Eventually, though, I was there as much as he could possibly have wanted.

If I didn't know something (and there were many techniques, and even products, that I had never seen before), I learned it. If I was given a box of carrots to turn (peel and shape into perfect cylinders), I did it. A case of tiny mushrooms to clean, no problem. I never rolled my eyes and never slumped my shoulders. It didn't matter what the work was—whether it was learning something complicated or doing the simplest thing that at other restaurants most people with my experience would have scoffed at—I did it as well as I could and as fast as I could. When I was done with one thing, I asked to do more. As soon as I finished my mise en place, I helped other people with theirs.

Eventually I worked so hard I barely noticed that I had been working six days a week and over fourteen hours on most days, with very few days off, for over a year. Slowly, I gained respect in the kitchen. I was the lowest guy above the African dishwashers when I walked in, and in a year I had become an important gear in the restaurant's machine.

We knew by late spring of 2001 (a year after we had opened) that the restaurant would be closed for about three weeks in August and that we'd all be on break. It would be a chance for me to get away, possibly see my family, who had all moved out of New York except Mike.

But when Ducasse unexpectedly granted my pleas to spend the break at his restaurant in Monaco, I no longer needed to stop working.

It was the middle of June and Ducasse was in town. While Ducasse spends time at all of his restaurants around the globe, he visited the Essex House often during that first year. When he wasn't there, Didier was his perfectionist stand-in. But when he was in town, perfection had to be exceeded. It had nothing to do with VIPs or reviewers coming in to eat. ADNY didn't rise to excellence; it was designed that way. This is Ducasse's way, and not just because this was one of his elite restaurants. This is true for all of his restaurants, even his bed-and-breakfast places.

I was now working on the fish station, and most of my mornings were spent in the always cool fish room downstairs. Having spent ten months at the meat station before moving to fish, I had made a half-turn of the kitchen, and now my mornings were spent cleaning fish. The fish room at ADNY is tiny and secluded. The guy who works the fish room works alone. It's the ultimate test of self-discipline and drive. If you want to prove your worth, if you want to move up the chain, you get the work done as quickly as possible. But it's not a simple, easy, or quick job. It takes a great deal of focus to get through everything that has to be done on time. Some cooks get lost in the fish room; whether it's because they're asleep on their feet or just can't handle the job, they don't get their work done, and they find themselves either back to working as a commis or out the door.

June comes right in the middle of the busiest time in the fish room. The restaurant has a shellfish menu during the late spring through early fall, so a lot of fish need to be cleaned on these mornings. I had arrived there a little before six, drunk a shot of espresso, and gotten to work. As always, there were two stacks of boxes taller than me waiting in the fish room. There was no way all of the uncleaned fish could fit in the fridges, so some had to be dressed—gutted and cleaned—right away. But before I even started opening the boxes, I put two pots on the stove to boil. There's only one stove in the prep kitchen and it's tiny. If I didn't get my pots on the stove, someone from the meat station would take it over for their stocks and sauces and I'd be left scrambling. Restaurants are competitive places and Ducasse is the major leagues. We were a team working to achieve Ducasse's high standards, but we were a team of individuals. Everyone wanted to be on the starting team, so the competition within stations and throughout the kitchen was intense.

I put up two large pots of heavily salted water for cooking lobsters. After that, I put away the fish that wouldn't be needed that morning, then started to clean the rest. I went to work on one of the striped basses first because I could get through these the quickest—wipe it down, take off the fins (which is an important but often skipped step to cleanly butchering the fish), scale it, and gut it. The other bass was next, then I began working on the halibut, when I saw Greenie walking into the prep kitchen. Even through the fish room window, it looked as though it hurt him to keep his eyes open and his feet were dragging a heavy weight. Mornings never got easier for Greenie. He had joined Ducasse a few months after me and was now with me on the fish station. But he was still a commis, while I had moved up to demi chef de partie.

I nodded to him as he slowly got to work, then my focus was back to getting through my mise en place. A few hours later, I was finished and carried the large container of lobster stock up the stairs to the kitchen.

The main kitchen at ADNY is immediately adjacent to the Essex House hotel's main kitchen. The conditions of even our prep kitchen were far better than their main kitchen. We had superior equipment even downstairs and kept our area noticeably cleaner. But the greatest difference between the two kitchens was the people. ADNY was staffed mostly with cooks in their twenties or thirties with serious ambitions; the Essex House, like many hotels of its kind, was staffed mostly by men in their forties and fifties who were all part of a union, all made a comfortable living serving hotel food, and all shared a common lack of aspiration for anything else. For obvious reasons, these differences sometimes resulted in confrontations.

But while the prep kitchen was measurably different from the Essex House's kitchen, the main kitchen at ADNY was in its own stratosphere. The first thing I noticed after I put the lobster stock on a burner at our station was that Ducasse was standing next to Didier and watching everyone. Erwin, a spidery French cook who was the fish station's chef de partie, was bent over the stove moving his long, skinny arms all over the place. He had to perform at the top of his game with Ducasse watching him, and it was obvious that he was feeling the heat despite the luxurious air-conditioning (a rarity in a restaurant kitchen). As soon as I put the stock pot down, he started ladling out the stock into a copper roasting pan filled with caramelized lobster bodies.

After setting up my station for service, I noticed Greenie was turning potatoes in a somewhat jerky rhythm, so I started helping him out. To turn a potato (or any other vegetable) takes a certain amount of skill. Your right hand with the knife or peeler is held at an angle and is rolled backward, counterclockwise, as your left hand continually rotates the potatoes in a clockwise direction. When a vegetable is turned properly it will no longer have any sides and can be rolled in a pan so that it cooks evenly—plus it looks damn impressive. Few restaurants turn their vegetables, most likely because few cooks are able to do it quickly. But it was one of the techniques I had mastered during my first few months on the entremetier station at Ducasse, and I could do a fast job of it.

As I was working on my second potato, I felt a presence behind me, and then a hand grabbed my arm. I stopped turning the potato and turned around to see Ducasse smiling at me.

"*Ça va?*" Ducasse asked.

"*Oui, chef.*"

"*Ça va,*" he said, then slapped my shoulder hard, like a punch, but with good intentions. Then he went over to another station. He went from cook to cook asking the same question. Around the room you could see small adjustments being made by everyone. Whether it was quickly wiping down their areas, making sure all spoons were in a bain-marie, or straightening a chef jacket, no one wanted to be called out, and Ducasse wouldn't hesitate to erupt if he saw the smallest of mistakes.

I went back to turning potatoes and refocused on getting the station's work done before service. Because of the seasonal shellfish menu offered in addition to fish courses on the prix fixe menus and à la carte, we were easily the busiest station. But there were five of us and this was lunch, not dinner. As the demi chef de partie, I did most of the actual cooking. Erwin, the chef de partie, did the saucing and plating. Our two commis did the veg for the plates and our stagiaire was there to run for every last-second thing we needed at all times.

When service was over we cleaned the kitchen until it was spotless again, then we all probably needed a break, but that didn't matter because we were on a forced break. It wasn't just offered—it was required. Everyone was strongly discouraged from staying in the kitchen or prep kitchen during the break. Anyone who did was there because he couldn't get his work done in time, and he stood out.

Most of the cooks went to the Essex House cafeteria during our break, because we ate for free. That we'd go from serving the highest-quality food to eating mediocre—or worse—food made it difficult to enjoy anything about the cafeteria, even if we didn't have to pay.

When I returned from the cafeteria, I went straight to the kitchen to begin preparing the station for dinner service. Didier was in the Aquarium but saw me as I walked in. In all three of Ducasse's gastros (short for *restaurant gastronomique*), his top restaurants, he has a private dining room in the kitchen called the Aquarium. (They're all named after the one in Monaco, the only one that even somewhat resembles a fishbowl.) ADNY's Aquarium is essentially a glass box with a door; a black tile floor; a blond-wood table; and a bookshelf with all of Ducasse's books, as well as many others. It's a beautiful room, with a great view of the kitchen, and is reserved only for the most important VIPs. And it's a place where Ducasse or Didier would have meetings. I assumed that Ducasse was still in the Aquarium as Didier came out to talk with me.

Didier was smiling his ear-to-ear smile. "Doog," he called to me. "So, Monaco, yes?" he asked.

At first I didn't understand what he was asking, but then I realized that he was talking about Louis XV, Ducasse's Michelin three-star restaurant in Monte Carlo. I had been asking about Monaco for the last several months. Everyone wanted to work there: it's the epitome of a Ducasse restaurant. But I suspect very few of the cooks would have been willing to give up their break to work somewhere else.

Didier smiled again and told me we'd talk soon. That I was going to Louis XV and had the honor of being the only cook in the kitchen offered this opportunity was virtually the only thing I thought about for the next month. This was a chance to work in one of the world's best restaurants, and even though I would be giving up my first vacation in over a year to do it, it was a tremendous opportunity. But

Didier and I didn't talk about it anytime soon after this conversation, and I was still in the dark about the details until almost the last minute.

As our August break approached, it became clear that a few of the cooks wouldn't be returning in September. ADNY was a difficult place to work and so many cooks didn't last more than a year. For most of these cooks, the kitchen team provided a memorable send-off.

A tradition common in a lot of restaurants in France and carried on in the kitchen at ADNY is to haze a cook when he leaves the kitchen for the final time. It was probably the most camaraderie displayed in ADNY's kitchen, but it wasn't pleasant for the departing cooks. It was a day that most of them would fear. The other cooks would often prepare in advance for the hazing, sometimes days in advance if they really liked or disliked the cook. When Greenie and Rustang had left on the same day a few weeks before our break, they were confronted with intense preparations, including a stock pot filled with a vile mixture of things like rotten fish guts, grease, old stock, and blue food coloring.

As we cleaned up the kitchen that night, I kept my eye on Greenie. He was telling everyone loudly that he was coming back, but we all knew he was returning to California. I wasn't going to let him miss this experience. As soon as I heard the commotion of people cornering Rustang behind me, I moved in on Greenie, who started backing away. Behind him was Didier, who looked at me as though we were about to feast on a suckling pig and yelled, "Get him!"

Greenie scrambled wildly to get away from us and collapsed to the floor as we grabbed him by the arms and legs. As we dragged him toward the stock pot, he fought us as though we meant real harm.

"I'm not leaving, I'm not leaving, I'm coming back," he screamed. I was deaf to his cries, but Didier seemed annoyed by his efforts to break free and was soon distracted by the group of cooks who were holding Rustang down on a tabletop. At first I didn't relent; I kept dragging Greenie by myself. But, I too got distracted by the sight of Armand spreading butter between Rustang's toes. I let go of Greenie, who scurried toward the locker room, and watched as the cooks gave Rustang a departure he wasn't likely to forget.

As I was leaving that night, Rustang ran past me in a hurry to get out of there. His entire head was Smurf blue from the food coloring and he stank like garbage on a hot day. Greenie escaped untouched, but without a proper send-off.

The trip to Monaco was going to be my first trip to Europe. I had never taken any real time off in all the years I had been working, and even if I had, I wouldn't have had the money to take such a trip. While I now had the time and a compelling reason to do so, there still was no way I could afford it. Ducasse had invited me, so I assumed there was a chance he'd pay for the trip. Otherwise it would likely take the salary I was being paid while ADNY was closed, and a good part of Mike's salary as well, to make the trip happen. I had no idea what a plane ticket would cost, or a hotel, and was concerned that I wouldn't be able to go unless Ducasse came through.

Two weeks before I was supposed to leave, these concerns were finally resolved. One of the business managers, who had only been in the U.S. for a few months and spoke very broken English, called me into the office. She had been put in charge of assisting me and was very friendly, in a dutiful way. I never asked why she had waited to act on this until two weeks before I was supposed to depart, and it didn't seem to cross her mind that I might be concerned. Regardless, by the next day she had booked a flight for me from JFK through London's Heathrow into Nice, and the hotel was taken care of.

"The only thing Mr. Ducasse asks," she explained, "is that you contribute two hundred toward the airfare." I had been prepared to shell out a lot more than that, and I knew the airfare must have been at least triple that amount, so this wasn't even a question.

It wasn't until hours later, when I was on an N train back to Astoria, that I realized why Ducasse had asked for the money. Obviously this small contribution meant nothing to him. But he knew how much I earned and he had asked for an amount that wouldn't strap me, yet wouldn't go unnoticed. The point, I figured, was that if I really wanted this, I'd be willing to give something up for it—more than just my time off. (I was also going to miss America's wedding. He had gone back to working on Long Island and was settling down with his longtime girl-friend, Nicole.) And even though I'd be working most of the time I was to be there and this was essentially a gift, nothing came without some sort of commitment. I respected him even more for this arrangement.

The two plane rides to Nice were mostly uneventful, though long and uncomfortable, with several hours between flights that I spent wandering around Heathrow Airport. The helicopter ride from Nice to Monaco was the extreme opposite. It was short and thrilling. As we approached Monaco over the intense blue waters of the Mediterranean, I knew that very few cooks would ever have the opportunity that lay before me.

Of course, a helicopter ride isn't the only way to get to Monaco from the airport, but Didier had suggested it before I left. I had arrived in Nice with a small duffel bag and little French, and my only clue as to how to get to Monaco was that a helicopter could take me there. I was completely exhausted but wide awake and somehow managed to figure out that my other options were an hour taxi ride or a taxi to a half-hour train ride. Despite my limited funds, the seven-minute helicopter ride for $100 was an obvious choice.

Back in New York, Didier had told me about Monaco and had drawn a completely ridiculous map showing how to get to the restaurant. "It's easy," he said, leaning on the black granite pass. "Get to the Hôtel de Paris, go through the main door, past the horse statue, and the restaurant doors will be on your right."

Sitting in the back of the town car that was waiting near the heliport (a dirt landing strip), I kept repeating "Hôtel de Paris" to the driver, but he gave no sign of understanding me. I must have said it five times, mixed in with "Monte Carlo," "restaurant," and finally "Ducasse," at which he perked up and sped off. Leaving the heliport, the driver spun around several curving roads. Then the bright blue water with large yachts everywhere lay before us.

A few minutes later, after a twisting and turning ride in and out of the hills, we stopped in front of the Hôtel de Paris in the Place du Casino—the actual casino was next door.

The building is massive, possibly better classified as a palace than anything else. Built in 1864, it's a luxury hotel the size of a city block. The sky was a perfect blue behind the gleaming white limestone building, and the air was heavy with the scent of the sea. Emerging from the taxi, I stood before the majestic edifice for several moments without moving. Then I remembered who and where I was and went to look for the restaurant.

Inside the hotel there didn't seem to be an inch of wall space where money hadn't been applied to elevate even the most ordinary element—a door handle or a wall switch—to an item worthy of a fine art collection. This wasn't anything like my world. Besides feeling groggy from the trip, I suddenly felt alert to the fact that all of the clothes I was wearing weren't worth an inch of the carpet I was walking on. And, like all intruders, I had the alarming feeling that someone was going to catch me and drag me out—the fact that I had a purpose for being there would neither be believable nor matter. I walked quickly and pretended to not be fazed by my surroundings.

Just as Didier had said, there was an equestrian statue in the lobby and the restaurant entrance was just to the right. I entered Louis XV, and a maître d' immediately led me to the business office and into one of the manager's offices. Vincent spoke English—if I had never seen him again, that would probably have been the only fact that I remembered. It was a huge comfort to be able to communicate with someone and finally be told some details, like where I was staying and when I was working. Vincent gave me a rundown and was walking me out when we ran into Ducasse.

I had departed New York early Saturday evening and arrived at the restaurant sometime in the middle of the afternoon on Sunday. I was bleary eyed and in need of a shower and a shave. Ducasse had left New York that morning (on the Concorde), so although he had left a day after me, he had arrived four hours before me. Though it was the first time I had seen him even somewhat unkempt (he was unshaven and had his suit jacket off), he was already working.

"*Bienvenue,*" he said.

"*Bonjour, chef,*" I responded as I followed him into his office. It was a cook's idea of a study more than an office. It had wood paneling, a bookshelf filled with cookbooks, a mahogany desk, and firm black leather chairs.

"*Ça va?*" he asked.

"*Oui, ça va bien,*" I replied.

Before he sat down, he stuck out his hand for me to shake and said, "*Ça va.* How are you? How was the flight?" I had never heard him speak English before. Most of the cooks at ADNY thought that he didn't know English. Unguarded, with his jacket off, he was speaking my language to me. That was it, though, and our meeting was over. As I left, I felt anxious to start working. And, while I had managed to get by on kitchen French for a while now, I decided that I'd learn the language for real.

Before leaving the office, I was given the details about my hotel and then was given a ride to it by a young French girl who smiled warmly but seemed to speak no English. I actually wasn't staying in Monte Carlo or even in the Principality of Monaco, which wasn't surprising, since the accommodations in Monte Carlo are mostly for the superwealthy, celebrities, and royalty. I was staying in Beausoleil, in France, which was just up the steep, winding road and only a ten-minute walk away. Once inside the hotel, I was pleased to find that I had my own bathroom and a balcony with a stunning view of the wide blue seascape. Then, I crashed.

When I woke up several hours later, it was dark and I was starving. My head felt hazy and I couldn't move any faster than slowly. From my balcony, I tried to spy some sort of restaurant or market where I could get some food, but I didn't see many lights on. My digital watch, which I paid way too much for at a store in Heathrow Airport because I had forgotten to bring a watch or clock with me, read 9:00. It wasn't very late, but the town looked asleep. Regardless, I had to find something to eat.

The hotel was tiny. It had only a few rooms and there appeared to be only one guy who worked there. He was middle-aged and seemed exhausted every time I saw him. His eyes were never fully opened, he was never clean shaven, and his hair was in an inverse mullet (long in the front and short in the back). He was asleep on the lobby's couch as I left the building.

Eventually I found a place with pizza, which was different from the pizza I grew up eating and not very satisfying. I asked for pepperoni and I got peppers. I asked for a beer and it was warm. Instead of parmesan for the pizza they gave me spicy olive oil. After that I gave up my search and realized I wasn't sure where the hotel was. It was dark and I had no idea which direction I had come from. It took a little while, but eventually I found the hotel by looking for buildings I had seen from my balcony. I was still tired, but I looked forward to getting to the restaurant in the morning. I wasn't supposed to be there until 7:00 A.M. But, considering how tired I was and that I hadn't regained my sense of time, I was worried that I might sleep the entire next day. So, I went to my room and studied my French book to learn how to ask for a wake-up call. When I went back downstairs, I found the clerk leaning on the counter with one arm stretched out holding a cigarette. He seemed to understand me when I asked for him to wake me at 6:00 A.M. When I returned to my room, I set my watch and my new alarm clock (also acquired at Heathrow for way too much) to be sure.

Waking up the next morning was not nearly as difficult as I thought it might be. I was awake with the first beep of my watch, before the alarm clock buzzed or the phone rang with the call from downstairs. The trio of alarms were unnecessary; I was ready to go. The lethargy I felt when I had awakened for the food hunt the night before was gone, replaced with a new alertness and eagerness to get going. I bounced out of bed, showered quickly (my first European garden-hose-style shower with no shower curtain), and dressed.

Once I got myself together, I headed down the hill that leads to Monte Carlo. I could see the sea in the distance and the sky meeting it in the lightest of light blues. It was as perfect a backdrop as I had seen yesterday when I stood gazing up at the Hôtel de Paris, and this beauty would impress me throughout my entire stay. Each morning, I felt energized by the magnificent setting, although most of my days were spent in the windowless kitchen at Louis XV.

Walking into that kitchen the first morning, I was struck by both its vastness and the army of men who were everywhere. Space was not an issue at Louis XV, as it is in most New York restaurants, and the place was nearly filled with the best equipment possible.

While the crew was of course dispersed throughout the stations, it was obvious as I made my way to the entremetier station, where I had been directed, there were more than enough cooks—and many of them shared my first-in attitude. I was early, but the kitchen was already filled. There were cooks of all ages from all over Europe and other parts of the world, like the sous chef, who was from Japan. There were so many cooks it was astonishing that there was enough work to go around. In fact, plenty of the so-called cooks in this kitchen never cook a thing. Any thoughts I may have had about being a significant and necessary part of this crew dissipated when I showed up at the overstaffed station, and the demi chef de partie made sure I comprehended this immediately (even if I couldn't understand his words).

François (though I wouldn't learn his name until much later in the day) said something in French while I followed his pointed finger, entrusting me to another cook on the station. The other cook, Michel, was obviously a commis. He looked younger than twenty and wore wire-rimmed glasses. Michel was actually the second commis on the station and, before I arrived, the lowest man in the chain.

I had just finished tying my apron and was opening my knife box when Michel put twenty artichokes in front of me. "Clean, yes?" he asked. I nodded and got to work.

When I was done cleaning the artichokes, he picked one up and said, "*Bon.*" I went to get my knife to turn them, but before I had returned he had placed a box of peas on my cutting board. He hadn't said a word. I put the knife down and began shelling the peas on the counter.

People were moving around me nonstop, but no one seemed to be rushing as at most New York restaurants. Everyone seemed to be on tracks that took them to set destinations to do exact tasks. No one leaned on counters or stood around joking. It was still early in the morning and this was the prep work, but everyone was serious and focused.

Michel stopped me from shelling the peas and asked me to get him lemon water for the artichokes to keep them from turning black. He spoke slowly and pointed several times before I understood where in the kitchen I could get the bowl and a lemon. As I made my way to the back of the kitchen, I noticed a cook setting up the humongous rotisserie across the room. This one piece of equipment was bigger than most stations at any other restaurant. It's made by Molteni, who also made our stove at ADNY, with two charcoal grills sitting in front of a rotisserie. It's easily the best rotisserie I've seen and certainly one of the markers that separates this kitchen from most others. As it heats up, you can smell the heat—it permeates the whole room. It's doubtful that many rotisseries like this exist; it's a rotisserie that most chefs just dream of.

The lone guy who works the grandiose rotisserie is responsible for everything that is grilled in that kitchen. He's alone at this island, away from the heart of the kitchen, grilling things like pigeon, foie gras, and beef with truffles. He was getting the grills ready for service when I returned to the entremetier station.

I put the lemon water in front of Michel. He picked up an artichoke and began turning it. Without saying anything, he made it clear that I should go back to shelling the peas. Throughout the morning I learned that my responsibility wouldn't be to do menial work; it was to do menial work for the guy doing the menial work. I wasn't there to cook and I wasn't there to learn by doing. I was there to learn by watching.

Just before service Michel had me set up butter with ice trays to keep it cold for everyone on the station, and during service my only responsibility would be to make sure everyone had enough butter or anything else they asked for. During lunch service, my observational skills went into high gear. The service was run in complete silence, except for the chef, and was clocklike in its precision. There were no crises and no mistakes. Everything was perfectly orchestrated and executed.

We were on break after lunch service, but no one told me this— not even Michel, who only spoke to me when he needed something. I knew it because soon after service was over and the kitchen was cleaned, everyone filed out. It was only when I directly asked Michel when we had to return that he told me we had two hours, and then he turned back to one of the other young cooks with whom he had been talking.

With nowhere else to go, I headed back toward my hotel. The whole town of Beausoleil seemed to be asleep again, so I went back to my room and took a nap myself. When I woke from my power nap and walked out onto the balcony, I realized the town had also awakened from its siesta. So, I showered and hit the streets in search of food. There were actually several markets within steps of the hotel and they were all open. I needed something to eat, as I hadn't eaten all day, but I momentarily forgot about my hunger as I came across a small butcher shop with several beautiful birds—completely intact with their heads and feet on—hanging in the window. Stepping into the shop, I saw neat rows of beef, veal, rabbit, and lamb behind the counter and sausages hanging from the ceiling. There were several men working—professional butchers, not kids. While this place seemed incredible and special, I quickly realized that there was nothing extraordinary about it. It was just another neighborhood butcher, one of many, including another one as good or better that I walked into just steps down the road.

I finally stopped gawking at food I desired and found some I could eat. I went into a takeout food store and ordered a croque monsieur several times until I was understood and had an involtini (fresh cheese wrapped in speck—smoked dry-cured pork—and marinated) while I waited. The sandwich was simple, cheap, and delicious. I devoured it in a few quick bites as I walked down the hill toward the restaurant. I must have been lost in the luscious ham or just not paying attention, because I didn't notice the car that had pulled up next to me until its horn beeped. I was startled when I heard the beep and then again when I saw Didier in the car.

He was smiling brightly. "It is beautiful, yes?" he asked. I looked down at the Place du Casino and the pastel blue sky behind it and laughed. He was from these parts and looked entirely at home. It was probably the first time I had seen him relaxed, even though he was getting married later in the week. I suppose that stress was nothing compared to what he was dealing with in New York. As he leaned out of the tiny car, he seemed pleased to see me. It was good to see a familiar face—especially the chef at ADNY—even if it was for just a moment.

That night's service went pretty much as the lunch service had, precise and orderly. There were rare moments when the intensity increased and even fewer lulls. After more than fourteen years in operation the restaurant ran like a finely tooled machine.

The next day was Tuesday and the restaurant was closed. In a completely foreign place with beautiful beaches and plenty of sights to see, the only thing I wanted to do was eat. I called the business office at Louis XV and asked Vincent if he could make a reservation for me at Bar & Boeuf, another Ducasse restaurant in Monte Carlo. I had heard great things about it and was excited to try it out.

Just walking into Bar & Boeuf it was clear that it was unlike either of the other Ducasse restaurants I had been to. The restaurant had opened around the same time as ADNY, but it was in an entirely different style. This wasn't elegant perfection; it was simple and modern, but also incredible in its own way. The restaurant is located in the "Sporting Monte-Carlo," the casino that is famous for both its beauty and exclusivity. I was welcomed in English as soon as I walked through the entrance and led to the terrace. On the way through the dining room we passed the open kitchen, and I noticed there were two huge coolers against the kitchen's back wall. One of the coolers contained a hanging bass (or *bar*, in French) and the other had a full rib eye (*boeuf*).

Seated close to the edge of the terrace, which is surrounded by rosemary bushes, I had a stunning view of the Bay of Monaco as the sun was going down. I was immediately served the first of several jazzed-up cocktails, this one with top-shelf whiskey, ginger ale, lemon, and triple sec. Looking over the menu, which was dominated by the restaurant's two namesake ingredients, it was clear that the concept was refined surf and turf, obviously with a heavy Mediterranean feel. I had never expected to see a restaurant like this from Ducasse, as I had really only known about his high-end places. I sat under the bright blue sky as it was just beginning to darken and looked out at, heard, and smelled the ocean. I was totally at ease—and not just because of the cocktails that arrived between each course. This was what vacation was meant to be: beautiful weather, great food, and no worries. I was totally transported and it seemed as if everyone seated around me was in the same frame of mind. But, unlike them, I was alone at my table and my vacation had a short shelf life. Tomorrow I'd be back to work.

Some time around the fourth or fifth cocktail (each one different), I started to think about how badly I had needed a vacation. But I had wanted to spend my break working six days a week, from seven in the morning until late at night each day. What kind of life was this, that it didn't bother me when I worked all the time? That my vacations, and even weekends, were spent working too? Then the next course arrived and the first bite of poached Mediterranean bass with bursts of lemon and olive oil put these thoughts out of mind.

When the meal was over and I had refused any more cocktails, it was dark. It had been a long meal and I was prepared to pay a staggering bill, but none was presented and the waiter refused to accept a tip. I still left cash on the table and then prepared myself for the walk back to the hotel. Other than the airport and heliport town cars, there were no taxis in Monaco. Bar & Boeuf was a fifteen-minute walk back to the hotel. It was still hot out, or I was feeling the warmth from all the food and drink, so I took off my dress shirt and walked in just an undershirt. That is, until the police stopped me and made me put my shirt back on. When I arrived at the hotel, I was ready for bed. I woke the guy sleeping on the couch and asked him to give me a wake-up call early the next morning. My first true vacation day was over.

Over the next few days, I continued to do very simple prep work and observed what everyone else did. It wasn't until Saturday that any of the cooks seemed to take notice of me.

As soon as I found the stores and the cafés near my hotel, I had started leaving even earlier in the morning to do some browsing and to grab a cappuccino and a pain au chocolat before going to the restaurant. Once in the restaurant that Saturday, I got to work cleaning the artichokes and then picked herbs.

While I had arrived even earlier than usual that morning and had gotten most of the simple tasks done, Michel was slightly late and was scrambling to get his work done. François noticed this and instead of making it easier for Michel to catch up on the work he needed to get done, he had him do additional work. Because of this, I got my first chance to move up from doing the least significant parts of the menial work to doing the main menial tasks: I started turning the artichokes, which was a job I would now take over.

During the break that day, I decided to check out the beach. The weather was still perfect, and sitting on the beach with a beer in my hand, a warm breeze blowing, and half-naked women everywhere was easily the most relaxing work break I've ever had. I decided I'd spend the rest of my breaks on the beach, possibly in the very spot where I was sitting.

On my way back to the restaurant, I slowly walked by the shop windows along the Place du Casino. There were no prices on any of the merchandise in the windows, but all of the jewelry seemed to glitter with dollar signs. I wasn't in awe of the jewelry—I felt more envious when I was staring at one of the deep red sides of beef in the butcher windows—but it was pretty entertaining. Standing in front of Cartier, I was about to make a joke to the guy next to me about how extreme and silly some of the jewelry was when I remembered I couldn't say what I wanted to in French, and then realized that the guy was Sir Elton John.

Walking back into the kitchen I wanted to tell someone what had just happened when I recognized a cook who was walking slightly ahead of me. Jim was probably a little older than me and was from California. He was working at the San Francisco Ritz-Carlton for Sylvain Portay, who had been Ducasse's chef de cuisine at Louis XV before running Le Cirque in New York. Portay had arranged for Jim to be a stagiaire at Louis XV for a week.

When I met up with Jim outside after dinner service, several of the French cooks gathered around us, even François. They had heard from Jim that I worked at ADNY, and because of that I was now more than just a pair of hands without a face. The group of us went out to a local bar and had a few beers. From what I understood, the others mainly talked about ADNY. Because it was Ducasse's first American restaurant and his only other gastro outside of Monte Carlo and Paris, they all wanted to work there.

Mostly I spoke with Jim, who made me laugh when he talked about having worked under Olivier, the original sous chef of ADNY who had also been a sous chef at the Ritz-Carlton. Olivier had scared him so much, he said, that he couldn't shit right for three weeks. American music was playing throughout the purple and black bar and everyone seemed into the music, even though they probably understood very little of the lyrics. I relaxed in the comfort of this facsimile of my own environment, while the other cooks talked about Ducasse and New York. It was clear that they envied my job at ADNY. I couldn't help but smile about this, as all week I had been envious of their jobs at Ducasse's palace in paradise.

The next morning I was busy doing my prep work when I noticed a quick change in the tenor of the kitchen. Ducasse had walked in and was standing next to the chef. Just as at ADNY, there were tiny adjustments being made throughout the kitchen to correct and perfect everything. I just continued turning the artichokes in my hand and focused on the work I was given.

I had done only a few artichokes when Michel stopped me to show me what was wrong with them. He indicated that I hadn't turned a few of them enough, so I trimmed these more and began turning the new ones to the same extent. The next time he stopped me he told me I had been turning the artichokes too much, so I went back to the way I was doing them initially. Then he came by and informed me I wasn't turning them enough. I just nodded, because I knew what was behind Michel's nonsensical instructions, and went back to work. He was giving me a hard time because he could.

This didn't bother me. I had seen this in almost every kitchen I had worked at, certainly at ADNY and even with Steve back in my grandfather's diner. No one wants to be at the bottom. Once cooks move up the line, some of them think the new job means busting the balls of the guy below them. I'm far from a saint and I won't hesitate to ride a cook mercilessly to work as he should, but I don't see the point in crushing someone's spirit just to feel like a boss.

Michel was pleased to have someone to ride and I didn't mind. I'd just do what I was told as well as I could and focus on the reason I was there: to observe and learn. It was clear that Ducasse hadn't arranged for this trip because he needed me to work. I was there to learn, and I was willing to do very menial work and be an ass to kick in exchange.

As I continued to turn artichokes, I felt a hand grab my arm. It was Ducasse.

"*Ça va, Doog?*" he said.

"*Oui, très bien, chef.*" All of the other cooks at the entremet station were still working, but I could tell that they were watching me. Ducasse then spoke in English and asked me if I had a reservation yet. I hadn't even thought about eating anywhere special after the great meal I had at Bar & Boeuf, and besides I didn't have a day off until Tuesday. He told me that he'd make a reservation for the restaurant and that I should see Vincent about it. I responded with just "*merci, chef,*" but I'm sure he read the excitement on my face.

Then he slapped my shoulder, said "*Ça va,*" and walked away. I went back to turning the artichokes, but I could tell that the other cooks were still watching me. Unlike in New York, Ducasse didn't go up to every cook in the kitchen. In Monte Carlo, he never spoke to any of the cooks except the chef de cuisine. Most of these cooks had never even spoken to him. So, the fact that he spoke to me, even knew my name, was probably a bit of a shock to them. From that point on, most of the cooks treated me differently, though I still wasn't given any significant work to do.

I had another day off on the following Tuesday but decided to postpone going to Louis XV until after I stopped working. Instead I spent the day wandering through the streets of Beausoleil and checking out all the markets and butchers. The day was one long walking meal, as I ate everything I could while I went from shop to shop, from small sandwiches and crepes to pieces of cheese and ham, pastries, and desserts. I had a food hangover when I woke up the next day and it took more than one espresso to feel okay again.

During the next week at Louis XV, I continued to work at the entremet station doing the menial work necessary for the menial work and some of the actual menial work. The other cooks occasionally gave me some small things to do and took some pains to show me what they were doing. And most nights after work I went out with a few of them to one of the local bars. I was definitely getting a feel for how the restaurant was run and what it would be like to work there, and I was impressed by both.

On my last day, I had the opportunity to work on the fish station, because they were down one commis and needed extra hands. Of course they didn't need me to cook, but I did get to do some simple tasks, like pulling the beards off mussels and washing scallop shells. The station was significantly bigger than the entremetier station and there were more people working on it. The fish station had huge lobster chambers at the station, and a fish room in the back where most of the cleaning was done. They used many local fish, like rouget, huge spiny lobsters, and some local fish no bigger than a quarter for the bouillabaisse.

One of the station's main dishes was a whole fish for two. The fish was a Mediterranean bass, which was washed down, cleaned, and roasted. But since the fish was served whole, it wasn't filleted and was somewhat difficult to clean. Also, it was somewhat painful, because it required making a small cut along the belly and using a toothbrush to clean along the bones, which tear apart the cook's hand. As I pulled the beards off mussels slightly bigger than a half-dollar, I watched

Jerome, the demi chef de partie on the fish station, clean the bass. He had gutted it, washed it thoroughly, and was now cleaning the inside with a toothbrush. Every few moments, he took his hand out and ran it under the water in the sink. The fish's blood washed off and I could see small cuts all over his hand. He shook the water off his hand and went back in with the toothbrush. His hands were enduring serious punishment. I doubt any cook would want this task for very long. Later that night, Jerome showed me his hands, which were covered with little cut marks, and in broken English tried to describe the pain when one of the tiny bones gets underneath a fingernail.

When the fish was fully cleaned, the cook washed it again and then prepared it for service. He repeated this with two more fish, so that the station was ready for three orders of this dish. When a table orders the fish for two, the bass is roasted and then placed on a serving tray with Provençal vegetables, and then the waiter provides table-side service, filleting the fish and portioning it out. I watched the cook prepare two of these for lunch and was amazed by the amount of work that went into such a simple dish.

On my way out of the kitchen for our break, my mind was probably already on the beach as I literally ran into Didier. He had been talking with the chef de cuisine and pretended to be upset that I had bumped into him.

"*Ah, putain!*" he sighed, and then he smiled. I laughed as he shook my hand vigorously. He seemed even happier than the last time I saw him, and I congratulated him, as he was now a married man.

He was in good spirits, but was in a rush. We only talked for a few minutes—mostly about the butcher block that Ducasse had given him as a wedding gift—and then he wished me *bon voyage* and told me he'd see me in New York. He then went back to talking in French with the chef and I left the kitchen. As I went out for my last break on my last day—one more trip to the beach and then a quick tour of the parts of the hotel I hadn't seen—I thought about Didier and how he was spending his honeymoon hanging around the kitchen at Louis XV.

After my last day of work, I spent two days in Nice with my friend Christophe, who also worked at ADNY and had gone home during our break. Christophe had started at the restaurant working on the bread station but then moved to the front of the house. He spoke English well, but with a heavy French accent and a voice that had an unmistakable resemblance to a low-pitched Kermit the Frog. Sometimes I couldn't understand what he said, and sometimes I couldn't help but laugh when he said certain things. We spent the two days by the pool and I slept most of the time. Then I returned for a final day in Monaco—basically to eat at Louis XV. I put on my only suit and walked as slowly as I could in the midday heat to stay as sweat-free as possible. I knew I couldn't fit in among the clientele—and not just because I was the youngest by fifteen years—but I didn't want to stand out too much. Of course this was impossible, since I was a young guy sitting by myself and getting VIP treatment at one of the most luxurious restaurants in the world.

Ducasse opened Louis XV in 1987. It was not only his first Michelin three-star restaurant, but the first hotel restaurant ever to be awarded this prestigious honor. The dining room is in the style of Versailles and as such is utterly decadent. The room is white with gold trim everywhere and has stratospherically high frescoed ceilings. Every thing on the table was either linen, crystal, or gold—even the silverware was gold-plated.

When the bread cart pulled up at the table, there were at least eight kinds of bread. Part of the kitchen at Louis XV is devoted to just this task, and each day that station turns out an array of fresh breads. I chose a mini baguette, which was as long as my longest finger, and fougasse au lard (a sweet country bread that's laced with salt pork). I cracked open the baguette and cut into the salted butter. Both salted and unsalted Beurre d'Echire (one of France's most highly regarded butters) were on the table.

After I ordered my food and then my water (there were eight different bottles of water), the sommelier came to the table and jokingly asked me if there was a special wine I would like to drink with my meal. He was joking with me because he had given me a tour of the wine cave the day before. This wasn't a cellar or a storage room; it was literally a cave dug into the building. Not surprisingly, the wine collection was vast. There were hundreds of bottles I had never seen before and will likely never see again. So, when the sommelier asked about the wine, I deferred to him.

I was served champagne to begin my meal and savored every sip. Soon after the meal, I'd be on my way back to New York, so this was the end of my vacation. The two days in Nice with Christophe had been entirely restful and had given me time to think about the trip. I had seen so much during the two weeks in the kitchen—it had been like a crash course in Ducasse. Louis XV was more organized than any other restaurant I had ever worked in, and while I hadn't really learned more about cooking, it had taught me a better way of working. I now had a clearer idea of what Ducasse's world was really like.

Was this experience worth two weeks of six days, six doubles instead of a real nonworking vacation like all of the other ADNY cooks had had? Was working all the time worth the reward? There is no answer. I realized that that question would always haunt me until I had achieved my goals. All my life I had been working for what my grandfather had—and a lot more. I knew that I'd likely never have anything like Ducasse's restaurants, but I also knew that one day I'd have my own place and it would fit my definition of perfection just as Ducasse's fit his.

Highlights of my meal were an incredibly exquisite bouillabaisse, made from the tiny fish I had worked with on the fish station, and a lamb dish with ricotta gnocchi and beignets of zucchini flowers, which were lightly battered and fried. All of the flavors were concentrated and true. Even if I hadn't seen these dishes prepared for the last two weeks, I would have admired the obvious amount of work and thought that had gone into them. The food of Louis XV is far from cutting edge. The cuisine doesn't showcase new flavors or inventive preparations; instead, it is traditional and representative of the region. I was wowed by the utter perfection of its strikingly simple menu.

As I watched the table next to me being served the bass for two, I thought about the many cooks who lined up for a spot in Louis XV, as they did in ADNY. There were just too many equally dedicated people competing for too few spots. It was highly improbable that I could ever move far up the ranks. I was fine with this, as I would continue to work relentlessly to understand Ducasse's perfection, so that one day I would be able to achieve my own.

When I left Louis XV at the end of my meal, I went to the casino and put a hundred dollars, the smallest bet allowed, on black number four. Feeling like a winner though I lost, I walked back to my hotel and fell asleep as contented as I had ever been.

The next day I returned to New York and went in to work for a half day of unpacking boxes and preparing the restaurant to reopen. It was September 4, 2001, just after Labor Day. It was great to be home. As Mike and I rode the train back to Astoria in the early evening, I thought about how rejuvenated I felt to be back in this vibrant city. The following day, arriving at the restaurant first thing in the morning and going right to the fish room, I was again in my own world. It was fine to be a floater while I was at Louis XV, but it felt better to be back at a place where I was necessary and important. I got to work tearing through the boxes and cleaning fish.

As I entered the kitchen with the lobster stock, I noticed Ducasse was in the Aquarium. As always, waves of small adjustments were being made throughout the kitchen. On our first day back, this was like a pop quiz. I hadn't seen Ducasse since his appearance in Louis XV's kitchen and hadn't had a chance to thank him. So, after I helped Erwin set up the station for lunch service, I decided to do just that.

I walked right into the Aquarium, where he was sitting at the table talking with Didier. He looked up as I entered. He was surprised that I had just walked in, and so was I.

"*Comment ça va, Doog?*" he asked.

"*Ça va bien, chef,*" I said, then I added, "*Merci beaucoup* . . . for everything, *chef.*"

"No," he said, and smiled. "Thank you."

I wanted to say more, but just nodded and returned to the kitchen.

This was the first time I had ever approached Ducasse, and the only time I knew any cook had done so. As I returned to the kitchen, it was obvious that everyone was shocked—especially the French cooks. I got back to work, even though I could sense that the chef de partie of the fish station, Erwin, was angry.

Weeks later when my role at ADNY started to change, I thought about how I had just walked right up to Ducasse. I had convinced myself while I was in Monaco that I'd always be lost in Ducasse's crowded kitchen, but as soon as I had a chance to change that, I did. I didn't want all my hard work to have been done so that I could learn and move on. Ducasse had some of the best restaurants in the world and I wanted to be a part of that—I wanted a lead role in it.

And then I thought about how running into Didier on the street in Monte Carlo and then at Louis XV on my last day seemed to be too much of a coincidence. He had worked there years before, so he knew when the kitchen went on break. That I was just some student in the back of the kitchen no longer seemed likely. I was being groomed for something more, but I had been blind to it.

In the coming months it would become clear I was going to be more than just another face in Ducasse's kitchen. After returning from Monaco, I was on a new path. A few days later, on September 10, I turned twenty-seven.

Chapter 13

Tour de Paris

After the horror of September 11, it was a welcome distraction to have the *New York Times* restaurant critic re-review ADNY and award it four stars, the paper's highest rating, in a rave review that ran just before Christmas. It had been just over a year since the first review, and we had worked harder than ever to reach the rarefied level at which the restaurant was intended to operate.

While we hadn't been working for the review, it was, finally, an acknowledgment from the generally unwelcoming media that ADNY was truly a great restaurant. This recognition was especially appreciated because it coincided with the end of what had been the toughest three months in New York's history. Following September 11, there was little on the city's mind besides how our world had been changed. There was tension constantly around us as palpable as the fighter planes circling through the skies. As with a lot of the service industry, ADNY was feeling the pain acutely. While the restaurant was in midtown and we could get back to work just a few days after the attacks, it certainly was not business as usual. This wasn't a time for celebration or luxury in the city. Hotels like the Essex House were facing severe conditions, as visitors stayed away from the city. There were days during the first couple of weeks after the attack when the restaurant couldn't open because there weren't enough reservations, and at those times our salaries suffered. Didier refused to lay off any of the cooks, as many of the restaurants were doing, but we certainly were affected. There were many restaurants, downtown especially, that were closed as a direct result of September 11. Besides our livelihoods, though, it seemed that we all lost something more—or someone.

For me it was a friend named Jeffrey Cole. He had made a small fortune in his twenties as a bond trader. Then he realized he wanted something else and started attending culinary school at nights. During his last semester, he won an essay contest that got him a stage at Louis XV. When he arrived at ADNY and I first met him, I knew him as a cook coming from Monaco and was relieved that I'd have someone working with me who knew French. It turned out he didn't, but he became a good friend.

In his previous career, Jeffrey had worked in Tower One, just a few floors below Windows on the World. He had given up a successful job, which probably had an office with a view like the one from Windows on the World, to work in windowless kitchens. Unknowingly, of course, he had taken himself out of harm's way, but in his journey to learn everything about restaurants he returned to that building—to Windows on the World—to learn about wine as an assistant to the sommelier. He was there early that morning, I later found out, to polish glasses.

It was hard to get over that. It was hard to go back to work chasing the same dream that Jeffrey had chased. Just like the rest of

New York, though, I had no intention of giving up. It took a few months, but eventually it seemed everyone was remarking on how soon the attacks had begun to move out of our primary focus (even the *New York Times* stopped running a special 9/11 section). We weathered the anthrax threat, bomb scares, police barricades, and a strong military presence (like the heavily armored truck that I passed by at the entrance of the Queensboro Bridge each morning), and then went back to living the way we always had. I like to believe that the return of the crowds to ADNY (and other restaurants) was an act of defiance. Like almost every other cook in ADNY's kitchen, I was in the city to cook and nothing was going to stop that.

Unlike the Halloween night a year before, when there was un-certainty—or perhaps denial—about how we would be reviewed, we knew several days in advance that we were going to receive four stars. If the newspaper sending a photographer to take a picture of the chef, which has become customary with the few four-star reviews that the paper has awarded, wasn't conclusive proof, the reviewer calling in a reservation under his own name the night before the re-view would be published was. For that meal, which he ate in the Aquarium, we went all out. Mostly it was the core group of cooks—Didier, Sylvestre (the sous chef who replaced Olivier), Jo-el, and me—working on the meal. It was one of the finer meals we had ever served: the epitome of what that kitchen could do. We knew by the time he was eating the meal that his article had likely already been submitted, but we pulled out all the stops anyway.

That night we went out as a team to celebrate at one of the fash-ionable brasseries a few blocks from the Essex House. Ducasse didn't join us, though he did hold a champagne toast in the kitchen before we left. Many of the cooks who had been a part of the success—such as Greenie, who was now back in California—weren't at the table with us, but the core group was and so were the new cooks, like Rory, who called himself R-dog; Jayson, a tough guy from Philly who was a very serious cook; and Ryan, a talented cook when he focused. At the brasserie we ate steaks and drank until late into the night. This was our private celebration; the next night was the real party

After cleaning up the kitchen the following night, we were asked to clean ourselves up, put on clean chef jackets if necessary, and then come into the dining room. Except when the restaurant was closed, the cooks never went into the dining room of ADNY. For that matter, neither did Didier or even Ducasse. In many restaurants the chef circles the dining room shaking hands, but in a Ducasse restaurant this is not done. The restaurant may be Ducasse's in every way, but in his own way he recognizes the importance of each cook in the kitchen. The face of the kitchen is the plate that arrives at the table. That night, though, the whole crew streamed out of the kitchen and into the dining room.

We were greeted by a crowd of familiar faces. Many of the chefs from all over town were there to celebrate the achievement. The chefs weren't necessarily friends of Ducasse or even those who had supported his efforts when he first opened ADNY. In fact many of the guests were competitors and detractors. I was surprised that one guest in particular was there. He was a well-known chef who had inherited a four-star French restaurant and had succeeded only in not screwing that up. He had been seen literally jumping up and down cheering when we had gotten our three-star review. He had celebrated our failure in his restaurant and he was there that night to celebrate our success.

Regardless of the reasons, the people were there that night as part of the community that Ducasse was now welcomed into—and had risen to the top of. For just this one night all of the chefs and restaurateurs who fought each day to be the best, to be better than those around them in the room, were celebrating together. Given free champagne and drinks, it was hardly a stretch for anyone to celebrate regardless of how they viewed the occasion. As I made my way around the crowd, I met many people who just a few years before wouldn't give me a stage in their kitchen but who now were shaking my hand.

One of the few people not wearing a chef jacket and not dressed up was David Bouley; he was wearing his typical outfit—designer jeans and a leather jacket—but he had so much style that he seemed better dressed than anyone else. I hadn't seen Bouley since I left Bouley Bakery for the last time. As I walked up to him, I wondered if he'd even recognize me.

When I returned to the Bakery after leaving for the first time, the first thing Bouley said to me when he saw me in the kitchen was "What are you doing here?" Other than his food, it seemed that few other things were really clear in his mind. The next day he remembered why I was there and came up to me. "Dougie," he said, "we have to show them how to do this right." I just nodded.

Before I had a chance to approach him, Bouley stopped me. He had a big smile. He was clearly happy to see me and to see where I was cooking now. It was a big moment for me: a sign of respect from a man whom I greatly admired. Even though I was at a lower position (I had recently been moved up to chef de partie) in Ducasse's kitchen than I would be in almost any other, I was obviously going in the right direction. I talked with Bouley for a few minutes. He would always be above me—my chef, my mentor—but I could tell that he approved of the level I was at. Before I moved back into the crowd, he grabbed my shoulder. "Don't take too long to come back home," he said, never losing his smile.

I continued to weave my way in and out of the crowd until I ran into another chef I had worked for: Wayne Nish, the chef of March. Wayne had always treated me as an equal, even when I was just a stagiaire in his kitchen, so our conversation that night didn't surprise me. We talked as peers. The rest of the night was pretty much the same. I ran into chefs I knew and others I had known only from afar. It was a great night, a celebration the kitchen needed. Normalcy—strict, determined, focused effort—returned as soon as we got back into the kitchen the next day. But instead of filing out of the kitchen during our break for the barely mediocre food served at the hotel cafeteria, we all feasted on sandwiches delivered by Katz's deli. Spread out on the black marble pass were corned beef, pastrami, rye bread, and pickles, all compliments of Mario Batali. It was a great gift from one of the city's (and country's) most beloved chefs.

In late November I knew I would be going to Paris in February during the week when ADNY would be closed. I had been talking with Didier about it for some time, as he thought it was important that I see Ducasse's restaurants in Paris. He urged Jo-el to go as well. Didier would also be in Paris that week and the three of us made plans to meet. But I was too busy to make any arrangements for the trip until just a few weeks before. My brother Mike was going with me, but while he normally managed our trips, he too was preoccupied with work. He was now working for a tiny literary agency, which he seemed dedicated to even though he was essentially running the small business for his nearly always absentee boss. When pushed (by me) he finally got us plane tickets and reservations at some of the restaurants that we wanted to hit on the trip. Some people go to Paris because it's romantic; some go for the museums; some for the architecture and history. We were going for food and we would get our fill.

Our last day at ADNY before the break was on Sunday, but

Mike and I departed for Paris on Wednesday evening so that he could work and only take off Thursday and Friday and I could just relax in New York and go out to eat, which I hadn't had a chance to do in some time. I was working all the time and rarely had the chance to enjoy the reason I got into cooking in the first place. For lunch on Wednesday, I went with Christophe to Rocco DiSpirito's Union Pacific, a restaurant where I had celebrated a few years before and once considered working.

The trip to Paris, which was just going to be a long weekend, would give me plenty of opportunity to eat in the best restaurants. We pored over maps during the first few hours of the flight and then were unconscious until it was morning and the plane touched down, which was the most sleep we'd get the entire trip.

We were staying with Christophe's friend Annette in her apartment in Montmartre. When the driver finally found her building, she met us at the door and then we followed her up a few flights of stairs to the apartment. Montmartre is an artsy neighborhood, almost like Soho before it was commercialized. It was a nice apartment, but it was of course small, maybe eight hundred square feet including the narrow hallways and a tiny bathroom. That morning we only had a few minutes in the apartment. As I talked with Annette as well as I could in French and organized our bags in the corner of her main room, Mike splashed water on his face and got dressed. We didn't have time for showers. We had a lunch reservation in less than a half hour.

Our lunch at a Michelin three-star restaurant was a disappointment. The service was impeccable, the decor was elegant, modern, and comfortable, but the food didn't meet our expectations. The restaurant had received its three-star rank just a few weeks before, and on our flight we had read a *New York Times* article about the restaurant and its acclaimed chef that was published the day we left for Paris. We were expecting a lot, but the long tasting menu we were served had few memorable dishes.

With no time for even a nap, we took quick showers back at the apartment, changed our clothes, and took a taxi that dropped us off just outside the Plaza Athénée on avenue Montaigne, the equivalent of Fifth Avenue in New York. It was raining lightly, as it had been most of the day, and it was already dark, though it was early in the evening.

ADPA (Alain Ducasse Plaza Athénée) is the marquee restaurant in one of the premier hotels in Paris. Opened in 1911, the hotel has an old-fashioned warmth and charm, and a sense of luxury, that is generally absent in New York. The lobby was gleaming marble with gold and brass, floral bouquets, and crystal chandeliers. In New York, Ducasse's restaurant enriched a large hotel in a good location; here, his restaurant was on a par with its surroundings.

We walked straight through the lobby to the entrance to ADPA and, soon after I introduced myself to the maître d', we were led through the dining room. The decor was an extension of the hotel. In the middle was a huge chandelier encased in a metal screen. I caught just a glimpse of this as we were led past all of the tables, along a corridor, and into the kitchen.

As waiters streamed past us, all nodding slightly and smiling or saying *"bonsoir"* the maître d' opened a glass door to our right and welcomed us into our dining room, the Aquarium. The room had just one round table in it, which was all that could fit in the small space. It was set for the two of us and we were seated side by side so we would both have a view of the kitchen. As soon as we were settled, the maître d' addressed us: "Gentleman, welcome to Restaurant Alain Ducasse. This will be your dining room for the evening. We have planned a special meal for you. We hope you enjoy it." He then nodded and started to leave. At the glass door, he paused. "Shall I leave the door open, so that you'll be a part of the kitchen?" he asked us, and then to me he said, "Perhaps you have enough of that already."

"For me, it's fine. For him, he should see, though," I said, gesturing to Mike and speaking in the kitchen English I had gotten used to using, so that the French cooks could understand what I was saying. I knew that Mike would enjoy the show. The excitement of a kitchen certainly wasn't something new to me, though I wanted to see how the service was run in this restaurant.

"Perhaps we'll start with open then and close it when it gets too noisy," the maître d' said. Then he backed out and immediately a waiter slid into the room, like an actor on cue. He held a bottle of champagne in one hand and a towel with two glasses in the other. He set the glasses down and then presented the bottle to us. It was the house champagne (which is the same at ADNY): Paul Drouet, Special Reserve Alain Ducasse. It was a perfect start to our meal and the first of several bottles presented to us, each matching a course. Though it was long and our second Michelin three-star meal within just a few hours, the dinner was extraordinary. It was a slow flawless progression of excellence. Being in a private room with the kitchen at work as a backdrop didn't hurt either.

While the maître d' had worried that we might find the kitchen too noisy, there was actually very little noise at all. Most kitchens are, in fact, noisy places. There's the constant banging and yelling. There's also the noise of cooks talking to each other, talking to cooks across the line, yelling out to waiters. There's joking and screaming.

It's frantic—sometimes fun, sometimes tense—and loud. Not in a Ducasse kitchen. As I knew from ADNY and Monaco, none of the cooks talked during service; only the chef, and maybe the sous chef, spoke. Having a chance to watch service from the spectator's box that we were in, I truly appreciated just how quiet the service was as compared to other restaurants.

The room was in constant motion—a fluid motion. The ADPA kitchen was run as tightly as Ducasse's in Monaco. Jean-François Piège, the chef de cuisine, stood behind the pass (a long counter) and called out the orders. In a strong, loud voice, he'd say, "*homard, bar*," and all of the cooks would reply, "*oui, chef*" in unison. Piège, who's a few inches over six feet and plenty of pounds over two hundred, paced back and forth behind the pass the whole time. He stopped moving only when he was talking to a waiter. At one point, he leaned over the counter reading the tickets and hammered his fist against the metal table the whole time. Bang, bang, bang, bang, bang. He was keeping a beat for the kitchen, a violent metronome at a very fast pace. He was a demonstrative and vocal orchestrator controlling a silent and focused team.

While I was watching Piège, I could tell that a cook had mistimed a dish. Piège turned to the cooks and yelled something in French and then pushed the plates that were sitting on the pass down the line, where another cook quickly removed them. Piège yelled again and then went back to banging out a rhythm.

After we were finished with our savory courses, Piège came into our dining room. We had eaten through the peak of the service and now it was beginning to slow down. I had spoken to Piège many times in the past when he called the ADNY kitchen at the end of his service (and the beginning of ours) to speak with Didier. The two chefs were very close friends. Other than that, the one thing I knew for sure about Piège was that he didn't speak a word of English. He held out his large hands to us palms up as though asking, "So?" Mike started telling Piège how much he loved everything and then started to ramble on about one of the great dishes we had been served: a potato marmalade. It arrived at the table in a bowl with a large black dome over it. The dome was actually thinly sliced rounds of black truffles. I had never seen truffles handled with as much care. Someone punched them into perfect circles, then overlaid them precisely, one over another. The first taste of truffle together with creamy potato was so simple, yet delicious and perfect.

Mike was trying to convey this in his rapid-fire New York accent to a man who didn't understand English. Piège opened his palms again, this time saying something like "I don't know what you're saying." Then I started talking to him in labored French, trying to thank him for the meal and express how incredible we thought it was. He left our room as a waiter was bringing in the first of our desserts. The cooks were beginning to break down the kitchen. They were carefully wrapping up items and wiping down counters, a routine I knew a lot about. As I watched, I noticed three cooks talking heatedly. One of them was just standing next to another who was doing some serious talking to the third cook, who just stood there motionless. I tapped Mike's hand, knocking the fork out of it before he could spear another piece of chocolate cake, as I saw another cook (the sous chef) walk toward the group. The cook who was being yelled at took a step back, but the other two cooks grabbed him by the arms. The sous chef walked right up to him, said something in French, and then gave him an open-palm punch in the chest. The other two cooks let the guy go and then they all went back to their work. This would never happen in New York, but the same level of control, discipline, and intimidation was common in many other, nonphysical ways.

While we were eating petits fours and drinking double espressos, Piège came back into the room. Sitting next to us, he seemed so much bigger than Mike or I. His dark-brown eyes were the only thing about him that wasn't big. He had a large, almost square, head and broad shoulders. He and I talked as best we could with the little French I knew while Mike sat between the two of us not understanding a word. Piège said that Didier had just gotten into Paris that night and that we would all go out the next night. Then he asked me what I was doing that night, even though it was already midnight. I don't think he understood much of what I said besides "Armand," and he responded just as everyone did when they heard his name—"Ah, Armand"—and then he shook his head in mock disbelief.

Armand was a real character. He was a long one-ended Q-Tip: tall and thin with a puff of curly brown hair on top. He was probably the only cook at ADNY who wasn't competitive. He was happy to work there (an opportunity arranged by his mom, who knew Ducasse personally), but had no desire to move up the ranks. His goals didn't go beyond working on a station—never running it—and just doing an okay job. He was one of the few cooks whom Didier hadn't handpicked, and he was a cook Didier had to watch over closely, because he would often make mistakes. They were friendly (as many of the French cooks who had come to work in New York together were), but they had traveled very different paths. Didier had worked hard to get to his place in the restaurant; Armand had been given a place. But while he was a thorn in Didier's side, he was one Didier didn't mind at all. No matter how badly he messed up, it was often just comic relief in an otherwise serious environment.

Mike and I met Armand at Man Ray on rue Marbeuf, a huge club and restaurant owned by celebrities. He showed up late and in head-to-toe designer gear. We had ordered one expensive drink each, never drank it, and then moved on to the next club.

In his small Peugeot, we raced around town, going from one bar to the next. The last one was in the eighth arrondissement near the U.S. embassy, the most heavily guarded building in the city. The club's entrance was very discreet with no sign anywhere. We went through the door, through a dark hallway that steadily descended, and then came to the bouncers. They said something to Armand and he replied angrily. The bouncer just shifted on his stool (or rather the stool shifted under him as it would if an elephant were sitting on it), and then Armand stormed back up the hallway and out the door. I would have been happy just calling it a night, but Armand—a descendant of Victor Hugo—wasn't having any rejection. With his pointy dress shoes clacking down the pavement, and Mike and me trailing him, he marched back to the car cursing in French. "They want to see dressed up," he said to me, "I'll have the best suit in the damn place." I didn't know what this would entail and I could tell that Mike was getting weary. It was pretty late and finding a suit didn't seem like it would be easy, but he went back to his car and popped the trunk. Inside was a suit worth more than double mine and Mike's suits together. Not caring that we were under a streetlight in the otherwise dark and empty street or that it was still lightly raining, Armand changed into a suit, and then we went right back to the club. It was the last stop in a long night. Mike and I both fell asleep as soon as we arrived back at the apartment in Montmartre.

We slept on the hardwood floor with blankets, as there wasn't a couch, or space for one. We had only slept a few hours, but we were running late when we woke up. We showered in rapid succession.

Minutes later, we were in new dress shirts and pants, then back out the door. We rushed through the streets until we got to the corner of boulevard de Clichy, just outside the Moulin Rouge, which Annette had told us was an easy spot from which to hail a cab. We found one immediately and told the driver to take us to rue de Marignan. *"Rue de Marignan, près de Montaigne, de Champs-Élysées,"* I told the driver. It was just around the corner from ADPA and I knew where we were going. But he didn't.

"Oui, oui," he said, then picked up the map on the seat next to him. Once he got going, it only took the driver a few minutes before he dropped us outside Alain Ducasse's Spoon, a Michelin two-star restaurant just a few blocks from ADPA. Spoon was not what I was expecting. From what I knew of Ducasse, everything was built on tradition. So much from the way the service was run—as quietly as possible—to the food could be traced back to his roots (to Alain Chapel, to Michel Guérard, to the farm he grew up on in Castelsarrasin, near Toulouse). This was a modern restaurant, more New York than ADNY. The decor wasn't refined and luxurious; it was fancy chic.

Already seated at our table were Jo-el and his wife and Didier. Everyone shook hands, then we all sat back down as Mike and I both uttered apologies for being late. Didier told us that he had already ordered for all of us, but we all picked up the menu anyway to read through it. Mike and I were both still looking around the room trying to take it all in. Mike was busy commenting on everything from the silverware, which was indeed cool and different, to the slot that ran along the edge of the table allowing the tablecloth to be tucked through it. Didier was obviously enjoying his enthusiasm. The two had met a few times before at ADNY's back door after work, but only briefly.

Didier pointed out other elements of the restaurant's design that had been his when it first opened in 1998. Its success was likely at least part of the reason that he was given the chef job at ADNY. Then Didier suddenly grew quiet. Only Mike was still talking when Ducasse approached the table. I had seen him sitting at a table not far from ours with a Japanese businessman but didn't know if he would come over to us. He put his hand on my shoulder as I turned to him.

"*Bienvenue*," he said and then shook my hand. Ducasse was of course wearing an elegant suit. I hadn't seen him since we toasted our fourth star in ADNY's kitchen. In all of the excitement around the kitchen, his was the one face that was unchanged. Even Didier had let a sense of relief show on his. But Ducasse had the same confident, content look he always had. In Spoon that morning the look seemed to say he was pleased I was there.

"This is the brother of Doog," Didier said, pointing to Mike.

Ducasse reached to shake Mike's hand. Then he smiled and nodded to the table and was gone. There was a brief pause, everyone took a sip of champagne, and then we relaxed.

The meal at Spoon was very good and fun. While it couldn't compare to ADPA (and didn't try to), it was just as enjoyable. For me, ADPA confirmed what I thought about Ducasse. Spoon opened my mind to a side of Ducasse I hadn't known. This more casual, globally influenced restaurant was unlike any of the others I'd seen or read about in his books. We ate things such as a clam soup—served in a large clamshell with a jelly of clam, thin slices of clam, and marinated vegetables—lacquered pork ribs, and a small rack of lamb. The meal might also have been enjoyable because it was the first meal Mike and I had eaten since we arrived that wasn't a few hours long. We were out of the restaurant after a little more than an hour and then we all jammed ourselves into Didier's tiny car. It was the same tiny car I had seen him driving when I was in Monaco. Seeing the five of us squeezing into the car that afternoon must have been like watching the clowns climbing into the little car in the circus.

As we stood on the sidewalk trying to figure out how we could all fit into the car, Jo-el caught my attention and said, "Nice suit." I just nodded; I knew that he was right. Jo-el was wearing a blue blazer, chambray shirt, red tie, and pressed khakis. Didier was wearing a seal slick gray suit. Mike and I should have worn jackets as well, but I hadn't expected that we'd see Ducasse.

"At least Ducasse acknowledged you," he said. I looked at him and shrugged. He wasn't finished with the conversation, but we were starting to cram ourselves into the car, and he just said, "Man!" with exasperation.

At first Didier just drove around the city showing us the major sights and then we hit the highway headed to Argenteuil, a small town about a half hour north of Paris. We were going to Ducasse's new cooking school: Le Centre de Formation d'Alain Ducasse (ADF). It was just a simple brick building that look liked an office building, on an ordinary-looking suburban street. Inside, though, it was impressive on many levels. Didier showed us around from top to bottom. There were two separate kitchens (one black, one white), both with equipment as good as we used in the restaurants—some of it, like an ice-cream maker that could turn just about anything into ice cream, we didn't even have. The school was set up for everyone, from the aspiring cook to the wealthy housewife who wanted to cook like Ducasse at home. Many culinary schools are utilitarian, but this was Ducasse through and through. Every detail was perfected, no costs had been cut. Our last stop was in one of the dining rooms, a beautiful room with a big black wooden table. There Didier opened another bottle of the Special Reserve Alain Ducasse champagne and we all had a glass.

On the ride back, Didier drove us around Paris pointing out more sights. Then he took us on a tour with Piège through ADPA's kitchen. There was a lot about that kitchen that was exceptional, but nothing was as impressive to me as the walk-in. The row of birds alone—all placed carefully in towels on a tray on a shelf, the same exact space between all of them—was amazing. The level of organization and care that went into maintaining the products was amazing. The quality of these animals was incredible, most of it better than what we received at ADNY. The chickens on these shelves were a beautiful white with dry skin. Each had its head (with feathers still on it) and feet and a tag on one leg identifying it as a poulet de Bresse— France's finest. Because of government regulations, it wasn't possible for us to import these chickens or any of the other birds that were precisely lined up on the shelves. But the discipline involved in maintaining this order and care was certainly possible. It was what we had been trying to achieve at ADNY. Then Piège showed us the meat and took us to the fish room and to the cheeses and the pastry room. It was clear that there was a lot to achieve at ADNY.

When we got back to the apartment, I crashed hard and then was awakened a short time later by Mike, who was standing over me. "We picked up cheese," he said. He had gone for a walk with Annette and had come back with about twenty dollars' worth of cheese, as well as some wine. In New York, this would get you a small piece of artisan cheese and no wine. In Paris, it got Mike several different types of cheese and a decent bottle of wine. I would have liked to sleep more, but eating young unpasteurized French cheeses, which are generally unavailable in the U.S., with a fresh baguette was irresistible.

Later that night Didier and Piège took us to a bistro owned by one of their friends, Yves Camdeborde. La Régalade had only a few tables, all of which were completely packed when we arrived. It was just one small room with a little bar by the door. There was a TV above the bar and rugby trophies next to the bottles of liquor. There were seven of us (Didier, Piège, one of their friends, Jo-el, his wife, Mike, and I) in the tight space, which meant none of us moved very much until we were all seated. While we waited, pâtés and a pork terrine—along with bread, cornichons, and mustard—and wine were passed around. It made the wait go quickly and increased my anticipation. When we finally sat down to eat (several glasses of Sancerre and a lot of pâté later), the food was unadorned and rustic and great. We put down a lot of it. I had thought that Mike and I ate quickly, but Didier and Piège put us to shame. They tore through a massive côte de boeuf (thick rib-eye steak) in less time than it took Mike to finish a whole roasted squab with lentils and foie gras. They ate like animals, but we did our best to keep up. At the end of the meal, they passed out shots of white Armagnac along with our espressos. Only Jo-el's wife was allowed to refuse the *pousse café*.

The liquor with the espresso actually worked wonders to help me digest and bounce back from the exhaustion that was taking over. I needed it as our next stop was Rungis, the wholesale food market. We arrived at the market a little after 2:00 A.M., without Jo-el and his wife, who had given up on the night after the bistro. Rungis consists of several large warehouses with each one dedicated to a particular segment of the market: fish, dairy and poultry, meat, fresh fruits and vegetables, and so on. Each building was massive, as big as a convention center. We started with the one dedicated to seafood. Inside it was like a giant supermarket with row after row of fish, many I had never seen before. This warehouse supplied fish for the markets, grocery stores, and restaurants of Paris.

Piège walked around Rungis like a king, knowing everyone, but paying attention only to the wholesalers he was interested in. At every stand we passed, people were anxious to show us the best they had. In one room, Piège picked his way through a huge basket of sea urchins until he found a nice big one. Then he whipped out a lock blade that was in his pocket and cut right into it. He handed us each bright-orange tongues on the edge of his knife. The taste was incredibly delicate, buttery, and powerfully briny. Then he wiped off the knife and opened a live scallop, handing us pieces that were still wiggling.

That night at Rungis was a highlight of our marathon study of the food of Paris and Ducasse. Didier had been a perfect guide; he had helped me to understand a lot more about the world of Ducasse, which I suspected was what he was supposed to do. I now had a greater appreciation for what Ducasse had accomplished and what he was trying to achieve. Just as when I returned from Monaco, I had gained a better sense of what ADNY was supposed to be.

I also finally understood why Ducasse's transition to the U.S. had been so difficult. There wasn't a single thing served at ADNY that wasn't the best possible ingredient that we could find. But by going with what the French cooks knew best, we also overlooked some American ingredients and at times served food that was in season or prized in France but not in the U.S. It was like ADNY not being open on Saturdays for its first few months. Much of the media interpreted this as arrogance, but it was just a poor translation. Most serious restaurants in Paris are closed on Saturdays, which is, of course, the biggest night of the week in the U.S. In New York, Ducasse had reproduced a French restaurant rather than creating an American one.

I was reinvigorated: more than ever, I wanted to be a major part of showing New York what Ducasse was really about. Not a translation of a Ducasse restaurant, but his principles in a New York restaurant. The fourth star we had received was deserved, but I knew we still had much to do.

A little over a month after the trip to Paris I knew what my role in the Ducasse empire would be. At the end of service, Didier let me know he wanted to talk to me after I was finished cleaning. As a chef de partie of the meat station, I was more than eager to delegate the job of cleaning the flattop, which meant stretching across it while running wet sandpaper over the hot sheet of metal. It was one of the worst of the cleaning jobs, in part because of the likelihood of getting burned (if the sandpaper slips, it's just your palm on the hot flattop) and the need to lean over the heat after a long night. That night, though, Ryan was moaning about having to clean the flattop every night, so I cooled the flattop down with ice and then pushed the sandpaper across it over and over again, until the metal was clean. By the time I was done, my entire face was sweaty and the rest of the station's cleanup was done. After all of the cooks had shaken Didier's hand and taken off for the night, I wiped off my face, pulled down my sleeves, and followed Didier into the Aquarium. If I thought the meeting would take long, I would have gotten cleaned up first. But I assumed that Didier just wanted to talk about changes to the meat station.

By the time I left the Aquarium, the kitchen was empty. There were few lights on, but even in the dim room I knew every step of the way to the locker room. In the all-gray room, one flight down, I opened up my locker and hung my chef jacket on the edge of the door. On a long journey through tough days, I had done this same thing at the end of each day. After so many months of work with so few days to rest—or even think—I would stop cooking in ADNY's kitchen soon. I had made two turns through the kitchen (worked on each station twice) and had learned a tremendous amount.

After putting on my jeans, I stood there for a second in the empty locker room and finally let myself smile. Everyone at ADNY knew that Ducasse was planning to open a new restaurant in New York. It would be modern and very New York, but still a Ducasse restaurant. The restaurant still didn't have a name or an opening date, but it was in the works. Didier had just told me that I would be the chef de cuisine.

Chapter 14

Mix in New York

When I first joined ADNY, I had worked at full force. I was running all the time. Now I felt I was just running in place. Slowly but surely, after achieving every award possible, ADNY was losing its incentive to become more. It was still one of the best restaurants in New York (if not the best), but it was no longer trying to be more than that. ADNY had reached a plateau and it was certainly a high one: the food we were serving was the same, the ingredients were still the best, and the service was still top notch. The effort was still there, but it seemed to me the intensity and determination were gone. Even though I was moving out of the restaurant "soon," this was frustrating.

Just two months after my Paris trip, which had inspired me to get back to working on making ADNY an even better restaurant (as good as ADPA), I came into the prep kitchen and saw that the pastry area was a complete mess. At some restaurants, the cooks clean at the end of the day, but not at ADNY. We worked clean and cleaned all day long. Leaving the station a mess was not the way the restaurant was supposed to be run. When I saw the pastry chef, I planned on saying something to him.

I went over to the meat table and tried to focus on my own work, but I was still heated up about the condition of the kitchen. I wasn't just frustrated with pastry. I was frustrated with the whole kitchen, at what it was becoming. This was just one instance of many. I cut through the meat—pushing the knife through with as much force as I could, as quickly as I could—until I nearly cut off half my ring finger.

I felt the cut but didn't know right away if it was bad. As soon as I lifted my hand off the veal, though, I almost got sick. There was blood streaming down my hand. My finger had been split right up the middle, from the top knuckle right through the nail. A part of it dangled loose, being held on by just a thin layer of skin. I got lightheaded and stumbled toward the walk-in, perhaps to get the blood away from the meat or just to get out of the way. The blood was streaming down my arm and pooling at the cuff of my rolled up jacket. I was lost in space, staring but not really seeing my hand, when Ben—a talented cook who was in his early twenties but was more disciplined than most people ten years older—came in and handed me a small Band-Aid. I looked down at my hand and then at him. A Band-Aid wasn't going to do it this time. There was no doubt I needed to go to the hospital.

The nurse who treated me when I first got to the emergency room didn't think it was a big deal. "Don't worry," she said, "the doctor will just snip off the piece and it will be fine." I came even closer to getting sick right then. As it turned out, the doctor decided to bandage up the wound and give the two pieces of my finger a chance to heal together and remain whole. A week later, he was amazed that this actually worked.

With a bandage covering my whole hand, I tried going back to work the next day. I couldn't use that one hand, but otherwise I was fine. Didier sent me home. "Your hand is your life. It's more important than tonight," he said. The next day I went back in and he sent me home again. He made me take the rest of the week off. When I finally returned, he talked to me. He understood why I had been frustrated but told me that everything I did should be under control. Being aggressive was good, but aggression without control was not.

Soon after my finger healed, I was moved off the meat station and became the chef de partie of the garde-manger station. In every kitchen that I had worked in before ADNY, garde-manger was the first station that cooks worked on (as I had at Panama Hatties and so many other places) because it is deemed less important than the others. But true to the traditional French system, the garde-manger at ADNY was one of the most important stations. At ADNY, it was usually overseen by the sous chef. It was the only station in the restaurant that had its own pass, so the chef rarely saw the food before it left the kitchen. For every other station, the plates were first sent to the chef, who moved it from the pass—one side of the stove—to the server's pass. Didier inspected every plate before it went out, though he saw what was happening with each well before it got to him. Since garde-manger was independent of this system, there had to be a lot of trust in the chef de partie running it. It was an important position. While there was a lot of responsibility running any station, becoming chef de partie de garde-manger was a step up in my leadership role in that kitchen.

For eight months very little changed for me. I was still running garde-manger, and the new restaurant was still scheduled to open "soon." While I no longer thought "soon" meant anything, Didier decided that my role at ADNY would have to be filled to prepare for the change. The problem with that, though, was that there were few people in the kitchen ready and willing to make the jump. For a few weeks, I trained Scotty-do to run garde-manger, but he was a slow learner and a reluctant one. He had never been very sure of himself, but now when we called him Scotty-do, he corrected us with "Scotty-don't." He had been one of the original American chefs and he was tired and battered from the journey. He eventually took over garde-manger without me, but he never got much better at handling the responsibility. A short time later, his threats of giving his notice, which had been sporadic, became frequent.

Besides me and Scotty-don't, Jo-el was the only other American left from the original team. But Jo-el was actively making his exit plans. He had grown tired of waiting for direction within the Ducasse organization. Soon after we returned from the Paris trip, there had been talk that he would run Ducasse's American cooking school, but "soon" for that project meant "maybe, if it happens." Like Scotty-don't, Jo-el had given a lot, had been through a lot, for the restaurant. (For the first year and a half, Jo-el had also commuted from Westchester and back each day.) Both had gone from learning how to work in a Ducasse kitchen to taking ADNY to the top of the New York food world. Eventually, though, they were both ready to move on.

As for the rest of the team, there was an ever-shrinking core group of French cooks—though many had returned to France or had plans to do so soon. Most of the new cooks in the kitchen were American, but few of them had been trained by cooks from the original team. They had learned from cooks who had been trained by the original team, and the message was beginning to become diluted.

Many of these new cooks had never seen another Ducasse restaurant or even ADNY when it was truly functioning at its best.

A little more than a year after the Paris trip, construction had begun on the new restaurant, so I began focusing on that project and moving out of ADNY. But by early spring the new restaurant was still in the planning stage and there was little that I could do. So, to fill my time until I would be working only on the new restaurant, I started helping out with the bread team. If I was going to be on the sidelines until the new place got going, at least I would have a chance to learn something new.

After the concept for the new restaurant was established, the next step was to write down ideas for the food. Ducasse wanted a restaurant that served refined comfort food, deriving from both French and American cuisines, in an elegant but not intimidating environment. It would be a place people could go to often to enjoy the quality of Ducasse in a fun, affordable place. Didier and I met often to work on the cuisine. I wrote down lists of comfort classics, dishes that we could refine and revitalize, things like clam chowder, pot au feu, and barbecue. Within a few days, Didier and I came up with a long list of possible dishes.

I cooked a few of the ideas for Didier as we were working through them, like barbecue and homemade pastrami. It was a challenge to develop a Ducasse interpretation of such homey dishes. Like his Spoon and Bar & Boeuf restaurants, the new restaurant was going to be a place that would change the way people thought about Ducasse. Working on these dishes was the most fun I had had in a kitchen in a long time. I was taking everything I had learned about cooking during my reprogramming in the Ducasse style and applying it to many of the things I had loved to eat all my life. Within a short time, we had a very solid list of possible dishes. Then we had to present our ideas. We started by cooking for Ducasse. Just Didier and I working together at the stove at ADNY.

The result of my training in an environment that was the equivalent of the military's basic training was that I was very sure of myself. I knew I could cook and I knew I could create. The rigidity, intimidation, and competition of working at ADNY had driven away many cooks. Some moved on to other restaurants in the city, where many of them excelled based on what they had learned at ADNY; some went back home or left to cook in less competitive cities; and some got out of cooking altogether. But the cooks who did make it in that kitchen were changed. If nothing else, I was confident that I could cook with the best under almost any circumstances.

Sitting in the Aquarium with Ducasse after he had eaten everything I had cooked, listening to him evaluate each dish (larger noodles for the macaroni and cheese, more black truffles for the elbow pasta, cleaner presentation for the pork barbecue), I was certain he was as confident in me as I was. At the end of his evaluations, he looked down at his empty bowl of clam chowder. He adjusted his glasses with his left hand and then, holding them slightly off his face, by the side of the frame and looking over them at me, he said, "*Très bien*, Doog. Now we get to work."

Didier and I cooked for Ducasse again and again. Then we cooked for him and some guests on several occasions until there was a strong menu that fit the restaurant's concept. Finally, we cooked for Ducasse along with his business partner on the new restaurant and his partner's family. By that time, I was confident in just about all of the dishes. We had developed something I was proud of and the partner was sold on the idea. Even his kid loved the chicken and shrimp gumbo. With smiles and handshakes, this was the final green light on the food.

When I met Didier in the Aquarium a few days later, Ducasse was already out of New York. Didier had a whole bunch of papers spread out on the table. They were the construction plans for the front of the house and the kitchen. There was work to do, he said, nodding his head and then closing his eyes for a long pause. He seemed overwhelmed by the prospect but assured me that the restaurant would be ready by the end of the summer.

It was only April and I would continue to help out on breads at ADNY for the next month while attending meetings for Mix, as the restaurant would be called, with people from the other side of the venture. Ducasse's partner on Mix was one of the biggest restaurant groups in the U.S. They were known for successful, money-making operations, but their restaurants were as much clubs as restaurants. The young, beautiful, and elite gathered at their restaurants to drink expensive drinks in hip modern rooms—and sometimes they ate the restaurant's food, which by design was flashy and simple. The management knew how to run a profitable operation, but not necessarily a restaurant where food was the principal priority. The partnership between this group and Ducasse, the master of haute cuisine, was odd, but it wasn't untested. They had already partnered on a Spoon in London, which was successful but considered by people in the Ducasse world as an outcast in the organization, not on par with any of the other restaurants. "I hear it has a great burger," they'd say when asked about it. Initially I wasn't thrilled by the company's involvement—I had spent much of my career steering clear of restaurants like theirs—but as we started to work together, they let us control what we knew best, the kitchen, while they controlled what they knew best, the front of the house.

By June, I had stopped working at ADNY and was just working on opening Mix. The site was under construction and wouldn't be finished for at least two months. Most of the work that I was doing on Mix at this time was attending meetings and conference calls.

At one of the first meetings between both sides of Mix, it seemed obvious that we weren't on the same page. There were several people at the meeting from each side, but Ducasse and his partner did most of the talking. I sat there, next to Ducasse and Didier, and for the most part kept quiet. The plans for Mix were finally taking shape. It was decided that the restaurant would be open seven days and serve lunch on five of those days. We had menus drafted and were going over the pricing at the meeting. The financial aspects of the restaurant (purchasing, accounts payable, the staff's salary, and so on) would all be handled by the other group, but we'd have a lot of say. For the kitchen, we'd handle the ordering of supplies and products and they would pay the bills.

I had already submitted a long list of kitchen equipment—steel frying pans, stainless-steel pans, sheet pans, hotel pans, stock pots, cast-iron pots, and copper pans were just part of it. When I had written the list, I had considered it a wish list and expected that we'd get most but not all of the items on it. When I showed it to Didier, though, he looked it over and told me that I would probably need more of most of the items. I thought about how when ADNY first opened we had unpacked more copper pans than we could possibly have used and how those pans were still in their original wrappings in storage. If I increased the equipment order, Mix would need storage space too. But I did as he suggested and that was just the beginning. We also ordered hand-crafted steak knives from Missouri; an incredible array of custom-made plates and bowls of all sizes; all kinds of custom flatware; and so much more. We spent without a care, even though this freewheeling spending was clearly in opposition to the other side of the restaurant's agenda.

At that meeting, as the other side studied their market research, cost analyses, and projections, I listened mostly to Ducasse. They would suggest a cost for a dish and he would push his upturned hand into the air and say, "More." They would suggest a price for one of our prix fixe menus and he would say, "More, more." The average cost for a diner, "More." The cost of a Ducasse meal has never been cheap. He was telling them that they were undervaluing a meal at Mix and they loved it. They would be happy to charge customers as much as Ducasse thought he could get them to pay. But I was concerned that we were constantly saying "more" on our side, while the other side was studying charts and graphs to best manage costs and profits. The agendas weren't the same.

This communication difficulty spilled over into the language of the menu. After I initially wrote out titles for the dishes and short descriptions of them, Didier, who wouldn't speak English when I first met him and now spoke broken English competently, made changes. Then we sent them to France to be translated into French for Ducasse's system, and then they were translated back into English. All of the initial menus for the restaurant (as with ADNY) would be printed in France and translated into French for their records, so it was necessary to send them the menu. But translating the French back to English instead of using the original English made no sense. I'd get e-mails that were like riddles without answers. A description of something like "low country gravy" would be translated into French as "sauce épice" (because, Didier would say, it sounded good); then translated back into English it would come back as "spicy sauce." It would take four or five times back and forth just to get back to the original.

Equally frustrating was that Didier was the point person on the project. Everything from and to me had to go through him, but then I could never get his attention. I respected Didier as much as I had any chef I'd ever worked for. He had been totally supportive of me and had gone out of his way for me. He was certainly significantly involved in the decision to make me the chef of Mix. But he was having his own problems. Didier had been asked to go to New York, to leave his home, to open ADNY for Ducasse. He had done that, and, despite intense difficulties, he had earned great praise for the restaurant (not just the four stars from the *New York Times*, but also the best new restaurant award from the James Beard Foundation, five stars from the *Mobil Travel Guide*, and much more). He had been the leading force behind the restaurant achieving its goals. Now he was being asked also to lead in opening Mix. That was a lot to ask. And while my name was going to be right behind Ducasse's with Mix, Didier had rarely gotten any public credit for his efforts. It was clear he was no longer happy.

As a result, Didier wasn't paying Mix much attention. This had been clear to me for a while. Even when we were first collaborating on the menu, his attention was wandering. Most of the dishes he suggested were taken straight from the Spoon cookbook, others we had served at ADNY as canapés or amuse-bouches. As gently as I could, I suggested that we didn't want to serve the same food at Mix that we did at ADNY. There were many reasons that this was so, but the easy rationale I used was that we couldn't charge the same thing for the same dish at both restaurants and we didn't want to devalue ADNY in any way. He agreed and we managed to shape a decent menu, but his lack of attention only got worse.

Several times I would show up for a meeting with Didier at ADNY and he was nowhere to be found. This was the guy who was in ADNY's kitchen at all hours, seemingly all the time. Now, I couldn't even find him. He was certainly coming into the kitchen, but not in the mornings and rarely when he said we would meet. I had a lot of respect for Didier; but, whether intentionally or not, he was sabotaging my opportunity with Mix.

Just before I left for a vacation in South Carolina to see my parents and my sister and her family, this all came to a boiling point. I had left several messages for Didier about problems with the construction at the site and hadn't heard back from him. Aside from the work being behind schedule, no electrical outlets were installed above the pass or the stations, there was no space for a lowboy fridge in the pastry station, and there was no ice maker for the kitchen. The last of these was unthinkable as the kitchen relied on ice for so much of what we did. In not planning for this the kitchen contractor had had a lapse in judgment, but there were also serious errors. They had installed cabinets above the tables, but at eye level and projecting out as far as the table. A cook working at the table would have a cabinet right in front of him and not be able to see below it—it would be like sticking your hands through a slot to work blindly, but with a sharp knife. Then there was the salamander and hood, which were installed backwards, so the salamander (a broiler that emits a tremendous amount of heat) would be right in the face of the chef working the pass, essentially making conditions impossible for him.

After I finally got Didier's attention and he went over to the site, he was enraged. When I met him at ADNY, his eyes looked bloodshot and his forehead was covered with sweat. He had immediately called the contractor and we were going to meet him at the site. Mix was a few blocks from **ADNY**, a short walk during which we said nothing to each other. As we descended the stairs into Mix's basement kitchen, there were a few men still working, even though it was late in the day. There were tarps over the counters, wires hanging loose, and dust everywhere. There was plenty of work left to do. At one of the tables, the blueprints for the kitchen were laid out. The contractor was standing next to the table. We all leaned over the plans and listened to him go through them. Several times—when talking about the placement of the salamander and the electrical outlets and the sinks—Didier questioned him.

Finally Didier, looking completely disgusted, said, "This is wrong. You have to get it right. You fix it."

"This is your problem," the contractor said.

Didier banged on the plans with two fingers hard enough to shake the table, "It's all messed up, you have to fix it." Then he pushed the plans off the table.

"You approved these plans," the contractor said. "That's your signature on those sheets. You approved those plans." Didier's face seem to expand. His eyes were bulging. I thought at any minute I would be trying to pull him off the guy. I had never seen him this angry. He pointed at the guy and then banged his fist down on the table. No one moved.

"*Putain!*" he screamed. Then we walked out of the kitchen.

A solution to this problem was achieved, but it took getting Ducasse involved. Alain Ducasse was not nearly as large as Didier or me, but he was more intimidating than either of us. Most cooks meet him and they remember him as a big man, but he's average-sized, maybe five foot eight, 175 pounds. His physical size has nothing to do with what makes him intimidating. His determination is fierce. A great demonstration of this happened during a meeting with the Essex House when he was finalizing his deal to open ADNY. As the story goes, everything was settled, but then they tried to change the deal on him, insisting that the restaurant be a union restaurant. Ducasse knew all about union problems in France. In the U.S., they are a significant reason why it is difficult to run a good restaurant in a hotel. The labor union is great for some cooks, but it makes things absolutely impossible for cooks who are willing to work long hours for little pay so that they can learn. Among other problems, union cooks have to get paid overtime after forty hours, which would often be halfway through the third day of the week, and they can only work a certain amount of hours a day. These are things that go against the nature of having apprentices and the reality of what a restaurant can afford. All of the best restaurants rely on cooks who fill the role of apprentices. Ducasse knew that he couldn't open ADNY with a union kitchen. Not having to was a vital part of his deal with the Essex House. In response to their trying to change the deal, he stood up, picked up the heavy wood chair that he had been sitting on, and smashed it on the floor. Then he straightened his suit and walked out. Cornering him had misfired. They needed him more than he needed them, and ADNY opened in the hotel without a union.

The contractor decided to make the necessary changes, and we had a meeting scheduled to go over them when I got back from South Carolina. But as I tried to relax at my parents' house seven hundred miles away, I wasn't comfortable at all. And one last infuriating episode occurred while I was on this long weekend break: the people on the other side of the project asked me to provide them with recipes for all of our dishes. Ducasse would never ask for anything like this, because he knew it would be ridiculous. We were still shaping our ideas, still developing the food, and probably wouldn't have a very good sense of what any one dish would consist of until we were in the restaurant and cooking for at least a few days. Some of the proposed dishes we had never even cooked before. They were just ideas on paper—potatoes with lobster, maybe basil with the potatoes, butter at the end, maybe garlic butter. Because they insisted, I wrote down several recipes for dishes that didn't yet exist.

As we sat in Dulles Airport waiting for a connection on the way home, Mike and I talked through all sorts of possible scenarios. Sitting on the plastic chair, staring at the faded carpet, I thought about walking away. The restaurant would be the first with my name as the chef. It could make me, or I could be associated with a failure. A few months earlier, I would never have believed that a Ducasse restaurant could be anything less than perfect. Now, I was having doubts. Mike listened to all of my complaints and my frustration. He knew that I was leaning toward turning it down. His advice was the same for everything I said, "I understand, but you should do it."

When I got home I called Greenie, who was in Los Angeles running a restaurant that had been on the top of most lists for years, and he repeated some of Mike's lines. "Dude," he said, "you'll never have an opportunity like this again. You have to do it."

I had a meeting with Ducasse when I got back to New York and I decided to talk directly to him about my concerns. I don't know if he suspected how close I was to not going ahead, but his response was simple. "Give me a year; I'll give you a career."

The problems with Mix didn't go away after that, but my indecisiveness did. I dedicated myself to the project. For the month of August none of the other principals was in New York. I had to coordinate decisions between Ducasse's offices in Paris and Monaco and his partner's in Miami. Right down to the last day, there were major problems. The wood floor of the dining room, which had been taken plank by plank from an old train station in France, arrived in America so wet that it had to be dried out for several weeks before it could be put down. Mix's dining room ceiling was glass (actually every wall was also a layer of thick glass), and the lights were suspended above the tables by a long metal wire that went through the glass and bolted into the actual ceiling. The problem was that a bulb couldn't be screwed in, as the wire would keep twirling with each turn.

Huge sums were being spent (reportedly around eight million dollars) on the restaurant—we were even getting a high-tech designer bathroom—but eventually the clamps started to come down on some of the spending. They decided that they wouldn't spend money on a sign, which was rationalized as a good thing since in New York this could be seen as an indication of exclusivity and chic. There was supposed to be a private chef's table in the dining room, which would be in the room but could be separated by a retractable metal curtain. The first curtain looked terrible and the second attempt didn't work at all, so the curtain was abandoned.

Most troubling to me was that the final concept was confusing and odd: "mixing the appreciation of past and present, cuisine and culture, and style and substance, Mix will bring the cuisine of the east coast of North America and the European Atlantic coast together." Our straightforward concept had gone through many channels and translations, finally becoming so convoluted that I could barely understand it. Plus, some of the English on the menu was ridiculous: First of Mix (for appetizers), Mix of Mix (a tasting menu),

Mix Prix Fixe (another tasting menu), and Must of Mix (house specialties).

But, despite all of this, this restaurant was still the opportunity that I had been working toward for so many years. While I couldn't control everything, I knew we were going to do some great food in an amazing room. I put together a serious team of very talented cooks. Eventually, everyone on all sides of the restaurant came together for the launch and Mix was born.

The week Mix in New York (as it was now called, since there were already plans for a Vegas version) opened I saw just how intense the media attention was going to be. To launch the restaurant, there was a major feature in the *New York Times* about me as Ducasse's protégé. In short order this would be followed by mentions, articles, and features in so many newspapers and magazines that I couldn't even keep track of them—not just New York publications or food or travel publications, but even men's magazines and design and architecture magazines. The attention was amazing, but the *New York Times* article mattered the most to me, and not because it was in the *Times,* or because it was published on my twenty-ninth birthday. In the article, Ducasse was quoted as choosing me for the position because "he's the best cook in my kitchen, he's ambitious and loyal." During my days at ADNY, I had worked as hard as I had ever worked, as hard as I had worked in my grandfather's diner. Only once did I get my grandfather's approval. This was a similar feeling.

Mix was located on 58th Street, just off the corner of Sixth Avenue. Our first week was a soft one, dedicated to just friends, family, and VIPs. On the very first day I got a sense of the struggle we'd face. We had served Alain Ducasse and Florence Fabricant of the *New York Times* a perfect meal in the afternoon. Just one table for a full team was a fairly casual walk in the park, no matter how important the diners were. That night we also had just one table: an eight-top with Ducasse, his partner, and six important future investors. This was just as easy for us and we prepared all of the food perfectly, but the waiter tripped on his way up the stairs and we lost a whole dish. We were forced to serve seven of the eight people and work like crazy to get another course out as soon as possible. I don't think the investors were impressed.

On our third day, we served a room of sixty-five journalists. Ducasse came up to my side early in the day, as I was working with a cook on preparing a chicken pot pie, and said, "Doog, tonight no, no stress, but no, no, no, no mistakes."

I nodded and said, "*Oui, chef.*"

Ducasse had spent most of the first two weeks with me in the kitchen while we were preparing to open to the public. On a few days, I had to serve him all of the food and then sit with him as he critiqued it. To the last minute, he was giving me instructions and advice. Right before service that day he told me how to handle the servers. It was as important to control the rhythm and flow of the kitchen as to manage the servers and their delivery of the food. Time was everything and both sides of the restaurant needed to work together smoothly. Ducasse pumped his fist in the air as he instructed me on how to keep the servers moving. "Kill, kill, kill, kill," he said. Then he pushed the air down with both hands. "But calm, relax, easy." He paused and then he pointed at me and added, "But kill." Then I dimmed the lights so that they would focus mostly on the areas where the cooks and I were working. We didn't have a hundred fiber-optic lights like ADNY, but the effect was similar. The lights guided our focus and limited our distractions. The room quieted. Then I started calling out the orders. At first just a few cooks were moving and then everyone was moving. Even so, there was little noise. Just total concentration. The show had begun.

On one of the last nights of the soft opening, Mike came in with our friend Ben, who was now an established investment lawyer. Mike had come by to check out the restaurant several times while it was under construction, so he knew exactly where it was. Many people probably walked right by at first, since there was no sign on the concrete facade and with the steel curtain closed across the front windows it was hard to tell that it was a restaurant. (With the steel curtain open, passersby could see through the restaurant's street-to-ceiling windows and into the dining room.) On the wall next to the doorman, who stood by the door that night, Mike and Ben may have seen a small monitor that was playing a video of a kitchen (not ours—it was of the Spoon in London). Pulling open the thick and unbelievably heavy cement door, they made their way to a hostess with startlingly beautiful eyes. Then the maître d', a Japanese man who was so buoyant it seemed he could float, led them to their table. They may have noticed the single round table by the front window near the coat-check girl, and the lighted bar, which changed colors throughout the night, and the different-sized podiums across from the bar—some with monitors in them playing the kitchen video—on their way into the dining room. They certainly noticed the glass walls, wood floor, and stylish seats and tables as they entered the dining room.

That night after their meal, I didn't come upstairs to the table. This was a Ducasse restaurant, so the chef stayed in the kitchen.

Ducasse had actually told me to stay out of the dining room, which I would have done anyway. (Ducasse's partner, on the other hand, walked through the dining room the whole night, often using his cell phone, sometimes sitting with one of his guests, who was opening his mail at the table, and sometimes kneeling next to a table of pretty girls.) Instead, Mike and Ben stumbled downstairs into the kitchen when they were done eating.

They had eaten a lot of food and drunk a lot of wine. I sent them a good sampling of the menu, including the clam chowder; the elbow macaroni with ham and black truffles; macaroni and cheese; duck ham served with a marmalade of cêpes; "tuna fish salad" (confit of tuna, cucumbers, citrus, and olives); "pot au feu" (poached bison, vegetables in bouillon, and country bread dressed with mustard pickles and onions); chicken pot pie; pastrami with potatoes, romaine lettuce, and mustard; and the "barbecue" dish (roasted pork, braised bitter greens, and corn bread in a casserole).

They both looked shot, but also ecstatic when they came down to the kitchen. As they stood by the pass for a few minutes, they were thanking everyone, including several of the cooks whom Mike knew well. In assembling the Mix team, I had chosen the most talented cooks I knew and those who I had confidence would be loyal and dedicated. At one point while we were putting together the restaurant, Didier had asked me which of the ADNY cooks I wanted to take with me and I told him none. He smiled his big smile, which could mean rage or amusement, and asked, "No, really, which cooks?" I again told him none. Rather than bring in ADNY cooks to train the new cooks, I planned to instill the Ducasse system in all of the cooks just the way it had been instilled in me. Eventually, I relented a little and asked to bring along R-dog, who had been on my case for months for me to bring him over as a chef de partie (though he had never been more than a commis at ADNY).

"That's not the guy you want to bring with you," Didier said. He had not been impressed by R-dog while he was working with me on garde-manger. But R-dog, if nothing else, was as ambitious and determined as I was. Plus, he was loyal. Despite my having to ride him mercilessly while we worked at ADNY, R-dog had become a good friend of mine. A study in contrasts, he sports three earrings in one ear but is a married Mormon who goes to church for most of the day every Sunday, even when he's been out drinking late the night before. I didn't know if he was ready, but I knew that if I gave him a chance it would break his heart to let me down.

While I hadn't brought any other ADNY cooks along, there were other cooks with Ducasse experience, including Jayson, the tough and talented kid from Philly; Ryan, who had been a commis for a year and was now crashing in our spare bedroom in Astoria; and Dagan, an upstate New York farm boy who had done a two-month stage at ADNY and retained some of what he saw. And in October, after leaving his L.A. restaurant, Greenie came aboard. The rest of the kitchen was filled with experienced cooks and guys I knew I could count on, like James, who had left a sous chef position at March, and Jimmy the Saint, who I had worked with at Bouley Bakery. It would be as strong a team as any I'd worked with, including the ones at ADNY and Louis XV. (Ironically, Michel, whom I had worked under at Louis XV, came to work under me a few weeks after we opened. Just like in Monaco, he was riding the guy under him, Ryan, over every little mistake—real and imagined. He was gone in a few days.)

I had handpicked most of the kitchen team. Two important exceptions were my sous chef, who had been selected by Ducasse, and my assistant, whom the other side of the operation had brought in. The sous chef, Massimo, was from Italy, but I had met him when we were both working at Louis XV. He was as talented and dedicated a cook as any of us. The assistant I was given was Julian, who turned out to be one of the most valuable people in the kitchen. He had never cooked in his life or run a restaurant, but he was thrown into the fire with me and performed like a champ. For the first two weeks we were open, Massimo was still on his way from Italy, so I had no choice but to rely on Julian for everything and that's what he did: he set up the computer in my office, showed people where they needed to be, spoke Spanish with the dishwashers we were hiring, and so much more. He was in a rough spot, but he handled it as though he'd been doing the job for years.

Before we got going, he asked me if it would be okay for him to have Saturday and Sunday off so he could hang out with his girl. He was from the office side of things, so he wasn't used to working on the weekends and wasn't needed during those busy days. I told him it was no problem, but he wanted to make sure that it didn't interfere with the days I wanted to take off.

"I'm not going to be taking days off, so you do what's best for you," I told him. He didn't believe me, but he would see I wasn't kidding.

Just about every cook had a significant amount of experience in serious restaurants, but many of them were being driven harder than they ever had been before. I was of course leading this effort and I was giving everything I had. I had once thought that the first few months at ADNY would be the hardest I ever worked, but I gave a lot more during the first few months at Mix. I was there every day from 6:30 in the morning until we were finished cleaning and ordering around midnight that night, every day from the day we opened in early September until my first vacation day—Thanksgiving. I was butchering a lot of the meat and fish, keeping the walk-in ordered and neat, watching over all of the ordering, working on the menu, managing the cooks and their schedule, and of course running every service.

After so many years of working every day to get this opportunity, I wasn't about to let up. I had anticipated that making Mix into a Ducasse restaurant would be a challenge, and I had expected there to be Ducasse detractors, but I hadn't expected that challenges would come from all sides or that I would be caught in the middle.

Chapter 15

Le Mess de Mix

The first few months of Mix were a blur. I did two things the entire time: work and sleep. Occasionally I ate, but not often. I probably lost twenty pounds, but I wouldn't know, because I didn't have time to weigh myself. I had given up so much to get to this point: few days off, fewer holidays off, little time with my family, little time with anyone outside of a kitchen, including girlfriends, who only lasted a month or two of my limited availability. I had lived on moments—a late-night dinner after work, the rare long weekend or even a Sunday off to watch football—but now I gave up one last thing: any life outside the kitchen. I didn't sleep in Mix's kitchen (during the few hours when I got any sleep), but just about every other minute was spent in the restaurant.

Mix was busy right from the start. The excitement of a new Ducasse restaurant and all of the media coverage that came with it filled up the sixty-seat dining room every night. Besides the journalists doing everything they could to get in, there were celebrities, chefs, and just about everyone I knew. The line of people coming into the kitchen each night was dizzying and a bit distracting—from Thomas Keller to a guy I went to high school with who now owned an Italian restaurant in our hometown. It was nice to meet a beautiful model, but the guests that mattered to me were the chefs, and the people who were there for the food—not those following the latest trends. On any given night, I would have a few major chefs in the room along with several journalists. One night it was Daniel Boulud and *New York Times* restaurant critic William Grimes. Normally the *Times* took precedence over everyone else, but not a chef of Daniel's caliber. For me the most important evaluations were from my peers.

One night Raphie, a good friend since we worked at Bouley Bakery together, came in. He was now a chef at the Four Seasons, and he brought along a bunch of chefs and general managers from the restaurant. He was unabashedly proud of me, and it was good to prove to his team that his praise was warranted. Another memorable visit was from Drew Nieporent, one of the most celebrated and respected New York restaurateurs. He came down to the kitchen and stood next to me at the pass. "Use this number when you want to go out," he said and handed me his business card with his cell phone number. "Everything was great," he added. Then he grabbed my shoulder as a sign of sincerity before walking back up the stairs.

But, as with all new restaurants, it wasn't all smooth sailing. We actually had some big problems. Ducasse, through me, had been in charge of everything involving the kitchen—the design, ordering, kitchen team—and everything about it represented what a Ducasse kitchen was like. The front of the house was managed by his partner and was another story altogether. One of the most embarrassing results of this disconnect between the two sides involved the reservationists. In any decent restaurant, handling reservations is extremely important and should be done by an experienced professional with an appealing voice and friendly disposition. Ducasse's partners wanted to pay our reservationists poorly and by the hour, which no professional would accept. So, they hired kids with no experience in restaurants. The result was that I had to keep an eye on the reservations. One day while I was looking over the reservations we had for that night I saw a 10:30 reservation for Pierre Hermé, one of the foremost pastry chefs in the world, with a note that he had asked for an early reservation. He must have had to spell his name for them, as they were prone to misspell names but got his right. Still, they hadn't a clue who he was and had given him an undesirable reservation, even though we could have accommodated him earlier in the evening. Another time I didn't know that Laurent Gras, a former chef at ADPA and Louis XV whose food I had enjoyed at Peacock Alley, was dining in the restaurant (the name they wrote down wasn't even close) until my spy and expeditor, Mr. Chen, whom I had worked with at March, told me that he had just been seated. Mr. Chen kept an eye on the waiters and the dining room for me and had recognized the chef before he ordered.

In a Ducasse restaurant, the front of the house is composed of dedicated, experienced professionals on the same level as the kitchen staff. At Mix, though, we had managers who might have been great with numbers but not at running a service, and servers who were chosen for aesthetics over competency. Most of the servers were young and inexperienced. They weren't professionals; they were college kids and actors making money on the side. Having a kitchen filled with experienced, dedicated cooks working extremely long hours for little pay on one side of the restaurant and well-intentioned but often incompetent servers on the other was an extremely bad fit. At first these seemed like difficulties that we could fix, a steeper than expected learning curve that we would overcome, but a serious rift was developing.

It didn't take long before we were battling the front of the house. The general manager came into my office one morning to tell me that all the cooks would have to start using the punch clock by the following Monday, as they were all going to be paid by the hour from then on. This was absurd. At first I didn't even understand their motivation for making this change. All of the cooks were on salary and working more hours than we could possibly pay them for on an hourly basis. When I suggested this to him, he said that they'd all have to start working thirty-five- to forty-hour weeks. I remained calm as I told him that would mean that we'd have to hire almost double the number of cooks we already had and wouldn't end up cutting any costs. But he smiled to show me that we were on the same side of the issue and then explained that they had gone through the calculations and it would work. Then he showed me the budget that had been approved. Like many of the numbers they ran, they were based in an imaginary world. A Ducasse kitchen is composed of positions like chef de cuisine, sous chef, chef de partie, demi chef de partie, and commis. They had positions like line cook, prep cook, and pasta cook. Maybe that was a system that worked well in some restaurants, but it had nothing to do with the way we were running Mix's kitchen. Without help from anyone else on the Ducasse side, it took me a couple of days of explaining why this wouldn't work before they relented. They agreed that only new cooks would be made to follow these rules and I just let it go.

I was sure that Ducasse would be as upset as I was about this, but I couldn't get a clear message to him. I would talk to Vito, Ducasse's manager of operations in America, and he would agree that we had some serious problems. He even told Didier about it before telling Ducasse directly. But Didier wasn't paying much attention to Mix. Ducasse would listen to Vito's complaints but would then ask Didier what was going on, and Didier would just say something like "Oh, Mix is fine, no problem." He didn't want to deal with it, so we had no way to explain the difficulties we were having, except to wait for the next Ducasse visit.

It was more than a week—a long time for a new restaurant—before I finally had the chance to tell Ducasse about some of the difficulties we were facing. He listened quietly to everything I told him and was even more livid than I had been. His response was to bring in his own guy, whose only job would be to watch their manager. But it turned out he wasn't there to build a system that would work, just to ridicule the one that was failing. Eventually the original general manager left the restaurant and was replaced by a new one, but nothing changed.

I was doing everything that I could from the kitchen to make the dining room resemble a Ducasse restaurant. At meetings I'd have to emphasize the most basic elements of service. Within a month of opening almost all our banquettes had been stained. They were supposed to be oil and stain resistant, but everything left marks on them. As soon as we got the new ones, the servers managed to leave ink markings on them from the pens that were kept behind the banquettes for order taking.

One night Raymond Blanc, a well-known and respected French chef, came down to see me in the kitchen. "The food is great," he told me, "but you need to watch the service. You have a lot of problems." I knew that we were having difficulties with the front-of-house staff but didn't know how bad it was. I had been mostly focusing on the one thing I could control, the food, but was getting killed by the service. As I started watching the servers more closely and asked Mr. Chen to tell me what was going on, I became more and more frustrated. Dishes were going to the wrong table, orders were being put in wrong, and finally one of the servers delivered a chicken pot pie to a restaurant critic for his dessert—not even thinking that was a little strange. The night that happened I was enraged but tried to remember what Didier had told me about controlling my frustration. We still had many covers left to do that night and I needed to keep my focus.

But our new general manager, Melissa, decided that we needed to talk about the situation right then. Unlike some of our hostesses, who could make anyone feel welcomed, Melissa had little warmth or charm.

"I don't know why you're so upset about this, Doug," she said. I was still keeping track of the orders—calling out what we needed and calculating when the next table's course would be ready—and trying not to get into this discussion at that moment. But she continued, "There are going to be mistakes. We have to expect that. It's just one table."

I slammed the plate I was holding down on the granite pass and turned to her. "It matters," I said. "Mistakes aren't okay. Let's at least try not to make them." Then I turned back to what I was doing and tried to pick up where I had left off. As the days went on, I would become adept at being able to switch from a dining room distraction to orchestrating the service. Mistakes and apologies were so common that I began to anticipate them.

At the end of that night, Melissa knocked on the door to my office while I was going over the ordering lists for the next day. She looked as though she had built up the courage to come to my door. I knew that I had been a little too harsh with her. She stood in the entranceway and pushed her long brown hair out of her face before speaking. "You know," she said, "when you talk to us like that, you're ruining our nights."

"When you make mistakes like that, you're ruining my life," I responded. I tried to explain how important this was to me, but she only got more upset. She was nearly in tears, but I felt my world was spinning out of control.

On a Wednesday in late October, I got up around 5:30 and took a shower. As I was shaving, I heard Ryan, who was still staying in our extra room, bouncing around. Ryan had a rough time with mornings and getting to the kitchen on time. He would hear me getting ready and would scramble to get himself together—trying to leave before me so he'd get to the kitchen first. I didn't waste much time myself. In just a few minutes, I was cleaned up and on my way out the door. I was dressed in a blue dress shirt, brown pants, and dress shoes. Didier had taught me a lot about being a chef and one of those things was looking decent. A slob—baggy jeans, unshaven, bags under the eyes—dragging himself in to work each day will never command respect.

I was still living in the same apartment in Astoria (and was even using my landlord's imported Greek olive oil, Athena, at Mix) and took the same route on my way to work. The only difference was that I got into a cab and not the subway. Since taking the chef job, one of the few things I granted myself was not taking the subway unless I absolutely had to. Besides, it was a lot quicker by cab. Ryan had raced out of the apartment to beat me to the restaurant, but thanks to the cab I arrived before him, just a little after 6:00. This was the ordinary way my day started even though this was no ordinary day, as I had been snidely reminded by one of the waitresses the day before: "Your review comes out tomorrow." She said it as though I would learn my lesson. They were constantly complaining about not being part of the team, but now she was separating herself further from the team.

In my office, I read over the orders James had done the night before and the lists that Julian, my assistant, had left for me. Julian was great at tracking down what orders were coming in, how many covers we had each day (and which were VIPs), and all of the paperwork. I took a quick scan of my e-mails. My in-box was inundated with "alerts" from the other organization's management team. The alerts would tell me to buy extra lettuce this weekend because prices were going up, but we didn't order like that. We bought on the basis of quality—what was best and freshest in the market that day—and ordered so that we would use the products only when they were best.

Then I heard someone out in the hallway. I took off my dress shirt and put on my chef jacket. Outside my office door was a deliveryman for one of the purveyors. He was stacking up Styrofoam boxes of fish along the wall. As he stood there, I opened each of the boxes to see what he was delivering. In one of the boxes was a special item I had been waiting for: live Japanese river crabs, each a little larger than a piece of popcorn. I had rarely used this purveyor, so I checked the order carefully. I went through the boxes and sorted out a few fish that didn't look good enough. I took a pen from the deliveryman and marked two of the boxes. "We're not taking these two," I said about the two boxes where I had put the fish of questionable quality.

Then I went into the kitchen. There were only a few cooks working, but there was already a lot of movement. In the walk-in, I went through all of our products. I had a beautiful whole pig hanging from the ceiling. In a few days, I'd butcher the pig and use just about every part. On the shelves, on towels on trays, was a row of gorgeous birds, followed by a whole side of beef that had been aged. Everything was in exact order, perfectly neat.

The kitchen was not nearly as big as the one at ADNY, but we had many of the same tools. In the middle of the room was a massive Molteni stove. It ran lengthwise through the room, and cooks worked on three sides of it while I stood on the fourth side closest to the stairs. On the wall that was farthest back when you faced into the kitchen from the pass, there was a rotisserie (complete with the Mix in New York logo on it) and then a combi oven, which allowed us to control the temperature and type of heat (moist or dry) for exact periods of time—an incredible tool that I relied on. The pastry station was to the left of the pass, with a counter that separated it from the rest of the kitchen, and the dish room was just ten feet or so to the right of the pass. Having the dish room so close was actually a good thing, as it provided me with a way to gauge how each guest was doing with his or her meal—a dish that came back into the kitchen barely touched, for example, could mean that a diner having a tasting menu didn't care for that dish or was just too full.

Through the dish room was a back hallway with a ceiling that had clearance of just over six feet and served as dry storage and pan storage (including many unused copper and cast-iron pans). Because we had a limited amount of space, we even used the hallway that led to my office, which was behind the kitchen's back wall, as a prep area. And because we didn't have enough stoves, we set up a table to the right of the main stove with a few portable induction stoves, which, like the induction wok at ADNY, use magnetism to produce a very efficient heat source.

When the kitchen was at full speed, just an hour or so later, the room would have a high people-to-square-foot ratio—sometimes an uncomfortably high ratio. Even so, it was big by the standards of many of the kitchens I had worked in and was without a doubt a beautiful kitchen. We kept it spotless. Everything from the black granite pass to the metal shelves was kept as clean as possible. There was never anything on the floor; there was never even anything on the countertops that didn't belong there. I instilled an ethos of cooking with one hand while cleaning with the other, though of course not literally.

After lunch was served, I went upstairs to sit down with Ducasse. When we met upstairs, it was almost always in the "lounge area," as it was mockingly called. (It was just one table in the narrow space between the bar and the front window. Ducasse restaurants don't have lounges; when his partner wanted a lounge, Ducasse's designer gave him one that could seat three people comfortably.) As I was walking to the table, where Ducasse was waiting, I thought about how when I had gotten back from Monaco I had surprised myself with my temerity in going into the Aquarium at ADNY to speak with Ducasse, about how, even in the last few months, I had gone from being quiet by his side to talking with him as I would with just about anyone else. This wasn't in any way because the great respect I had for him had diminished at all. It was just that I had grown familiar with being one on one with him.

I also dealt directly with Ducasse more now because Didier was often missing in action. He came through at the end to open Mix, but once it was open his involvement changed. He didn't act like my boss; he acted like an advisor. When he came by, which wasn't often, he'd just ask me about what I was doing and make some suggestions. I appreciated and valued his input as much as I ever had. However, while my focus was on Mix, I was hearing from a lot of the ADNY cooks, including some who were getting ready to leave, that Didier's attention at the restaurant was spotty and then I saw Ducasse confront him.

It was a few weeks earlier, and I had been sitting in Mix's lounge with Ducasse going over the menu when Didier sat down to join us. He was several minutes late for our meeting. Ducasse looked at his watch and then turned to me. "Doog, what time were you here today?"

I told him around 6:00. Then he asked Didier, who paused and then said, "Just now."

"Chef," Ducasse said, as if to say, "*voilà.*" He nodded his head as though in agreement and said, "Chef," and once again, "Chef," the final time letting in some anger and making it clear what he thought about that fact by looking directly at Didier. It was an uncomfortable couple of moments.

Like other reviews of Mix—most were published within a month of the restaurant opening—there was a lot that was positive and a lot that was negative about the *New York Times* review. The review began:

> *Somewhere deep in the kitchen of Mix in New York, a chef is struggling to get some attention. His name is Douglas Psaltis, and he has talent. His instincts are wholesome and honest. But he has a lot of visual and conceptual clutter to break through.*

The review then went on to critique the concept, the dishes, the design, and just about everything else. But the "good news," William Grimes concluded, was that "after all the effort, there is a reward. It's the food." And he ended the article with some advice: "allow Mr. Psaltis his well-deserved share of the spotlight."

While I never hesitated to separate myself from the other owner and would have been the first to suggest that the front of the house was holding the restaurant back, when I was in the restaurant I was Ducasse. I was certainly the creator of much of the food, but I did so in a manner I had learned from Ducasse and that he wanted. Separating the two of us was impossible.

Our meeting at the table didn't last long. He asked me if I was happy about the review and I told him no. We never discussed the reviewer praising me while attacking him and his partner. I never knew what he thought about that. But, from what I knew about him, I thought he saw the review as a challenge to overcome and would use it to become more determined and focused on our goals.

Following all of the reviews critiquing the restaurant, the problems only got worse. Because of all the media exposure, we were very busy, but it was never enough. Rather than working to fix our problems, the focus shifted to increasing the number of covers we did. The other half of the partnership set a goal of 180 covers a night, but then we were doing 210 (before we even handled 180 well). In a sixty-five-seat dining room, turning the tables three times in a day was a lot of stress on everyone. This wasn't a restaurant where people went to have an appetizer and entrée. The menu favored tasting menus (there was an option to order à la carte, but there were two tasting menu options), and the majority of orders were menus. This means that the kitchen is cooking multiple courses for most tables, and the servers are serving and clearing multiple times. It is difficult to speed this process up without really herding customers in and pushing them out. But when we started doing 210 regularly, management wanted to do even more. They wanted to do 240 covers and eventually 300. It seemed like a joke to me. There was no way we could do the food we were doing or control quality at that level. And the space didn't allow for these numbers, which accounted for all the damage that was being done to the dining room. That wasn't a concern for the management, though. Their other restaurants were rarely reviewed, so this was a unique opportunity for them. Their response was to milk Mix for all it was worth.

There was nothing I could do about this. They took the reservations and filled the house as much as they could. I tried just to focus on the food, and for most of November and December that's what I did. Then they announced the plans for New Year's Eve. Traditionally this is one of the biggest nights of the year for a restaurant. It's a huge moneymaker, because of the sky-high prices that the market will bear. Most fine dining restaurants, which are providing top quality in exchange for top prices all year long, either provide something very special on that night for a premium or just close for the night (as ADNY did the first year). In devising Mix's plans, the other side's management team looked down the road at Ducasse's other restaurant and decided that if Ducasse could charge more than $300 a person at ADNY, then they could do something similar at Mix. When Didier and I heard this, we were both furious. This was preposterous. It showed how little they understood about Ducasse's restaurants or even about Mix. ADNY was a super high-end restaurant, the finest of fine dining, whereas Mix was a casual upscale restaurant. The reviews often described Mix as "Ducasse on a dime."

New Year's Eve was an opportunity for Mix to do something special without robbing our customers. I tried everything I could to prevent this mistake but again had difficulty getting the message to Ducasse. A couple of months after Mix opened, Vito left the organization, a new manager of operations in America was named, and an assistant position below him was added. With the loss of Vito, the organization took on another layer between me and Ducasse with this assistant, Jean François. He was a French guy in his early twenties who acted like a forty-five-year-old who had seen every situation five times over. When I pleaded with Jean François to address the New Year's situation, he just assured me, "Don't worry, don't worry, just cook, don't worry." Didier was also trying to get Ducasse to intervene, but he was unsuccessful too.

The New Year's plan went forward and was a debacle. Soon after they tried selling the idea, they realized that they would have to justify the cost, so they asked me to write up a special menu with luxury ingredients. I did what I could, but I refused to turn the restaurant into their catering hall for the night. We would do the restaurant's food, but adapt it as best as we could for their ridiculous price tag. A few days before the big day, they were nearly hysterical. They only had reservations for about twenty people for the entire night. All of their efforts would end up costing them money. Then they came to me on the day of the impending disaster and asked me what we could do. "Do you think your brother or any of your friends will come for half price?" Melissa asked me. I told her no, without asking anyone. There was no way I was going to sell this terrible idea to any of my friends.

New Year's Eve was our first true disaster, but it wasn't our last.

I was miserable after the episode, disappointed and embarrassed. It was just one night (witnessed mercifully by only a dozen or so people), though, and I hoped that the management had learned something about Mix from it. But the only thing they learned was that this particular approach to milking the restaurant was wrong, and come Valentine's Day they were back at it again. This time their scheme wasn't to try and get as much as they could out of each guest; it was to bring in as many covers as they possibly could. This was, of course, a business and that's normally a perfectly acceptable initiative. But they overbooked the restaurant to nearly double its capacity. Having so few guests for New Year's Eve, they weren't going to have another holiday with an empty dining room. They went with a reasonable approach to entice diners—a special menu, not too expensive, three different seatings throughout the night—and then made reservations for forty-two parties for the first seating when we only had twenty-two tables. We could only accommodate half the parties that arrived for the first seating. Some left, but many waited for a table to open up, knowing they wouldn't find an empty table elsewhere on such a busy night for restaurants. Because of the people waiting, the situation cascaded through the rest of the night.

In overbooking the restaurant the management also added tables anywhere they could. They pressed all the tables together and squeezed in extras in every open space, and then used the same number of waiters and runners that they did for 180 covers. What ensued was nothing less than chaos. It should have been a simple service—a set menu with everyone getting essentially the same food—but the dining room was as packed as a high school cafeteria. Some of the diners were getting the same course twice while others missed a course. We were cooking in waves—garde-manger would do ten salads for one group of tables, then fish would do ten lobsters for that group while garde-manger was doing the next ten salads for the next ten tables—so having the waiters come into the kitchen to tell us to redo courses over and over was unbelievable—it was a nightmare that wouldn't end. Because the waiters made so many mistakes, the kitchen got backed up with orders and was nearly out of control.

By the end of the night, Melissa, who had planned every aspect of this—the concept, the reservations, the preparations—was standing next to me in the kitchen. She was too embarrassed to go upstairs into the dining room. But what was a bad day in the office for her was crushing for me. On the way home, I questioned whether I was the one in the wrong place. This wasn't a Ducasse restaurant; it was his partner's and we were in the way by trying to do something respectable.

It was clear by this time that the two sides of the venture were locked in battle. We didn't just have different agendas for the same restaurant; we were trying to pull the restaurant in two different directions. While they were trying to make it into another of their lounge restaurants, I was still trying to make it a Ducasse restaurant. But I was alone in this fight. Jean François was useless, Didier was dealing with his own problems, and Ducasse hadn't been in the restaurant in a while. When I spoke with Ducasse, he would just tell me to push them to do things right and be patient. It was difficult to be patient, though, as the conditions were deteriorating by the day.

Ever since Ducasse essentially forced out one of their managers (by bringing in the guy whose sole job was to watch over their manager), I had sensed that a struggle for control over the restaurant was coming. During the planning stages, they had sat back and let us do just about whatever we wanted. They hadn't even curbed our aggressive spending until the very last few weeks—after the eight million of their money had been spent. As it was explained to me, it was a fifty–fifty partnership, but Ducasse's investment was the value of his name, plus a limited financial commitment. The big money side had been responsible for the rest. This is a common arrangement with a chef who can command attention because of his reputation. Considering this, though, their allowing us to control so much about the launch of the restaurant showed a tremendous amount of faith in Ducasse and, in retrospect, was at odds with their dollars-and-cents approach to everything.

Then there was another major catastrophe. This time it had nothing to do with the front of the house, even though it occurred in the service area of the dining room. Before service began on a Sunday night, one of the servers rushed down the stairs into the kitchen. "Chef," she said, "there's a flood upstairs."

When I got upstairs, I couldn't believe what I saw: in the service area, an open space tucked behind one of the dining room walls, there were cracks in the glass ceiling with water coming through. The water had already filled up a huge plastic tub and was overflowing. I told the server to get another tub to replace this one and stood back to get a better look at what was going on. Mix's ceiling was glass with a true ceiling a foot or two above it. Somehow the leak was coming from above us and it was heavy. I could hear the stress on the glass: an ominous creaking. Then I saw that there was another leak right in the middle of the dining room. No tub was going to fix this problem. I wasn't as worried about the water as about the glass. I backed up slowly and went back downstairs.

Tony, the only manager working that night, came into the kitchen to ask me what I thought we should do. I told him that I thought we should close. There was no way I was going back up there under breaking glass and I wasn't sending anyone else. He agreed with me and started making calls. When Tony finally got through to someone in the management office and told him what we wanted to do, he responded that we didn't have the authority to close the restaurant. Ignoring their orders, I started sending everyone home and got all of the patrons out of the building.

The next day I discovered that the cracks in the ceiling were the result of a massive flood that had passed through several floors before working its way to us. It took some time before they were able to stop the leaks and there was considerable damage. The restaurant would be closed for a few days because of it. Included in the damage from the flooding was a large section of the precious wood planks that had been taken from the train station in France. They were ruined and would eventually have to be replaced.

Despite all of the money that had been spent, Mix was not built to last. In addition to the banquettes that would need to be replaced again, and now part of the floor, we kept having problems with the front door. It was an extremely heavy door, one that many patrons struggled to open, especially when it was windy. One night it came completely off its hinge and couldn't be opened. This was after we had a roomful of guests. Everyone in our ultramodern dining room had to be led down the stairs, through our kitchen, down the hallway past my office, and up another flight of stairs to the back entrance. Then there were the high-tech bathrooms that rarely worked. One thing or another went wrong with them, including a reviewer's wife falling off a toilet when the seat came off. We had to keep someone by the bathrooms at all times to monitor all of the potential problems.

The heating was another example of design run amok. The restaurant had been built so that it would get all of its heat from the kitchen. This was necessary partly because there was no way to put vents into the panels of glass. Unfortunately we were using a Molteni stove at least in part because it gave off so little heat. The designer had calculated the heat an average kitchen would give off, not ours. This problem was intensified by the fact that the hostess stand and coat check were right near the large front window. They had to drape an ugly curtain over part of the window just to provide some insulation and even used space heaters around the door and bar.

In early March, I decided to get away for a little break. I went to Umbria, Italy, to get up close and personal with the truffle industry, on a trip organized by Johnny Magazino, one of the purveyors I relied on and a good friend. Some of the world's best black truffles come out of this region and Johnny is a major U.S. representative (as he is of caviar as well). Besides me and his lovely assistant, Celine, Johnny also brought along a few other chefs and people in the industry. We had truffles with every single meal, went on a truffle hunt (which turned out not to be very fruitful), and ate pretty much the entire time. Going to small restaurants and seeing how happy the chefs and waiters were reminded me of why I had gotten into cooking in the first place. But when I got back from the trip, I lost my newfound energy almost immediately.

On a Wednesday in late March, I woke up around 8:30, got ready, and then waited for Mike. I had stopped going in so early because the kitchen was now functioning without me having to be there every minute. Now I left the apartment with Mike, though I took a cab after I got coffee, and he took the subway all the way downtown. We were quiet that morning on our way to jobs that we both were beginning to question. Working all the time for an absentee boss had taken a lot of the passion out of something Mike once loved. For me, Mix wasn't much different.

With so much going wrong at Mix, management had begun to focus on the kitchen. They again tried to force the point about changing all of the cooks over to being paid by the hour. We had agreed that all new cooks would be switched to this system, and they questioned me as to why there were no cooks yet on the system. The answer was easy: few cooks had left and no new ones had been hired. This was just the beginning of their putting pressure on me and the kitchen. We were no longer untouchable.

I had been ignoring e-mail alerts about food purchasing from Ducasse's partner since before we even opened our doors. But now they started to remind me about the alerts in person and even asked me why I didn't follow the advice. It was important to them that I purchase something perishable in mass quantities when it was slightly cheaper than it would be in a day or a week. This went against everything Ducasse stood for. I was using small farms and organic and artisanal ingredients when possible. The food we cooked with was grown or raised with care, which is an important distinction in general and particularly important for a restaurant that is supposed to be serving food of the highest quality.

Trying to convert nonbelievers, I argued about the importance of quality, but we were speaking different languages. Quality meant nothing to them; they only cared about price and about using their purveyors. They had a system and couldn't understand why we didn't follow it. I tried to explain our system, which—by using whole animals, for example—actually was just as cost-effective as theirs, but they just didn't get it. They would tell me they could get me frozen pork loins that were cheaper than the whole pigs we were ordering.

And I'd explain that if we had been throwing everything but the loin out, they would have been right. But we were using every part of those pigs.

Over and over, everything was questioned. When they were just nagging me, it was easy for me to brush them off. Then they started to insist. When I refused to lower our standards, they began making the changes anyway. Perhaps the pettiest action was their holding off paying my stone-ground grit supplier, Nora Mill. All the grits we could use in a few months cost us seventy dollars, but they made the small mill make several requests for payment. They finally paid the invoice, but only partially, as they decided that they weren't going to pay the thirteen dollars for shipping. After a while I started to expect the calls from our purveyors, almost all of whom were getting screwed. I cringed every time the phone rang.

By that Wednesday in late March, I had been fighting for so long I was growing weary. And Ducasse, who had been behind me the whole time, pushing me to fight, was no longer there. He was gone from the picture. It was just me versus an unstoppable force that was shaping the restaurant into the epitome of what I had avoided my entire career. There had clearly been a disconnect between the two forces that had put Mix together. We had envisioned a Ducasse restaurant like any other, where quality was everything, while they had wanted it to be another hot spot, like some of their other restaurants where people were eager to go, but not necessarily because the food was great. Now I was alone, as they were winning out. They were insisting on every cost-cutting method possible to squeeze the place as hard as they could.

Just before dinner service that final day in March, I was in my office waiting for a phone call from Ducasse. I hadn't seen him in several weeks. As I waited for his call, I thought about the last time he visited the restaurant. It was a cold, gray day in New York after our disastrous New Year's, but before Valentine's Day. Things were going downhill, but we hadn't come close to the bottom yet. That morning, while the kitchen was working on our misc en place, Ducasse came in through the back. I was surprised to see him and I was surprised that he had come through the back. He stepped into the kitchen, I suppose to let me know he was there, and then went back down the hallway toward my office. I left the stove and followed him to the office. A new stagiaire passed me in the hallway, muttering "Chef."

Ducasse looked cold and angry. At ADNY, Ducasse never showed anger. He may have been angry, but he was always in control. That morning, he was ready to kill. The first thing he said to me was, "Who are these people?" Then he said a few words in French that weren't quite as kind. From what he explained to me, between words of disgust, and what I heard from the stagiaire I had just passed in the hallway, his anger was justifiable.

Ducasse had gone to the front door of Mix, but it was too early and the door was locked. He then looked through the big glass facade and saw a hostess setting up the stand. So, he tapped his finger on the window a few times to get her attention. She looked up and smiled at him, then waved her first finger in a playful no. I doubt he smiled back when he tapped on the window a little bit harder. She looked up again, a little annoyed this time, tapped her wrist to show him that they weren't open yet, and gestured "no" to him with her whole hand. She smiled again and walked away. Ducasse was left standing out in the cold staring into his restaurant.

He hadn't come back after that. He was now in New York, though, and had set up a time for me to expect his call. I knew what I wanted to say when he called, but I just listened. Ducasse explained to me that the restaurant was losing too much money and because of this his partner was going to make a lot of changes. It was mostly their money—his investment had mostly been his name—and they weren't willing to wait any longer to start earning it back. He could no longer protect me, he said, and it was no longer good that I was there. I agreed on the last part. He asked me what I thought and I said, "Thank you for the opportunity, Chef."

I walked out of the office and into the kitchen, and thanked the whole crew for their intense effort and determination. As I left, Jimmy the Saint and Jayson threw down their aprons. They were out the door before me. They were the first cooks on the team to leave, but within a month almost everyone would be gone.

The next day I spoke with Ducasse again. He wanted me to come to France, to spend six months in Monaco and then spend another six months in Paris. After that, I'd help him write a book. I told him I would think about it, but he and I both knew I would not be going to France. I had learned more from Ducasse than I had from anyone else, but what opportunity did he have left to give to me? He had given me the best he could—a chance to run a restaurant in New York.

This was not a good time for Ducasse. Mix was not his only problem. Soon after I was removed from Mix, Didier was gone from ADNY. The restaurant in the Essex House had been struggling for some time, and they were now facing a challenge that would put them in serious jeopardy. Just before I left ADNY, the hotel's union had finally managed to force the restaurant to change over to a union staff. All the cooks (except for those in management positions) were forced to join the union and abide by the benefits of membership. This was a serious obstacle for the restaurant to overcome, but more taxing was the staggering amount of back pay that Ducasse would be responsible for. Running the union kitchen made Didier's position even more difficult, and he was already unhappy. Finally, Ducasse announced that Didier would no longer be the chef de cuisine. It was one of the few times that he had publicly given him the credit he deserved. Didier would stay with the organization, though. He apparently took a deal similar to the one I refused. (But, less than a year later, he left Ducasse to take over Les Crayères, a Michelin two-star restaurant in the Champagne region of France.)

Spinning the change as though it were an attempt to appease some of his critics, Ducasse announced he had hired a chef who was nearly his equal to helm ADNY. He suggested that while he couldn't spend enough time in New York, this new chef, who was successful in his own right (though he was known mostly for a restaurant that had already earned four stars before he got there), would be a good replacement in his absence. Clearly, though, Ducasse moving in an experienced chef was a sign that he was giving up on New York. (Less than a year later, the *New York Times* reviewed ADNY again and downgraded it to three stars, and soon after, that experienced chef was removed as well.) Ducasse would focus on building his restaurants in the rest of the world, where there weren't as many obstacles and difficulties. One astute food writer called it "Ducasse's Bay of Pigs," but I cringed when I heard this. The thought that America was losing one of the greatest chefs of our time was extremely depressing.

Within a week, I was offered the opportunity to take over as chef and eventually buy into one of New York's oldest French restaurants. Then I was offered the chance to open a major restaurant in a new hotel with another established chef. These seemed like strong options, but then I got a call that intrigued me the most. It was from R-dog, who had left Mix in January to help open another new restaurant.

R-dog had struggled mightily at Mix, but he had given me his all. I would have to tell him to go home at the end of the night because he would stay there much later than he should have trying to get his work done. He's a solid cook and dedicated to the profession, but moving from commis at ADNY to chef de partie at Mix was too big a jump. He wasn't ready and it was a painful few months for him (and for me, too). When he saw the opportunity to jump ship, to go work for a restaurant that would surely capture all of New York's attention when it opened, he took it. The rule of leaving a Ducasse restaurant and thriving anywhere else still applied. He was made a sous chef at Per Se, Thomas Keller's first New York restaurant since he opened the French Laundry in Napa Valley. R-dog was relaying a message from his new boss: "Tell him not to do anything before he speaks to me."

Chapter 16

The French Laundry

With black eighties-style Ray•Bans on and my head tilted all the way back against the leather seat, I enjoyed the bright sunshine and warm, dry air with both of the thick, tinted windows rolled down. I was the only one in the back of the limousine as it moved slowly down the street that leads out of Yountville, California. The town is essentially just one street, quaint and quiet. There are several restaurants along the main street and a few stores. In the distance and in almost every space that isn't occupied by a building, there are fields of grapes. Toward the end of town, we paused briefly at a stop sign alongside a field. Anchored to posts and strung together, vines hung four feet from the ground and formed perfect rows that stretched the length of the field. Each row was followed by another perfect row a few feet away. It was late spring, and hanging from most of these vines were tiny green grapes.

As we turned off Washington Street and headed south on Highway 29, our speed increased, the space between the rows seemed to disappear, and it all became an expanse of green vines—rolling hills of grapes. Against bright-blue cloudless skies, it was as perfect a setting as I've ever seen.

I had just come from the restaurant that embodies this perfection. The French Laundry is located in an old building resembling one that might be found in the French countryside, complete with vines crawling up the side of its strong facade. In front of the restaurant is a two-foot-high wall that creates a passageway to the restaurant's entrance on the right side of the building and runs the entire length of the front property. Hanging to the ground from the two-story building's wooden balcony are several clusters of flowering vines, adding to the stone building's beauty and privacy. To the right of the building is a small, immaculate courtyard, where diners luxuriate before, after, or even during their meals. Small trees hang over the stone wall and effectively stand guard in front of the street, protecting the serenity of the courtyard, which has flowers and bushes strategically scattered around the square of grass. Parallel to the street are several windows that look into the restaurant's kitchen. The intention behind the open kitchen, however, isn't to provide diners with a view inside the kitchen; it's to provide the cooks with a view of the beauty outside the kitchen, which they would otherwise rarely see in daylight.

From the small bi-level dining room, which accommodates approximately sixty people, to the garden across the street, where some of the ingredients that will be served grow, this is an awe-inspiring restaurant. While it isn't perfect—the dining room, for example, isn't nearly as impressive as many of New York's—it is very close to ideal. There are no slow days or real business concerns. The restaurant is packed every day. Diners travel the world to eat there and reservations are booked two months out to the day. Would-be diners fight through busy signals like kids trying to get tickets to a concert that will sell out in minutes. It's a cook's dream, and I was deciding if I wanted to become a part of it.

With sunlight streaming through the partly rolled-down window and onto the slightly worn black seats, I was totally relaxed and looking forward to returning to New York. The trip had been a good one—a whirlwind tour through Yountville, the town that Thomas Keller put on the map. I wasn't convinced that this was the right next step for me, though I was leaning toward it, and I wasn't certain that I'd get the offer. The trip was both an introduction to Keller's restaurants and a series of interviews with just about everyone in his organization, from his human resources people to the general manager of the French Laundry to the chef of Bouchon, his bistro. I had been flown out and taken care of the entire way. After so many years of struggling, of working all the time while not having anything, it felt good to be treated as though I was valuable. I knew better than to count on this kind of treatment lasting, but I was luxuriating in it.

Following my first trip out to Yountville, Thomas and I had met again and spoke several times. We were both still feeling each other out, trying to determine if it would be the right fit for each of us. It was not a simple matter for either of us. For me, it would be the first time I had even considered working for anyone but Alain Ducasse in years. Before I joined ADNY, I thought I had exhausted all of the possibilities that were right for me in terms of being an apprentice. Now that I had graduated from that level within the Ducasse organization, I was even more skeptical. This wouldn't be a step down, as Thomas wanted me to help run the French Laundry, but it would still mean being a part of another chef's kitchen—and not my own.

There are very few restaurants in the country that are on the same level as ADNY, but the French Laundry intrigued me. It had won a lot of awards and was considered to be nothing short of miraculous by many people. A little more than an hour outside of San Francisco and thousands of miles from New York, it was considered to be among the world's best restaurants, even though most people (including me) had never had the chance to judge for ourselves.

After more conversations and e-mails, I went back to Yountville and worked at the French Laundry for a few days. I hadn't been as dazzled by the kitchen or the food as I expected to be, which is not to suggest they weren't at a high level, it was just hard to be blown away after working for Ducasse. But I was definitely impressed by the way the kitchen team worked together. I had worked in so many kitchens that were all about competition and working to be the best cook, at times inadvertently to the detriment of the restaurant itself. Starting at Panama Hatties, I learned that competitive cooks sometimes work hard to prove not just that they can do a great job, but that they're doing better than the other cooks around them. At the French Laundry, I saw none of this. There was a true team working for the same goal and there was respect among the cooks. Plus the chef worked along with everyone else: not just yelling out orders and motivating the cooks to perform, but actually involved in the process. That this great chef worked in the kitchen alongside his team—unlike any of the other great chefs I had worked with including Ducasse—sold me on the restaurant.

While I knew living in the Napa Valley would be a huge change from New York, I also knew that it would be good for me to get out of the city for at least a little while. Besides, the weather in Yountville was unreal. I was told that it rained in the winter (though it rarely ever snowed), but most of the year every day was essentially the same—either perfect or not far off. In late May, it was somewhat chilly in the morning, then the sun rose in a clear blue sky and got brighter throughout the day. It was hot by afternoon, but in the late afternoon it started to cool down and by evening it was cool, almost cold. With the idyllic grape fields everywhere and the almost oddly friendly people, this was a real-life Pleasantville.

When I returned from that trip, I still hadn't received an official offer, but I had no doubts. The next step was for me to cook for Thomas, and the chef de cuisine and a sous chef at Per Se, his new restaurant in New York. If nothing else, I had absolute confidence at this point in my life in my ability to cook. I went to the restaurant early in the morning, checked out what products they had available in the kitchen, and devised a menu on the spot.

Per Se is a swank, modern restaurant on the fourth floor of the recently opened Time Warner mall. It is part of a collection of fine dining restaurants in an otherwise unremarkable addition to the city. The dining room manages to transport diners from the intensity of the city into a serene and elegant environment. Through a narrow entrance, past a hostess stand, on one side there's a long, open, and uncluttered room, with couches and glass tables atop fine carpets, and on the other a small bar. The dining room is just around the corner but essentially out of sight. By the time one arrives at one's table in the small modern dining room with a fireplace and a view of Columbus Circle, the stress of the day has begun to lift.

The kitchen is beautiful, with white tile and blue trim and huge hanging lamps (the same kind that hang in the French Laundry kitchen), although the equipment, and the stove in particular, isn't as good as the top-of-the-line equipment, like the Molteni stove, I had in Mix. That morning I cooked just a few dishes. All of them had just been ideas that morning and were created on the spot. I didn't use luxury ingredients and I didn't cook any dishes based on those I did at Mix, ADNY, or any other restaurant. I cooked just two dishes: one with sweetbreads and one with lobster and asparagus. I was confident that Thomas would enjoy the dishes, and he did. That was it. I met with him the next day (after meeting with his business advisor), and we started to discuss in earnest my joining the French Laundry.

A week or so later, in the beginning of June, I packed up my apartment in Astoria and prepared to move to the other side of the country, to a place that seemed like another world. The decision had been the most difficult one I had had to make about choosing a restaurant to work in. Perhaps I was just being overly cautious after what had happened with Mix, but even as I prepared to leave that day I had some doubts. Besides moving out of the city and my home and into a rural area, the situation I was going into worried me. It was not what we had originally discussed. I was putting a lot of faith in Thomas Keller.

While I wasn't certain that this was the right move for me, I was confident that no matter what, there would be something for me to learn from Thomas Keller, as there had to be a reason he was as successful as he was. Perhaps I'd be back in a week or a month or six. Or maybe I'd become a part of something that would make me stay out there for years. Maybe I'd find something that I was no longer certain I'd find in New York.

By late August, I had lost a lot of this optimism. I had been in Yountville, a very small town (population less than three thousand), essentially by myself the entire time, except for Soda Pop. During an all-staff orientation that included all three Keller operations in Yountville—the Laundry, Bouchon, and Bouchon Bakery—we all introduced ourselves and said a few words to the group (it was California after all). After the meeting was over, the guy who had run the slide show came over to talk to me. It was Brendan (Soda Pop), a cook I had worked with at ADNY when it first opened. He had left soon after and when he returned home to California, he took a job at the French Laundry and now was running the Bouchon Bakery. During the first few weeks out in California he was the only person I could hang out with. He was the only person I knew who didn't work at the Laundry.

That changed all at once when three of my friends came to town. When I first arrived, the Laundry had a serious need of cooks with some experience. Most of the cooks there had never worked in any other kitchen and many of them were struggling. Within just a week, the idea that I was taking on a smoothly running machine was over. I kept suggesting that I could bring in some experienced cooks, but they would just show me the stack of résumés they had and brag that they had no shortage of people dying to work there. But they were in fact struggling to bring in talented cooks, and finally they came to me to see if I knew a cook who could come in to contribute right away. My first thought was Andrew, a young guy with talent and dedication. He had come from L.A. with Greenie to work at Mix and was back in L.A. when I called him. Most cooks who come to the Laundry for a day—get a feel for the area, get a sense for the restaurant—want to work there. This is the way it was for me and Andrew was no different.

Another Mix alum, Dagan, was also coming to cook. He was working at Per Se on the banquet side and had arranged to come to Yountville for most of August, since New York is generally dead in August (certainly at least as far as big restaurant parties go). It would have been a good opportunity for him to spend the month at the Laundry, which would have related to what he did at Per Se (which, despite its name, serves almost exactly the same food as the French Laundry), but it was arranged for him to work at Bouchon. The month would turn out to be mostly a vacation for him, even though he was working at the bistro five days a week. He provided us with a lot of laughs as he complained about working at a level that he hadn't seen since he first started cooking. It wasn't that it was bistro food; it was that he was working with a bunch of kids, most just a year or two out of high school, and he was in charge of frying fries and searing steak all day.

The last one to come out was my brother Mike. He had finally moved all of our stuff out of the apartment in Astoria and into storage. He was taking a break from New York for a month before going back and getting another apartment. He was no longer working at the small literary agency, which was getting smaller by the day. He decided that there was no reason to keep working for someone else and was taking the first steps to open his own business.

We all stayed in a small house about twenty feet from the edge of the Laundry's property. The house had three bedrooms, two bathrooms, a main room, a kitchen, and a deck in the backyard. It was bare and in disrepair—like a college frat house—but my staying there was courtesy of Thomas. He owned the house and the one next to it, which was between us and the Laundry. He also owned all of the property across the street from both houses and the Laundry, where there was a garden (in front of our house were little green pumpkins that were still a few months from being big and orange). He also had his own house directly behind the Laundry. At least part of the reason for owning all of this was to keep his restaurant insulated. There was no chance that anyone could build anything close to it if he owned the land.

The house was great for me when I first showed up, since I didn't have to look for a place to stay right away and it was right next to the restaurant. The last of these benefits, I realized quickly, was also a shortcoming. The first time a cook barged into my bedroom and woke me up to ask an ordering question was the last time that I was entirely comfortable in the house. After Andrew got himself a place and Mike and Dagan went back to New York, I was going to move out of the house and into one in St. Helena (a nearby town). During those last few weeks I stayed in Yountville, though, it was good for me to come home to friends hanging out on the back porch. It helped me calm down when I left the kitchen, as I was growing frustrated at the restaurant.

The two obvious reasons that Keller wanted me to join the restaurant in the first place were because he had lost his chef de cuisine, who left to run his own kitchen in D.C., and because he had had a major setback in opening Per Se. To open his first major restaurant in New York, after failing with a restaurant in the city over ten years before, Thomas had planned to close the Laundry for renovations for the first couple of months, when his attention would be needed the most in Per Se. Once Per Se was up and running, he'd have a chance to focus on some of the other projects that he was working on before reopening the Laundry. This plan was derailed when a fire caused major damage to Per Se's kitchen on the sixth day that it was open. Now he was needed at Per Se and would have to split his time between that restaurant and his reopening of the Laundry.

Another reason he needed me was that he had moved many of his best cooks from the Laundry to Per Se and had few strong cooks left in Yountville. He hadn't told me that before I joined the Laundry, but he spoke candidly about it as soon as I had a chance to get a feel for the team. He had a few sous chefs at the Laundry, but none of them was ready for the chef position. The Laundry certainly had some solid cooks at this time, but not enough.

While the Laundry is a top restaurant in the grand scheme of things, it is also a restaurant in the middle of a rural area inundated with tourists. A difficulty in getting good cooks to work there is that not only do you have to attract the cooks to the restaurant, but also to a place that offers very little for people used to city life. Since most of the country's best restaurants are in large cities, it's a major change for a cook with experience in one of these restaurants to move to Yountville.

Pleasantville might be ideal for a family man, but not for someone used to some nightlife. I had to drive to Napa, a fifteen-minute drive each way, just to get a bite to eat after work. (The only restaurant open late was a Denny's.) You can only stare up at the stars or watch spiders fight in webs hanging over you on the deck for so many nights in a row without going crazy. While I may have rarely had the opportunity to get out when I was in New York, there's a huge difference between choosing to go home and relax and not having anywhere to go *but* home.

Because of the difficulty in getting experienced cooks to move to the area, the Laundry mainly had cooks who were right out of culinary school or had had only a little experience working in restaurants. Very few of them had experience outside of the Keller system. They were some of the most loyal cooks I have ever met, but because of their inexperience they had no objectivity. I know what was great about Bouley, Ducasse, and every other chef I've worked for, and I know what wasn't great about them as well. Going into Thomas's kitchen was no different. There were things that impressed me and other things that I just didn't agree with. Even if you're learning from a chef, it is important to have a sense of balance and perspective. Most of these cooks had neither. They did what they were supposed to do because that was all they knew. This was frustrating for me because whenever I suggested anything I would receive the same response: "Well that's not the way we've been doing it, so I'd have to ask the chef."

This was the excuse for why they did just about anything. If pressed, many of them wouldn't be able to explain why they did most of what they did. "It's just the way we do it." I also heard a lot of excuses about the state of the kitchen. I'd ask why the cooks didn't work clean, which I'd always heard Thomas was fanatical about, and Thomas would say, "I know, this isn't the way it used to be." I'd ask why the cooks were ordering produce that was readily available from the farm across the street or the one a few blocks away, and was, in fact, rotting on the ground because it wasn't being used, and I'd hear the same thing. "You know, Doug," Thomas said to me, "if you think this frustrates you, imagine how frustrated I am." While I understood why Thomas was frustrated—he was no longer able to control every aspect of the Laundry, as he had gone from watching over that one restaurant every hour of every day to managing a group of restaurants, which already faced a major setback with the fire at Per Se—it didn't make it any easier on me.

One night I came back to the house and almost packed my stuff to leave. I was so frustrated I didn't know if I wanted to stay. Thomas had been telling me to stay patient after just the first month, but this was two months later and I was losing patience. I went out to the deck at the back of the house and tried to talk through it. Andrew was in a chair looking about as miserable as I was. It had been a bad night—an embarrassing night. We were behind on orders most of the service, which made the kitchen hectic, and some of the cooks did a very poor job cooking the dishes for which they were responsible.

Mike looked tired, like he had been staring at his laptop screen all day. Only Dagan looked alert. He had worked too, but there was no stress at the bistro.

I started complaining about the night when Dagan interrupted me, "Man!" he exclaimed. "I'm frying fries. How bad could it be? I mean, I'm frying fries!"

I laughed and then continued to rant about all the things I didn't agree with in the restaurant. I hadn't talked about these much, partly hoping to change most of them. Everything from the way they cooked certain things (like lobster) to how they stored products (like beef) bothered me. But I had a really difficult time with their stocks and sauces. I first learned the importance of sauces at Bouley Bakery and had this reinforced in the Ducasse system, where the chef de partie was in charge of sauces. At the Laundry, many of the sauces were made by the lowest-level cook, a commis, in the morning. Also in the Ducasse system I learned a whole new level of preparing stocks, in which their preparation involved using the highest-quality ingredients and was exacting in every way. Now I was in a kitchen where some of the stocks were outsourced, and those that were made in the kitchen weren't even close to Ducasse's standards.

Then I talked about the way they kept their walk-in, which I had cleaned and organized just the week before and came back to find a complete mess. Since being shown around the ADPA walk-in, I've done everything I could to maintain the walk-ins I've worked with at this level of efficiency and order. The Laundry's walk-in wasn't nearly as clean or organized. I already sensed that no matter what I did, I wouldn't be able to change that.

Dagan had thought I was just complaining about nothing, but now he understood some of the things that were bothering me. He thought about it for a few seconds and then said, "Man! I'm frying fries."

We all laughed and then ripped into Dagan a little. Fry Boy, as Andrew dubbed him, was an easy target. But he gave me a sense of perspective. I couldn't expect that everything would be exactly the way I wanted it. I needed to be patient. Eventually I'd be able to influence the kitchen and improve on some of the methods I didn't agree with. As the weeks passed, though, my patience would continue to be tested. There were many bad days, when I never thought the kitchen would get to a functional level, and then there were a few good days.

By the end of September, almost all of the grapes had been picked. I was told it was an unusually early harvest, and it was over by early October. I had moved to St. Helena and had been wondering what the fields I drove by on my ten-minute drive to Yountville each day would look like without grapes. I soon learned that the Napa Valley is as beautiful in the fall as it is in the summer. Replacing the endless rows of grapes is the array of colors on the leaves of the vines and trees. Not only is it spectacular visually; the scent of wine in the air is almost overpowering. It's like having your nose buried in a glass of merlot. The first few days it was intoxicating, but after a few days it was too much. On one stretch of Route 29, between Yountville and the house I was staying in, the smell was so intense that it felt as if I was breathing wine. And when I got home, it would be even stronger.

I was living with two great guys, Mario and Giancarlo, who were both Napa Valley born and raised. They were in their early twenties but educated and generally mature beyond their age. They both loved the outdoors, especially Giancarlo, who had grown up in Yountville, where his father owned several grape fields. After the harvest that year, Mario and Giancarlo decided to make some wine of their own. They had a huge plastic tub, which is used for picking grapes, set up in our garage. Part of the process in making the wine is to remove all of the sugar from it before it is barreled. On a regular schedule, we'd check the wine's sugar content and then press the pumice down with our hands and arms so that the solids wouldn't sit on top of the liquid. My shift was late at night, usually around 1:30 A.M. when I got off work. Coming home to check on the wine may have been the only thing that I looked forward to for the week and a half that we were waiting for the natural sugar to turn into alcohol. But the smell of grapes in the house was almost too intense.

On the way home during the first week of October, I had the windows rolled up and the vent off, but the smell of wine was inescapable. I was being trapped by something wonderful. Thomas had not been in the kitchen that night, so I was running the service. When Thomas was there, he worked the pass and I worked the SAS (stand-around station), which is a second pass run by a sous chef, a position unique to the Laundry. He would be responsible for the canapés, first course, and fish. I would be responsible for the meat, cheese, and desserts. The kitchen was run by two chefs working in cooperation, and I worked with Thomas as well as I had ever worked with any other cook. From the first day, I was as comfortable working with him as I had been with Americo at Panama Hatties or Greenie at Bouley and ADNY.

Thomas impressed me more than anything about the Laundry. I was impressed by what he had accomplished with the restaurant, bringing it from an ordinary restaurant in the middle of nowhere to the top of most lists. Not only did he work the pass and run service, which just about no other chef of his stature could claim, but he'd come into work with a whole bunch of vegetables that he had picked from the garden or do anything that was necessary in the kitchen. One night I watched him on his hands and knees cleaning the floor.

He worked hard—some may say too hard considering all that he had taken on with adding New York and Las Vegas restaurants to his expanding group—and I respected him for it. We were very similar.

I think an aspect of my personality that Thomas hadn't expected was that I am completely outspoken, admittedly sometimes to a fault. After I'd worked at the Laundry for about a month, he asked me when I thought I'd start contributing to the menu and I told him I didn't feel comfortable doing so.

"I just don't think about food in the same way," I told him.

"What does that mean?" Thomas asked me. And I explained to him that I thought a lot of the dishes were created with aesthetics as the primary goal and how enticingly they could be explained to a guest as the second consideration, that the sauces were meant to look bright and beautiful and that sometimes they ended up flavorless in this pursuit. While I understood that other elements are important, I always think of food in terms of flavor and taste first.

He was clearly taken aback. I doubt anyone associated with the Laundry had ever addressed him as directly and honestly. Most of the time the cooks there told Thomas only what they thought he wanted to hear and nothing else. They were all so determined to please him and overly worried about making mistakes, but none of them more so than Jeffrey. He was about thirty-five years old, wild-eyed, and almost always disheveled.

One night as I was walking back to the house next to the Laundry, a figure jumped out of the bushes. We never locked the front door; sometimes we left without even closing it, so I wasn't nervous. Out of instinct, though, I almost hit the figure, until I realized it was Jeffrey. Jeffrey had worked the day shift and had been off work for at least eight hours. It was after one in the morning, so I was surprised to see him. Under the streetlight, I could see that he was smoking a cigarette but still had his uniform on, even his heavy blue apron. "Has everyone left?" he asked. I nodded. "Good," he said, "I've got to get an early start on something." He was at least four and a half hours early.

Jeffrey was the chef de commis (in charge of all the commis) and had held that position for two years. He had asked to be moved up several times, including that past summer with a written formal request. In early October, he was moved to the bakery. It was a move essentially to push him aside. I had told him so many times, but he would never believe it. He refused to believe that the chef wouldn't one day recognize him and move him onto the line at the Laundry. Although not to this extreme, this sort of desperation to please Thomas was common.

It took a very big man to listen to another chef criticize his food and not kick me out of his kitchen. I respected Thomas for being able to listen, whether he agreed or not. All the same, I was becoming increasingly frustrated with the restaurant. While Thomas kept telling me to be patient—that things would change even though they hadn't yet—there was also a double standard in his expectations. Thomas was constantly on me about when I was going to get more committed to the restaurant. He questioned me as to why I had moved to St. Helena, which was partly because I felt it was good for me to not be so close to the restaurant, but also because he made it clear that he didn't want me to stay in the vacant house, which was part of his original offer. More important, though, was the fact that I was expected to do the job of the chef de cuisine, but that wasn't really my position.

When Thomas first contacted me about the Laundry, it was with the possibility of becoming the new chef de cuisine. He wanted me for the job and ultimately I wanted the job too. Then I met with his business advisor and the story changed. Thomas told me that it would be wiser for both of us if I went out to California for six months and then we both decided whether it was the right move. He told me that he had a delicate situation at the Laundry and was worried that he might lose some of his key guys, who had been there for years but certainly weren't ready to be chefs. His sous chefs in particular might not take it well if Thomas brought in an outside guy to run the kitchen and to be their boss. I understood his dilemma.

The problem was that I was brought out there to be one of the sous chefs for six months to see how it would go, but was asked to do the job of the chef. When Thomas wasn't there, I worked the pass. When he was there, I worked the SAS. I did the chef's job but didn't have the title, and I didn't have the respect of his kitchen. What Thomas probably hadn't anticipated, as I didn't, was that this put me in an untenable position.

That night during the first week of October, with the windows up and my shirt over my nose to try to filter out some of the wine, I decided I was wasting my time.

Earlier, while one of the cooks was preparing a rabbit loin with its silver skin on, I suggested that he take the skin off before cooking so that it wouldn't curl up on him as it had done each time he'd done it that week. The cook looked at me skeptically. "I don't know," he said. "This is the way we've always done it. I'd have to ask the chef before changing." I just nodded. I'd heard that line enough.

I was powerless in this kitchen. There was so much I wanted to change, that Thomas was pushing me to change. But if I couldn't even get a cook to do the simplest kind of food preparation, I was convinced I'd never have any control of the kitchen. Maybe it was resentment because I hadn't moved up the ranks. Or maybe it was because I was put in the position of trying to be the boss of cooks who had the same title I had. There was nothing that could be done in six months or a year to change the attitude toward me. Even if I had the chef title, I would still hear that they had to ask Thomas before doing something.

Uniquely in Thomas's restaurants everyone is called chef, even the front of the house staff. I refused to follow this practice, as I found it objectionable, almost offensive. In every other kitchen, chef was a term of respect. I had worked very hard to earn the title of chef in the Ducasse world; in Keller's universe I was called chef but it meant nothing.

As I saw it, it was an impossible dream that Thomas and I had. No matter how we might have proceeded (giving me the full position and possibly losing many important guys or having me go on without the title and not really be able to do the job), it wasn't going to work. Perhaps if I had been at another stage in my career or the restaurant in a different state (not so talent deficient and with a strong chain of command), it might have worked. But the more I thought about it the more I questioned if it even mattered whether I truly became the chef de cuisine of the French Laundry. Perhaps the restaurant had been different during a previous time, but the way it was while I was there was not right for me. As much as I respected Thomas, I did not agree with the way the Laundry cooked. If Ducasse was 60 percent ingredients and 40 percent technique (a common claim of his), Keller was 40 percent ingredients, 40 percent technique, and 20 percent theatrics. The Laundry seemed intent on keeping the focus off the food—with gimmicks like serving a course on a small plate that was stacked on top of several increasingly larger plates, so a stack of plates was used for an item that took maybe two bites to eat—and served portions so small that it would be difficult to truly judge how well a piece of meat or fish had been cooked.

While our styles were different, there were several things that I learned from Thomas in just a handful of months. It took me a little while, but I figured out what it was that Thomas did better than any other chef I had ever been around. He knew how to provide a fine dining experience, American-style. The reason that his patrons are so devoted to him is that he knows how to please them better than most chefs.

Americans don't necessarily enjoy the formal, sometimes stuffy, atmosphere of the traditional French restaurant. They want to have fun, and Thomas gives it to them, with his playfully named dishes—such as a dish with oysters, tapioca, osetra caviar, and a sabayon called Oysters and Pearls and one called Peas and Carrots, which is lobster, a ginger carrot sauce, pearls of carrots, and pea shoots—and with a staff that is efficient but relaxed and somewhat informal, even though they wear formal attire. He is the equivalent of a pop musician in the fine dining world. He provides meals with many small courses, and some of the dishes are incredible hits. With enough of these in any meal, after so many courses (more than a dozen at times) few people remember anything but the hits.

While I'll never try to emulate his approach, Thomas did make me appreciate that cooking in a windowless basement didn't always allow me to keep the diner in focus. He has some smart strategies for pleasing people, and at the end of the day that's what we're supposed to do. No matter what I thought about Thomas's techniques and style as opposed to Ducasse's, there was no doubt that he was running one of the best restaurants in the country.

Despite my frustration while working at the French Laundry, the quiet days in Napa Valley helped me realize where I belonged and where I was headed. I was ready to return home.

Chapter 17

Seasoned

In the middle of November, I got in my new used Chevy Blazer and headed back across the country. I had left Napa a couple of weeks before and had gone to help Greenie open a new restaurant in L.A. Greenie had come to help me at Mix for our first few months, so I figured I owed the little fella when he opened his new restaurant. As I left L.A. and returned to New York (with a stop in the South to see my parents and my sister's family and to eat barbecue), I was confident that Greenie, who had already been described by the *Los Angeles Times* as being as compact as a fireplug, would have people calling him a "Yoda in the kitchen" one day, just as they once said when he worked an espresso machine.

Even before I left the Laundry at the end of October, I was contemplating my exit plan. I had been talking with investors and restaurateurs for months. After I left Mix, there were several options presented to me. I wasn't sure what was the best course of action and ended up making a quick decision to be a part of the Laundry. Now I was going to take my time and make the right move. Driving my truck back home, I turned up the radio when I heard a song by Harry Chapin, who had lived in my hometown: *All my life's a circle, sunrise and sundown . . . seasons spinning around again, years keep rolling by.*

Running into Soda Pop in Yountville was a great surprise. Then down in San Francisco I ran into Brent "Sugar" Johnson. Sugar was working at a small shop that serves wood-oven pizza. It was the first restaurant he had worked in since leaving ADNY. For a few years, he told me, he just didn't think it was healthy for him to be in that sort of competitive atmosphere. As for Soda Pop, he left Keller's organization soon after I joined (so we only worked around each other for a few weeks again) and then went to Colorado to work in a restaurant there.

In Colorado, Gibb Long, whose bagel shop I helped open many years ago, before I even knew that I wanted to work in a restaurant my entire life, now owns three shops in different towns. I haven't spoken with Gibb in a long time, but I talk often with one of his best friends, Johnny Magazino, the purveyor and friend who had organized the trip to Umbria in the spring. Johnny also provides truffles and caviar for many of my other friends, like Raphie, who is still a chef at the Four Seasons Hotel in New York. He's still braving the New York winter, but being in a hotel, in a controlled environment, with more or less set hours, easier work, and great pay suits Raphie very well. He had never done well with the high-pressure low-reward life of an apprentice. At the hotel, he thrives. Working with him at the hotel, though, is one of the Mix soldiers, James, with whom I first worked at March. James is making good money for the first time in his career, but I hope one day he'll set off to open his own restaurant, like the one that Mr. Chen, my partner at March and expeditor at Mix, is working on.

When Ducasse named his new chef at ADNY, he gave that chef

the opportunity to return to the Essex House hotel, where he had once been a chef at a restaurant that closed and was replaced by ADNY. That restaurant was Les Célébrités. It was the restaurant where Blake, the first chef to show me the possibilities of food at Panama Hatties, had worked in the city. He had gone there and then decided that chasing the dream in the city wasn't for him. Americo, my partner at Panama Hatties, has also given up on the city of dreams. He's a family man now and working on turning a good restaurant on the eastern end of Long Island into a great one.

Soon after I left the Laundry, Dagan left Per Se. We were both figuring out what we were going to do, and he had an idea: we should go out to Las Vegas and join the first American restaurant of a world-famous Michelin three-star French chef. It didn't take me a minute to turn him down. The apprentice life—always chasing that next restaurant, always going after the next opportunity to learn—was over for me. I had done my time trying to be Bouley and Ducasse and so many other chefs.

I had started in my grandfather's diner in Queens and had risen to the top of some of the world's best restaurants. The whole time I kept telling myself that I wanted more than Poppy's diner, and as I set off to be a chef in my own right, that's still mostly true. I haven't come full circle; I'll never open an old-style diner, which is a dying breed even in New York. But I have the same goal that he once had: running my own restaurant. For him, it was a profession that allowed him to provide for his family. For me, it's a passion. There is no doubt that the food I serve will be vastly different from what he once served. I've learned so much from so many since my diner days. My cuisine will reflect the influence of all these talented people, as together they are what has made me a chef. Now the hard work begins.

Glossary

bain-marie. A type of double boiler that can be placed in a pan filled with water and heated gently; also, spoons are commonly kept in a bain-marie to keep them clean and warm during service.

brunoise. A very tiny dice, a precise and laborious task.

checks. Black-and-white checkered cook's pants.

chef. Responsible for all aspects of the kitchen's operation, and often for the entire restaurant.

chef de cuisine. The head cook in a kitchen where the chef is not involved in the daily operations. He manages all aspects of the kitchen, from the menu to food costs.

chef de partie. The chef of a particular station, such as "chef de partie de garde-manger."

chinois. A cone-shaped strainer made of fine stainless mesh. Something is said to be "passed" through a chinois.

combi oven (or combination oven). An oven that can produce either moist or dry heat, or a combination of both.

commis. The lowest level of cook assigned to a station in a French kitchen.

confit. Meat (traditionally goose or duck) cooked in its own fat at a low temperature until it is falling-off-the-bone tender. The term is also now used for other items, including vegetables, cooked very slowly.

demi chef de partie. The second in command on a station.

double. Two consecutive shifts—usually from early morning through lunch service and then dinner service through closing.

en place. French kitchen phrase asked as a question essentially meaning, "Are you ready for service?"

entremetier station. Often responsible for vegetables and hot appetizers.

expedite. To oversee the progression of orders coming into the kitchen, being prepared by the cooks, and being sent to the tables by the servers.

fabricate. Terms for butchering meat, poultry, or fish and preparing cuts for a specific purpose.

garde-manger station. Responsible for all cold foods.

gastro (or *restaurant gastronomique*). A French term that describes the finest restaurants.

glaçage. A French term for a glaze.

induction. A cooking method that uses magnetism to heat a ferrous pan. Induction stove tops are capable of reaching high temperatures without giving off as much heat as a typical stove-top burner.

line. The kitchen crew that does the actual cooking, as opposed to the work of a chef, expeditor (who oversees orders), or prep cook (who prepares the mise en place). Cooks who work on the line are called line cooks.

lowboy. A small refrigerator that is often kept near a station and holds essentials necessary for service.

mise en place. The prepared ingredients needed to make a dish. Also the prep work each cook and station needs to do to be ready for service.

pass. An area of the kitchen, often a table of some sort, where the chef inspects, finishes, and expedites the dishes to be served.

plancha. A fine metal griddle on which food is cooked (as opposed to a flat-top, on which food is cooked in pots and pans and not directly on the metal surface).

poisson. "Fish" in French; the fish station is called the *poissonier* station.

pousse café. A French dining custom of drinking a shot of liqueur (usually Armagnac) following a coffee or espresso at the end of a meal to aid digestion.

proof. A step in making bread that allows the dough one final rise after it has been shaped and before it is baked.

rondeau. A deep round pan that can be used for several types of cooking.

rotisseur **station.** Responsible for meat dishes.

salamander. An open-faced broiler that emits a lot of heat.

service. The time when a restaurant serves customers, as opposed to the time it spends preparing (prepping) to do so.

sous chef. The second in command in the kitchen. The responsibilities of a sous chef vary, but it is always a management position.

sous vide. Cooking in vacuum-sealed plastic pouches, often for several hours at a very low temperature.

stage. An often unpaid apprenticeship that can serve as a trial run for a permanent position in a restaurant.

stagiaire. A cook who does a stage.

stations. Areas in a kitchen that are devoted to particular parts of a meal, including appetizers and salads, meat, fish, and dessert.

walk-in. A commercial refrigerator that is large enough to walk into.

Acknowledgments

First and foremost we thank our parents and the rest of our family, whose never-ending support has allowed us to survive while trying to make something out of our dreams.

We also collectively thank everyone at Doubleday Broadway for their expertise and encouragement throughout the process. In particular, we thank Jennifer Josephy—who proposed the idea for the project—for her guidance, wisdom, enthusiasm, and patience, and Steve Rubin for believing in this project so strongly and for all of his sage advice.

Doug

There are many people who have helped me along the way. First, of course, my brother Michael and my friends, among them Marc Arner (whom I know I can count on no matter what), Tim Colbert, Kirby, Ben Gruder (for being a fan and an advisor), Nora, Jeff Nelson, Menacho, Cito, and Melissa (whose sweetness and kindness have made me a gentler person).

I'd like to thank the cooks and servers and other people in the restaurant world I've worked with, including Greenie and America (both of whom have never been more than a phone call away), James Orteaga, Tim and Veronica Chen, R-dog, Leslie, Christophe, Ryan, Dagan, Hugh, Ben Roux, Andrew (Sleepy), Julian, Johnny Magazino, Massimo, Joel, Jay Hook, Chris Putnik, Jimmy the Saint, Raphael, Brian Bistrong, Mike Anthony, Paul Liebrandt, Alex Urena, Blake Verity, Matt Hisiger, Kent, Nicky, Danny-boy, Ron Labo, and Olivier (who has always had pointed advice and the strongest opinions).

I'd also like to thank the chefs who have helped shape me into the chef I am today, most especially Alain Ducasse, Didier Elena, Wayne Nish, and David Bouley.

Michael

I've learned from, leaned on, and owe so much to many people in the book world, but none more than Judy Appelbaum, Florence Janovic, and Selma Shaprio and Jim Silberman. I would also like to acknowledge the writers I've worked with and, in particular, Steven Shaw, an invaluable source of information on all things gastronomic and a good friend.

I'd like to acknowledge all of my friends, who have been an invaluable source of encouragement and support, in particular, Alison Abrams for being one of the first people to believe in me. Special thanks to Elizabeth Hanslik, who played many roles during the writing of this book: my rough draft editor, my cheerleader, and most important, my sweet Elizabeth. Thanks also to my brother Andrew for always being an instant message away no matter how late it was, and to all of the chefs who have treated me kindly and all the cooks who have shown me what their lives are like.

Finally, thanks to Doug, who gave me the chance to put his tale into words and has kept me food rich for years.